See Me
More
Clearly

by the same author

The Guide to College Life (Prentice Hall)
The Guide to Canadian Universities (Simon and
   Schuster)
*I Can Be Anything: Careers and Colleges for Young
   Women* (The College Board)
Other Choices for Becoming a Woman (Dell)
Free to Choose: Decision Making for Young Men
   (Dell)
The Work Book: A Guide to Skilled Jobs (Bantam)
*The Men's Career Book: Work and Life Planning for
   a New Age* (Bantam)
Stopout! Working Ways to Learn (Avon)
*The Classroom Teacher's Workbook for Career
   Education* (Avon)
What's Where: The Official Guide to College Majors
   (Avon)
Be a Mother . . . and More: Career and Life Planning
   (Bantam, in press)

Joyce
Slayton
Mitchell

With a special section,

Charting Your Course:

Life Career Skills

by Ellen J. Wallach

HBJ

See Me More Clearly

Career and Life Planning for Teens with Physical Disabilities

Harcourt Brace Jovanovich

New York and London

Requests for permission to make copies of
any part of the work should be mailed to:
Permissions, Harcourt Brace Jovanovich, Inc.,
757 Third Avenue, New York, New York 10017

Printed in the United States of America

Library of Congress Cataloging in Publication Data

Mitchell, Joyce Slayton.
See me more clearly.

Includes index.
SUMMARY: A guide designed to help disabled
teenage students make constructive and
positive decisions about their lives,
education, and careers.
1. Physically handicapped—Juvenile literature.
2. Physically handicapped—Education—Juvenile
literature. 3. Vocational guidance—Juvenile
literature.
[1. Physically handicapped. 2. Physically
handicapped—Education. 3. Vocational
guidance] I. Title.
HV3011.M55   362.4'088055   79-3768
ISBN 0-15-272460-5

First edition
B C D E

*"You are the light of the world—a city on a hill,
glowing in the night for all to see. Don't hide
your light! Let it shine for all; let your good
deeds glow for all to see . . ."*

—Matthew 5:14–16

Contents

Sources and Acknowledgments   xi
Definitions   xv

I / Teens with Physical Disabilities

1 / Getting Out from Under   3
2 / Teenage Sexuality   11
3 / Coping: Your Physical Differences—Their
    Handicapism   18

II / Specific Physical Disabilities

4 / Visual   31
5 / Hearing   38
6 / Diabetes   51
7 / Muscular Dystrophy   56
8 / Cerebral Palsy   60
9 / Spinal Cord Injuries   67
10 / Epilepsy   74
11 / Getting Tested for Physical Disabilities   81

III / Beyond Your Disability

12 / Fight Handicapism: The Disability Rights
    Movement   101
13 / Getting Around   110
14 / Friends   116
15 / Sports   128
16 / Life Survival Skills   142

IV / Independence

17 / It's the Law   161
18 / Educational and Career Decisions, Strategies,
    and Goals   171
19 / Making Money Feels Good!   195

V / Special Section

Charting Your Course: Life Career Skills
by Ellen J. Wallach   205

Appendix   241
Index   275

Sources and Acknowledgments

The primary source of information for *See Me More Clearly* is *Guidance, Counseling, and Support Services for High School Students with Physical Disabilities*, 1978. The publication is a federally funded project from the United States Office of Education, Department of Health, Education, and Welfare (HEW).

The "disability" and "handicap" definitions are adapted from Frank Bowe, Director of the American Coalition of Citizens with Disabilities, Inc. (ACCD), as described in his book, *Handicapping America* (Harper and Row), 1978.

Many interviews in the book were quoted or adapted from *What Happens After School? A Study of Disabled Women and Education*, published by the Women's Educational Equity Communications Network (WEECN), 1978.

Newsletters that helped to shape the book include *Advocate* and *Disabled in Action Speaks* from Disabled in Action of Metro New York; *The Coalition* from the American Coalition of Citizens with Disabilities, Inc., Washington; *Complete Elegance* edited by Neil Marcus, Rational Island Publishers, Seattle, Washington; *Mainstream*, from Mainstream, Inc., Washington; and *Resource Roundup: Disabled Women and Equal Opportunity* from the Women's Educational Equity Communications Network, San Francisco.

Excerpts from *On the Move* by Harriet May Savitz (Copyright © 1973 by Harriet May Savitz. A John Day Book. By permission of Thomas Y. Crowell, Publishers) are quoted in the spinal cord injuries and sports chapters.

Douglas D. Dillenbeck's chapter, "Tests Are One Measure," in *Free to Choose: Decision Making for Young Men* by J. S. Mitchell (Dell) is quoted and adapted with permission in the testing chapter.

The concept of handicapism was instructively described in a special issue of the *Bulletin*, "Fight Handicapism," Vol. 8, 1977, published by the Council on Interracial Books for Children.

Individualized Driver Education for the Handicapped in Vermont from the State Department of Education and *Rehabilitation World* and *1978–1979 International Directory of Access Guides* published by Rehabilitation World are the sources for "Getting Around."

Quotes from Margaret Mead's chapter, "Learning for Friendship," in *Other Choices for Becoming a Woman* by J. S. Mitchell (Dell) and Harold N. Boris's chapter, "Choosing Friends," in *Free to Choose: Decision Making for Young Men* by J. S. Mitchell (Dell) were adapted with permission for the friends chapter.

Dr. Natalie M. Shepard gave her permission to adapt from "Discovery Through Sports," in *Free to Choose: Decision Making for Young Men* by J. S. Mitchell (Dell) for the sports chapter. Also, the action section of games and sports in the sports chapter came from *Vocationally Oriented School Planning for the Handicapped.* The publication was developed under a federal grant of Title III of the Elementary and Secondary Education Act in conjunction with the Windham Southeast Supervisory Union, Brattleboro, Vermont. Emily Sheldon was the Project Coordinator of this grant and publication.

The National Easter Seal Society's selection of "Books about Persons with Handicaps," 1978, is adapted for the survival skills chapter.

The New Education Law: What Does It Mean?, a report from Closer Look, the National Information Center for the Handicapped, is the primary source for the law chapter.

The skills chart in the special section by Ellen J. Wallach is from "The Quick Job-Hunting Map: Beginning Version" by Richard N. Bolles and Victoria B. Zenoff, © copyright 1977 by Richard N. Bolles and the National Career Development Project. Used by special permission. Those desiring a copy of the complete map may obtain it from the publisher, Ten Speed Press, P.O. Box 7123, Berkeley, California 94707, $1.25, plus postage and handling.

I am forever grateful to each of the following people for teaching me an awareness about what it's like to be a person with physical disabilities.

Chester P. Avery, Director, Office of Handicapped Concerns, United States Office of Education, shared what it was like to go blind as a young man in high school, and the consequences of blindness in his career development.

Edward V. Roberts, Director, Department of Rehabilitation for the State of California, gave the keynote address at the first national Career Education Conference for Students with Disabilities. The address is often quoted and adapted in this book.

Judy Egelston Dodd, Coordinator, Career Education Project, The National Technical Institute of the Deaf, Rochester, New York, put me in touch with people and publications and her own research about stereotypes of the disabled and their career choice.

Jean Garvin, Director, Special Education and Pupil Personnel Services for the State of Vermont, encouraged me in my project and started my groundwork when she gave me a copy of *Vocationally Oriented School Planning for the Handicapped.*

Helenmarie H. Hofman, senior editor of *Sourcebook: Science Education and the Physically Handicapped,* published by the National Science Teachers Association, 1979, helped me to understand the school's lack of expectation for excellence for children with disabilities.

Anna Kolodner, TAPS Project Coordinator, Epilepsy Society of Massachusetts met with me, read, and made several good suggestions for the epilepsy chapter.

Leslie B. Milk, Executive Director, Mainstream, Inc., spent time sharing materials and cases of people with disabilities who face employment barriers and the ways in which they are learning to overcome them.

J. Corbett O'Toole, a Training Specialist at the Center for Independent Living (CIL), affirmed the need for this book and opened the communications door beyond her book, *What Happens after High School? A Study of Disabled Women and Education.*

I want to especially thank Editor-in-Chief Barbara Lucas at Harcourt Brace Jovanovich, who started it all by asking me, "Won't you do a career book for teenagers with physical disabilities?"

Joyce Slayton Mitchell
October 1979

**SPECIAL SECTION ACKNOWLEDGMENTS BY
ELLEN J. WALLACH**

My deep appreciation to Fred, Jonathan, and Cathy for their encouragement and support. We are truly a family of people who root for each other! And, to Dick Bolles, for sharing his genius and his friendship with me.

Definitions

Physical Disability

A physical disability is a physical impairment that lasts for at least six months and interferes with major tasks of daily living like walking, seeing, hearing, lifting, talking, and going to work or school.

Handicap

A handicap is the result of a barrier or obstacle in the environment that prevents people with physical disabilities from performing daily tasks. If we remove the barrier from the environment by using large print or a reading machine or braille for the legally blind, or if we provide an interpreter for the deaf or a ramp in place of steps for the disabled person in a wheelchair, then the disabled person is no longer handicapped for that particular activity.

In other words, by this definition, *you* are not handicapped. The environment and our society handicap you by constructing obstacles and barriers that prevent you from access to independence in your daily living tasks.

I / Teens with Physical Disabilities

1 | Getting Out from Under

"I went blind my junior year in high school.

"I was seventeen when I went to the rehabilitation center for the blind. I was the youngest guy they had ever had there; most were in their forties and older. I thought I was going to be the original hotshot blind guy. I had a terrible time. I didn't type well; I failed it every time. I didn't use my cane well. I had a typing and caning course, and it was a complete surprise to me that I wasn't good at either of those things—they tested me to death, and I just kept flunking and flunking. I went around getting really depressed. After all, I used my typewriter every night, I wrote to the kids back home, wrote four or five letters every night. And here I was using it well enough to write and still flunking the course. Just before that I had entered the hospital at five feet seven inches tall for eye operations and came out some months later six feet one inch and blind. I had no idea what I looked like. I was depressed and just felt blind. Then one day a group of high school girls came over to sing to the 'blindies.' They were singing away, and I was listening; then, after it was all over and they all were standing together,

I overheard one say to another, 'Hey, look at that boy over there; he's a yum!' Well, I knew it was me, because six feet or not, I was the only boy—the only one there under forty years old! I really had a moment of truth. I went from a blind guy to being special—a yum. I'll never forget that moment of truth when I realized for the first time since I went blind that I was more than a blind guy . . . I was a yum."

More than a blind guy. When everyone wants to put a label on you, wants to know you're just like all the other blind gals and guys, you've got to find something more; you've got to set yourself straight. You aren't just like all the rest of the "blindies" or "wheelies" or deaf or people with diabetes or epilepsy. You are you. And you can be everything there is to be. The more clearly you see yourself, the clearer you can be as you teach others to see you.

Seeing yourself more clearly is the purpose of this book. Helping you set up your own moment of truth—when you know that you are more than your disability, when you are a "yum" or a something else that has nothing whatever to do with your disability—is what the book is about.

Getting out from under the stereotype—the disability label that others say you are like—is what you have to do. You have to get out of the box that implies you need the same things, have the same joys, have the same fears, need the same education, and go into the same careers as all the others with your particular disability.

Stereotypes

Leslie B. Milk, the executive director of Mainstream, Inc., an agency to help the disabled with employment, has heard all the stereotypes. She says there are negative stereotypes, and there are positive ones. But whichever they are, they still put you in a box and label the box, and that label prevents people from getting to know what you are really like. The common stereotypes heard at Mainstream are: The disabled can't take stress; they will break; they will get too tired; they are fragile. On the other side, the disabled are very loyal, they will never quit a job, they have super character, and they are very admirable. . . . All these labels, negative or positive, assume that all disabled are alike, just as they all are loyal and all get too tired. Connected to stereotypes for the disabled are the ones for the special education teachers and counselors who work with the disabled. For example, they are wonderful, they are willing to work with these children, it's a gift to work with the disabled, it's a special talent to work with the disabled. In other words, the disabled are so stereotyped that even the professionals working with them get in a special box, too!

You have probably already had people say to you, "You ought to be a rehab counselor or a teacher of the deaf or blind," or one of the careers that go with a particular disability. The big problem for students is that career stereotyping limits your aspirations. Just when you have a chance to develop career skills in school, career stereotypes limit what you think you can do, what you will explore as a possibility for you. Here are some students who have felt the pressures of stereotypes.

Mary, who works from a wheelchair because of a spinal cord injury, says:

> "Just because I'm disabled doesn't mean I'm going to work with disabled people. First of all, I'm an Indian counselor, and that's where I choose to stay. I think that will be true for quite some time. If I chose to work with disabled Indians, they would have to come into the regular school system. I would not go into a special program."

Ann, who has been legally blind since seven, feels the same way:

> "After I got my B.A. degree in speech, I realized I did not want to correct people's lisps. I did not want to help a stutterer not stutter. I did not care to work with non-

verbal people because being blind, I depended upon verbal responses to know what people were feeling. At that point I was very verbally dependent. When aphasic [speech-impaired] and deaf people came in, I found I couldn't cope. So I decided to get my graduate degree in social work."

The first careers that many of you may think of are in the disability field mainly because those are the jobs that you see most often. Those are also the jobs that many counselors expect you to be interested in.

Some students go into careers with the disabled because they are the easiest places to go. With little muscle control since birth, Alice speaks about how she got into her college major:

"When I first went to Hunter College in New York City, I found out that the education department was very hard to get into if you had a disability. I decided I would become a rehabilitation counselor so I could help other disabled adults. In college I became active in the disability rights movement, and then I started getting support from the disabled community."

Even though working with the disabled seems the best job for you now, or if it is the last place you want to be, read Ellen Wallach's Special Section at the end of this book to find ways to explore all careers, the ones people try to steer you to and the ones they never mention. Chester Pike Avery is the director of the United States Department of Health, Education, and Welfare's Office of Handicapped Concerns. Probably Chet's career development has a lot in common with the problems and issues that many of you will have to deal with. This is what he says:

"I was a teacher in a private boys' school for three years; then a Harvard friend told me to come to Washington and take the civil service exam. When I first got to

Washington, I worked for the handicapped. I was stereo-typed into that job. After a while I got to feeling uncer-tain, guilty, and depressed. I felt as if I were cashing in on being blind, and the only reason I had the job was that I was blind. I wondered if I could do a regular job—one that blindness had nothing to do with.

"I finally left that first job with the handicapped and went to work in another area altogether—financial aid and research in education. My job was going really well: My boss loved my work; they thought I was bright; they liked the way I put things together; I worked indepen-dently and really felt good. I was doing a super job, and the job had nothing to do with my disability. My boss was the nicest guy anyone could work for: never judgmental, never critical, always appreciating my work.

"Then the Office of Education opened this office [Office of Handicapped Concerns]. When it started look-ing for a director, I didn't want the job. I loved where I was. But then I decided I had to pay my dues. I had to give something back to others who are handicapped. I had to help others to a better life with good educational opportunities like those I had been given. I began to get involved. I was very pleased with the work I was doing, but I looked at the list of people whom they were going to select to direct this office, and I really became a di-vided man. I finally decided to go with it. I took the directorship. After all, I had proved myself in research, in financial aid, in work outside of the handicapped. I had proved to everyone else that I could work anywhere, so it felt OK to work again with the handicapped."

For you to be stereotyped into a job for the disabled is like having to go to work for the family business. It's *not* OK if it's because you can't do anything else. But it *is* OK after you've left the family for a while, worked for someone else, and proved to yourself and your family that you are qualified for the job.

Charting Your Course

Once you get the idea that you may be programmed for certain careers because of your disability, you will want to spend some time undoing all that. The Special Section in this book that will help you assess your skills the most is called "Charting Your Course: Life Career Skills." This section consists of a group of exercises that will help you see your skills and abilities and interests in ways that will make career planning much clearer for you. If it seems like more than you want to tackle when you first look it over, go back some other time, and plan to read the beginning of the chapter and to do only the first exercise. Or the first and second ones. Or go over the exercises with a friend; each of you do your own and then discuss your results with the other. Or take the book to school or to a group you are in, and use this chapter for a workshop idea to find your career skills. When you get through all these exercises, you will have a good basis for decision making. You will see yourself more clearly.

Accepting Your Limits

The first thing that Leslie Milk, from Mainstream, Inc., likes to be clear about when she is helping people find a job is that they accept their limits. She feels that everyone who works with the disabled is so eager to tell them they can do anything that the job hunters aren't realistic about their limits.

Milk points out, for example, that there is no such thing as a blind bus driver. She also points out that everyone has limits, and often career counselors mix up your disability with an ordinary limit. For instance, Milk tells the story about the rehab counselor who told the deaf man he should be an accountant. The man kept saying, "I can't be an accountant." The counselor kept insisting, "Of course you can; you can be anything; lots of deaf people are accountants." Finally, the deaf guy replied, "But I can't add." Disabled or not, everyone has their limits: brains, personality, looks, height, dexterity, persistence, ambition, concentration. You name the trait, and you'll find people without it or with too much of it.

As you chart your course and learn about your skills, you will learn to see your limits. Some of them are tied into your disability. Some are not.

Schools and colleges are not always as accepting as you may expect them to be. When Milk was a senior at college just about to be graduated with a degree in journalism, she was told two weeks before graduation that she would not be able to get her degree because she could not type fast enough. She can't lift her left arm and types with one hand. She was told that the world won't accept people with disabilities, so the college couldn't give her a degree. Lucky for everyone, Milk was an assertive young woman and got that policy changed in a hurry. But her point is that the world *does* accept limits—because everyone has them.

Driving and Sex

Driving and sex have a lot to do with stereotyping and limits. One of the outstanding surprises about talking to adults who work with disabled teenagers is that no one talks about sex and driving. One reason is that a lot of people think the disabled are not interested in sex. They think, too, that driving is out of the question for teens with physical disabilities. Being a teenager, you know of course, that few issues interest you, like all your contemporaries, more than sex and driving.

It may help, as you read the sexuality chapter (Chapter 2) in the book to know that your parents are not the only ones avoiding the issue. There is nothing wrong with *you* that prevents them from talking about sex. Parents don't like to talk about sex with their children because it's a hard issue for all of us to talk about, whatever our ages. And many parents dread the time when their teenaged children get their driving licenses and start the hassle of wanting to use the car, and they dread the possibility of an accident. Both sex and driving are signs of growing up, of having control over your life. As much as they would like to be, parents aren't always ready for you to take more control of your life.

Whatever the issue—sex, your particular disability, handicapism, getting around, the law, or placement testing—you will want to take some time to work out where you are. Work out what these concerns have to do with your life and your life planning. In some cases, what you read here will be all you want to know; for others, it will be more than you want to know, for still others there will be issues you will want to learn much more about. Explore, write to the resources cited, and use this book as a starter for your exploration of an issue. There are addresses and organizations and advocacy groups (support groups that represent *your* interests) to which you can write for more information. There are groups to join, films to see, and books to read. Get in on all or some of it. Talk about what you learn and where you are on these issues. Talk to your parents and friends and teachers and counselors and whomever it is you talk to about things. If it's hard to get started on some topics, suggest that a friend read whichever chapter you just read and then talk about it. Take your time; put these issues on a back burner as you go through current homework and rehab sessions that you have to give priority to. It all will fit together over the years. To see yourself more clearly is a lifelong process, and every single one of us is in on the same process.

2 | Teenage Sexuality

It's true. You *are* physically disabled. It's true. You are NOT *sexually* disabled! There is no such thing as being sexually disabled. Sexuality, like other birthrights, cannot be taken away regardless of an accident or an injury or illness. A very few physical disabilities directly affect the genitals, but most do not. Even in those few cases, the people who cannot actually have intercourse are still sexual beings, who feel, love, and express their sexuality in other ways.

Most of you became aware of sex in our world just as all kids do, through watching TV, going to movies, and reading advertisements that are loaded with sexual messages—selling everything from cars to chain saws. But most of you havon't had the freedom from your parents and teachers in sixth and seventh grades to join in the kissing games—post office and spin the bottle—to try things out for yourself. More often you have found yourself an outsider in the social and sexual lives of other teens.

Even worse, some of you have believed society's nonsexual stereotype for teenagers with disabilities, and you apply it to yourself. At least for a time.

Your sexual birthright means that you have the right to be curious, to experience, and to learn about sex to the extent that you want to learn about it. Others cannot take away or give you your sexuality; all they can do is to help you understand your sexuality, to help you take responsibility for it and make choices based on information and on freedom from fear.

Regardless what you do about it, *you are a sexual being.* You are a sexual being from birth to death with the right to express your sexuality. There is no disability that can take sexuality away from you any more than spiritual, emotional, or intellectual aspects of you can be taken away. These are all parts of you that make you whole and human. Everyone is born a sexual being, and that means that we all need love and affection all our lives.

Parents and teachers are often uncomfortable talking about sex to teenagers because they deny that their children are sexual. From their attitude about your sexuality and with the stereotypes about the disabled being asexual, it's hard for you to know what to believe.

You are a sexual being whether you have a girlfriend or boyfriend or not. You are a sexual being whether anyone else is sexually attracted to you or not. You don't have to be sexually active to be a sexual being. Your decision about what you are going to do sexually is easier to make when you accept the fact that you are a sexual being regardless of how you do or do not express it.

Stereotypes

You may be painfully aware of the stereotype that labels people with disabilities as asexual, not sexual, not interested in sex, or too disabled to be into sex. Edith Schneider, director of a cerebral palsy group in Boston, writes that "everyone thinks the disabled are 'too good' or 'too different' to be interested in sex." The problem with stereotypes is that people believe them —even the people who are stereotyped. For example, the stereotype that girls cry and boys don't means that little girls grow up to cry and boys grow up not to cry even when they are scared to death. Because of the asexual stereotype, people with disabilities often kid themselves into thinking that sex and interest in friends for sex are unimportant or unnecessary. If you act as if the stereotype is true, that means people will treat you by the stereotype. In that case, no one has to teach you anything about sex. It's a good way out for everyone else involved, a way out from teaching you about sex and birth control. Being treated as if you weren't a sexual being is a put-down that no one needs.

In their article about stereotypes, Drs. Douglas Biklen and Robert Bogdan write in the Interracial Books for Children *Bulletin:*

> Disabled people are almost always portrayed as totally incapable of sexual activity. A common way to show this is by omission of the sexual dimension from characterizations of people who are disabled. In fact, they are rarely shown in a loving relationship of any kind. Detective Ironsides is portrayed as having *had* a love life once upon a time before he was shot in the spine, and thus, put out of commission. His 'old flames' turn up occasionally to join him in soulful reminiscences about their lost love, but nothing's happening in the here and now.

The flip side of this stereotype shows that the disabled person is sex-starved or sexually degenerate—especially in comic books. Another reversal is that *men* with certain mild disabilities—especially ones sustained in war—are often viewed as exceptionally brave and sexy. This image has been exploited in the ads for Hathaway shirts featuring a man with an eyepatch. Moshe Dayan is a real-life example. In a macho society, women similarly disabled are *never* seen in such a glamorous light.

Who's Physically Perfect?

Denial of your sexuality is not the only sex-related problem you may have. You may also be frustrated because you aren't physically perfect. Physical growth and change, awareness of biological urges, development of sexual friendships, and sexual exploration are normal for everybody. Doubts in these areas of sexuality are kept alive by the rigid standards of what others think you should look like. Males should be big, strong, and athletic, and females should have beautiful legs and boobs.

With these physical standards for sexual attraction, it's easy to blame your physical differences for the difficulty you are having with sexuality. It may be easier to work it all out when you realize that for all adolescents, there is a tremendous pressure to conform to the expectations of your peers in terms of sex, what a male and female should look like and how they should act with each other.

Our society's emphasis on the physically attractive female and the strong, independent, and dominant male may be standards that you simply cannot meet. Some of you may consider dating and eventual marriage as experiences you do not dare think about realistically. Others admit that sex is uppermost on their minds. Like Bob:

> "I'll tell you, I was a crazy guy—always had a broken heart. I can remember the very first kiss after I went blind. I was eighteen. Oh, I was a panting puppy in those days—I missed her mouth and hit her glasses! All I could think of was girls, girls, girls. I wanted to kiss them and hold them and be close to them all the time. I used to go down to the beach every single night and take some beer and walk up and down the beach, looking for girls to talk with and girls to kiss.
>
> "I had a deep longing for love and sex, to show that I was accepted—even if I was blind. I must have had five or six girlfriends that first year back from the rehab center, my last year in high school. Everyone else went steady—not I; I had to have more than one. I wasn't macho; it was a need to have people accept me, a need to be loved, a need to be able to love. I didn't know the difference until I met my wife."

Learning about Sex

Students with disabilities experience very trying times, but so do most teenagers. Disabled teens who are convinced that their difficulties in forming sexual attachments are only the result of their disability would do well to realize that many, if not all, teenagers have problems with sexuality which may be no lighter than your own. And it doesn't end with the teen years. They don't often admit it, but most adults are still learning what sexuality means to them, too.

You can be almost sure that your parents and teachers aren't going to talk about sexuality to overcome the stereotypes. As you must well know, parents and teachers have all kinds of reasons never to talk about sex with their children and students —regardless of whether they are disabled or not. Some parents don't want to talk about sex or teach you about birth control because they think that if they teach you the truth about sex, you'll go and try it. It isn't just a matter of talking about anatomy and the biological reproductive system and birth control that teens need and want. It's attitudes about sex, stereotypes about sex, and myths about sex that young men and young women would like to know more about. Things weren't much different with your parents; no matter which generation it is, disabled or not, parents and children have always had a hard time talking about sex. As one pregnant sixteen-year-old said, "You know, my mother was always self-conscious about talking about things like that [sex]."

If you are a teenager who would like to get a conversation going about sex with your parents, one way to do it is to give them something to read about teenage sexuality or sexuality and the disabled teenager. You could show them this chapter to start with. Or some of the books about sex and your specific disability may be good, too. Get a book listed on page 241 that you might like to read. If it makes sense, show it to your parents as a way to open a conversation.

Talking with your parents or some other adults about sex is important because it's the only way you can learn fact from myth. Anything kept as secret as sex is loaded with myths! The trouble with myths is that you get the wrong information. Another trouble with them is that they make you feel as if something were wrong with you because the myths may be different from what you are doing or thinking or fantasizing about. It's important to learn how you feel about sex. You already know how your family or school or church or friends feel. Because you feel one way about sex doesn't mean, of course, that you have to *do* everything you are thinking about or even that you would have the opportunity to do everything you are thinking about. You should know that there is no such thing as wrong things to *think* about. You can read the facts about masturbation, fantasy, virginity, homosexuality, contraceptives, and VD in some of the sex books for teenagers. You can't read about your own attitudes and how to make decisions about what you are going to choose to do sexually. You have to figure that out for yourself, knowing what you know about yourself and all your relationships.

Teenage Pregnancy

No matter what facts you know or don't know, no matter what your parents and teachers may think about sex being only for married couples, teenage pregnancy can and does occur. It can easily result from the first time you have sex. Pregnancy may have nothing to do with love and have everything to do with curiosity and being turned on by your partner. Starting a baby may be the last thing on your mind, but there are more than a million teenage pregnancies a year. If getting independence is what you are after, having a baby is not the road to independence. The one fact that you must always be aware of is that sexual intercourse, no matter what the time of the month, can result in pregnancy unless you use contraception. Contraceptives vary in their efficiency. Saran wrap does not count. Withdrawal (removing the penis before ejaculation) does not count. The first time does not count. Not being in love does not count as a contraceptive. Many teenagers get pregnant trying all these makeshift or mythical contraceptives. Magic does not count. Hope does not count. Condoms (rubbers) and foam, used together, without a doctor's prescription count and work very well.

Most teenage pregnancies occur because no one bothered to decide (1) to have sex (they just did it on the spur of the moment) and (2) to use contraceptives.

As you decide what you are going to do about sex, what are your options? You can masturbate, you can pet, you can repress your sexual urges through sports and cold showers, you can dream and fantasize, or you can have sexual intercourse with or without contraceptives.

How can you decide what's best for you? The best sex has to do with relationships. Talk it over; spend some time thinking through what you want from your friend right now and how that fits in with the rest of your life: your rehabilitation life, your school life, your home life, and your other friends as well. Keep in mind that what you decide to do now with the friend you are deciding with can change. So what you decide for now is for now, not forever. As you learn more about yourself and your relationship, you can decide again as things change. Teenagers, just like everyone else, change. Your friend changes, and you change. As you grow, your needs are different; as you understand more about what is going on and where you are going, as you make school and career decisions, you also have to make sexual decisions. It's good to change your mind; it shows you are growing and changing and not stuck in a rigid position.

Young women or young men can keep their choices and options open as long as they respect themselves enough to protect against pregnancy. You can accept your sexuality and still decide that a sexual life with another person would not be good for you at this time. Remember it's your body. It's your life. And it's a sexual body, and you are a sexual being with the possibility of a sexual life no matter what your physical differences are. You decide what's important to you. Accepting your sexuality regardless of what you do about it is important to everybody.

For a list of more things to read about sex, see page 241.

3 | Coping:
Your Physical
Differences—Their
Handicapism

Coping means dealing with and working through the difficulties. Not to cope is like sitting in a fog or spending your life in front of the TV. Not coping also means managing by living in a dreamworld and not noticing your disability—an "ignorance is bliss" attitude. The opposite of coping is giving up. This book is about coping with the difficulty.

No matter how severe your disability, you have within yourself the potential for coping with your disability and for self-fulfillment. Coping is easier if you can learn to:

1. Achieve whatever degree of physical independence is possible.
2. Have good friendships.
3. Accept your limitations without feeling worthless.
4. Center on your abilities more than on your disabilities.
5. Take responsibility for yourself.

Acceptance of Physical Differences

For many of you, the teen years may be the first time that you realize that your physical condition is permanent. You may have just caught on that you are *not* going to outgrow your epilepsy, paralysis, or hearing loss. You may just have realized that you don't come off as well as a teenager with a physical disability as you did as a six-year-old; after all, it's not as unusual to see a six-year-old stumble as she walks as it is to see a sixteen-year-old who stumbles! A hearing aid on a three-year-old may look like fun—like a toy—but on a fourteen-year-old boy, there is no mistaking the physical difference. Tony, with leg braces since seven, tells us how he felt when he finally realized he was different:

> "It wasn't until ninth grade that I began putting together what I was, how I was different, and really coming to grips with the fact that I was not the same as other people. I desperately needed to prove to myself that despite the difference, there was really something of value in my being alive. . . . The school started a wheelchair sports program, and for the first time in my life I had a reason to go to school. For the first time in my life I wanted to be there. Prior to that I was just cruising, making it from year to year without learning much of what was intended to be learned in school. My mind had been in a vacuum in terms of academic learning until I started sports and found a new interest in school. Everything was new; everything was exciting; everything was challenging to the point of sometimes being overwhelming. It was an incredible door. . . ."

The severity of your disability has a lot to do with your choice for coping with it. For example, a young woman with epilepsy which is controlled by medication can hide and deny her disability and try to compete with everyone else, never facing the issue that she has anything more to cope with than the other kids in her class. On the other hand, a young man without arms has little choice but to cope with the problem of accepting himself as a person with a disability.

Getting Used to Dependency

If you are severely disabled, one fact of your life is that you will have to ask for help from people around you. How much help you will need to ask for depends on how disabled you are and what kinds of aids you need and what kinds of skills you can develop on your own. One skill you have to learn is how to say no when you don't need the help of others—those who have no idea what you can do and what you can't do. And another skill to learn is how to accept help when you need it—in a way that makes you feel OK about it. One way to accept help, of course, is to give help in other ways. No one wants to be a taker all the time and never a giver. And no one has nothing to give! Even if you can't help the person who is helping you, you can always help someone else. If your parents are always helping you, you could help someone else in the family, for example, by playing a game with, or reading to, a younger brother or sister, by offering to do something that needs to be done in your family, or by volunteering in your community with other disabled people.

Coping with needing help—at a time when most of the kids you know are acting as if they don't need any help from their parents—means dealing with taking your medicine, using the aid that helps you most, sticking to a diet, and getting the rest that you need. As long as you don't get these things mixed up with real dependency, as long as you find ways for others to need you, too, you will be able to deal with and accept the help you need because of your particular disability.

A Recent Disability

Some of you were not born with a physical disability; it has come later in your life. Coping with a whole new image of yourself all of a sudden *is* something new for you.

Even if you got the clues that you were going to be permanently disabled, you really didn't believe it could happen to *you.* So you didn't really see it coming. When Michael, a sophomore in high school who had a detached retina (just like his partially blind mother), went blind in one eye, he was later asked, "Then you expected to be blind?" He exploded and roared:

"Are you kidding? NO! I was *invulnerable.* There was no way a good guy like me, who followed doctor's orders, could turn into a blind guy. Or so I believed at the time. I did everything the doctor said to do; he even told me about all kinds of behavior, 'Don't bend over,' 'Don't blow your nose too hard,' 'Don't cough.' I was the good guy; I felt guilty if I did the least thing that would have upset those eyes. What I found out later, of course, was that seeing was a matter of the retina's healing and had nothing to do with my behavior. I thought if I was really good, just as the doctor said, I would get all my sight back again. The doctor led me to believe that, too. The whole medical scene was really bad. It took years for me to accept my blindness."

Rehabilitation

Rehabilitation is the process of learning to live with a disability in your own environment. In other words, it means learning to cope—to find enough satisfactions and rewards to make life worthwhile. Rehabilitation does not end at the moment of discharge from the hospital, but it begins when people practice the techniques they have learned in the hospital and apply them in coping with their own worlds. Other people's attitudes toward you influence how you cope, so that if everyone around you is treating you as if it were the end of your world, it will be harder for you to get a start on coping. If you have been disabled from birth, but are just beginning to accept that you won't outgrow it—and it's here to stay—or if you have been disabled in the past few years, one approach for coping is to have a "mourning" time: a time of grief for your loss—your lost image of your body and what you wanted for a body image. Losing an image of ourselves, whether a body image, a career image, or an image of where we wanted to go to college, is not so different from losing a friend or a parent. It hurts. And it takes time to get over the loss. Taking time to grieve for your lost vision, limb, or perfect health can be the beginning of your healing, the beginning of your rehabilitation. Losing your identity with a perfect body is something to cry about—something to be depressed about. Go ahead and *be* upset. When things hurt, you *should* be upset. And a lost image counts, too.

What you know by now is that if you are severely disabled, you must adapt, in many ways, your former self-image. Your aspirations, your friendships, your body image, your concept of self, and your relationships with the physical world may be strongly affected, if not completely changed. You may refuse to accept your disability for a million reasons. It may be hard to accept because you feel as if it's a punishment for something you did wrong—getting paid back for your sins. You may feel the disability means an end to your acceptance by society as a worthwhile person. You may refuse to accept it because it means the end of the career plans you had, or you may not be able to accept your disability because you can't stand the resentment you feel from the pity that others show toward you.

One thing we know is that after mourning for your loss, you must give up all the reasons you can't accept your disability if you are going to be healed. It is basic to any rehabilitation that you accept the change in you. Acceptance of the change must exist before you can effectively accomplish the new learning that is essential for your future development, essential for learning to cope.

One of the things that acceptance of your disability means is that you may have to reevaluate your goals. You may *not* be able to do the things you thought you could do without a disability. If you had important sources of feeling good that could happen only before your disability, then you need to give them up and find *new* sources for feeling good. If you were a downhill skier and lost a leg, you will have to get special equipment and switch to an easier slope until you get your sense of balance and can be safely out on the trail, where everyone else can run into you as well as you run into them! Your ability to cope with the stress and pain you feel at having to change your goals, your ability to modify activities that you were crazy about, and your ability to make new plans and actions that you will also be crazy about are necessary for successful rehabilitation. Actually it's these very things that everyone, disabled and nondisabled, has to learn to do: set goals; learn about options; learn about limits; change goals; set them again and again.

OK. So by now, in your teen years, you have learned that you have to cope with your disability. The problem remains, for some of you, of how to cope with the handicapism that goes along with it, how to get past other people's attitudes about what a disabled person is like, what you can do, what you can't do. After all, it's hard enough to be responsible for your own attitudes without figuring out how to take on everybody else's ideas and attitudes and put-downs about the disabled. As you know by now, other people's negative attitudes don't come only from the nondisabled. You have also had to learn how to cope with put-downs from the other kids with disabilities. Nicci tells what it was like for her:

> "High school was a school for the mentally and physically disabled. They segregated us so we wouldn't be ridiculed by regular high school students. Yet we had our own divisions in high school. The people that limped were better than the people on crutches. The people on crutches were better than the people in wheelchairs. And the only way that someone in a wheelchair was better than anyone else was if he had clear speech. If a kid had cerebral palsy and couldn't speak clearly, it didn't make any difference if she had an IQ of two thousand. It wasn't being grouped together with disabled kids that affected me; it was the absence of nondisabled kids."

You will feel handicapism at work when other people focus on your disability rather than on your ability. Sometimes overprotection and underestimating what you can do are basic to the beliefs that people have about the disabled—that you are really not like other (nondisabled) people—and like sexism and racism, "not like the others" means not quite as good. "Not like the others" means that you are dependent both physically and psychologically, that you are not a sexual person with the sexual dreams and drives of the rest of the world, that your disability takes over your whole life space. If you buy any or all of these beliefs about the disabled, you will have to give in to the disability rather than learn to cope with it.

Deaf since birth, Ron describes how handicapism worked against him in school:

> "In high school, people judged me because of my disability, and that was where I had the most problems. People didn't see me as a Puerto Rican or a man; they saw me as a deaf person. If I hadn't been disabled, school would have been a lot easier. I would have gotten a better education if I had not been disabled. The resource teachers didn't really try to teach us. They felt they could pass us on, letting us get away with minimum work instead of making us meet the same standards that nondisabled children had to meet. As a result, when I graduated from high school and wanted to go to college, I wasn't prepared; I had to take remedial courses. If it weren't for my rehab counselors, I never would have made it."

If you are overprotected or not much is expected of you from your family or school, if others have a tendency to pity you, then you won't get a chance to make the decisions you need to make. You won't get the honest feedback about how you act and what you say that all teenagers need to test their growing against the world. Parents and teachers who believe that you are doomed to dependency are not about to expect much independence from you. If your family or school doesn't insist on independence, *your* job, then, must be to get all the coping and independent living skills that you can get somewhere else, in spite of others. Maybe a good place to start would be with a friend or two. Reading the chapters in this book on friendship and life survival skills (Chapters 14 and 16) is a good beginning toward independence.

What on Earth Makes People Afraid of You?

The myths about the disabled prevent others from knowing you. Nondisabled people are usually uneasy with any disabled person, not just you. They don't know whether to offer assistance, to use the word "see" with a blind person or "walk" with someone in a wheelchair, or to use exaggerated facial and lip movements when speaking to a deaf person. Because of this uneasiness, people avoid contact with the person who is physically different, even when it is only through contact that both people can get over their anxieties. If a blind friend is coming to dinner, you don't know if you should change the candlelight for a 200-watt bulb, put a reading light at the table by his or her plate, or just act as if you didn't notice how dark it is in your house.

It's not only "other" people who are afraid of you. Your own parents can be, too! Roger became paralyzed at seventeen. He says:

"It took my father four years after my accident finally to be alone with me in a room. My mother wasn't much better. But I was a hero in my town. I came from a very small midwestern town, so everyone was good to me and encouraged me and knew all about me. They wrote thirty or forty letters a week to me when I was in the rehab center. The support of my community helped to make up for the fright of my parents."

Self-Concept

To develop, restore, and maintain a positive self-concept has to be your primary goal in life. A by-product of a positive self-concept is that it's the way out of everyone's myths and fears about the disabled. The nondisabled best learn their attitudes about the disabled by your attitudes. It's not so easy for a teenager to build a positive self-concept. If you set up in your mind that you are going to cope—you are going to deal with your difficulties, rather than give in—then you can take one step at a time. And having a positive self-concept *part of the time* counts as one step at a time. One way to take a step toward a good self-concept is to get started on developing survival attitudes such as these:

1. Broaden your range of values beyond the physical. Your body may seem like everything to you, but it isn't. There are other aspects of you worthwhile, too, like your head (thinking) and heart (feelings), that are you as much as your body is.
2. Put the physical down. Don't let society's value of the perfect body (which *no one* has for long anyway—ads just make it seem that way) take over your values about yourself.
3. Contain the disability. Keep it separate. Don't let it spread. When some people look at others who are deaf or blind, they often spread that concept to "not bright" or "not feeling." The one disability takes over the whole person. Keep your disability within its boundaries. You can teach others by your attitudes what your limits are. You can teach others what your limits are *not* as you get beyond them.
4. Emphasize your abilities. Think about what you *can* do, not about what you can't do. It's those interests and skills you can concentrate on and build on year by year.

Another step toward a good self-concept is to begin some of these activities:

1. Read about other disabled people who have learned to cope with their disabilities. If you read, you will learn that you are not alone with your disability. You don't have to be living in a city with ten other kids who have epilepsy or fifteen kids who are blind. Look on page 270 for a reading list of books about other kids with disabilities.

2. Meet some disabled adults in your area. Talk with them about how they cope. You don't have to act as if coping isn't a problem to some people; you can be sure it is for everyone. If you start talking about how you cope, you can depend on someone else's taking over the conversation and telling you how he pulled it off or is in the process of coping.

3. Join a group of disabled and nondisabled students to understand and cope better with common teenage and student problems.

4. Improve your daily living skills. Reduce your dependency as much as you can.

5. Get in on school activities. Really try, even though other kids act as if they don't want you there. Give them a chance to learn about your abilities, to see beyond your disabilities.

6. Volunteer your time at an agency for disabled children or at your church. Find a group that needs your time and abilities. Keep looking. Be persistent; there *will* be one!

7. Tutor your friends who need your help with their studying and homework.

8. Meet adults in your community who are in advocacy (support) groups for the physically disabled. Help them work actively to get rid of handicapism.

9. Join a group of students with disabilities or parents and teachers to work on community problems for the disabled.

You have a physical disability. You are physically different. You can choose to deal with the difficulties your disability brings to you. You can choose not to let the world handicap you because of your disability. You can choose to cope. You can accept the fact that you have the same emotional, social, and psychological needs as nondisabled people. You can accept the fact that a disability in *no way* displaces your need for love, respect, productivity, and independence.

II / Specific Physical Disabilities

4 | Visual

"The first year I was mainstreamed and walked alone in the halls of our school . . . I found that whenever I had to pass three or four students together, if I happened to be alone, they would whisper about me; . . . sometimes they laughed at me, calling me names and cracking jokes. This was something I didn't know how to handle, and it seemed as if I couldn't bear it. . . . It was in school that I started to learn what the sighted world thinks of people who are blind. Besides being blind, people think I'm deaf. Like they shout at me or speak to my friend as if he were my interpreter, instead of speaking directly to me. People act as if I have a 'sixth sense' or unusual smelling, hearing, and feeling senses."

Gary McArthur, eighth grade

It's really hard to live under the blind man's stereotype because it isn't you. You aren't like all the other blind men, besides that, half of you are blind women! One way out of the box or stereotype is to know as much as you can about your own blindness and to let people know where you are, what you can see and what you can't see, and what that means to you and to them. Blinded at birth, Alice found out that lots of people didn't even realize she was blind:

"I was a super oddball bookworm. Some people thought I was snobbish until they realized I couldn't see because I didn't wave to them across the street. I didn't even know they were waving to me. When they smiled at me, I didn't smile back. Once they realized that I couldn't see, they started saying hello. Others just avoided me altogether because they didn't know quite what to do or say."

Teenagers don't like to appear different from their friends. Yet blindness does not exactly allow you to blend in with the crowd if you use a cane or a guide dog, or require special assistance from the teacher, or use adapted aids or equipment. Some of you have been to special schools for the blind. Some of you have been overprotected by your parents and teachers, and they don't always tell you how you look compared to the other kids in your class. Find out how you come off: in looks, hair, eating, dressing. Ask a trusted friend to help you with understanding how you look.

Teenagers who can see how they look, worry about it, so it's not surprising that you would worry about your looks even more. Of course, you have to be dependent and protected in some areas in your life, but you certainly can be independent in others, and finding out from your friends how you look is one way to take the responsibility for your clothes, hair, and style.

Coming off blind or coming off different from other kids in your class is sometimes even more difficult for you if you have borderline low vision. While you are not blind, you are not sighted either. It's hard for you to try to meet the school standards of a sighted person without the aids you really need. Your classmates may tease you about the aids that would make your work easier for you. For example, many of you need telescopic spectacles, which look like jeweler's lenses mounted on the frames of glasses. Or hand-held and table model magnifiers, optical enlargers which project printed matter into a built-in viewing screen, or glare shields, which reduce the glare from white paper, may be necessary in class. You may need large-type textbooks and reference books. When you think how kids tease someone for just wearing glasses, it may seem outrageous to ask you to use these aids in school. One thing you have to do is to decide. You have to make a conscious decision to use aids because you can get along without the aids. One thing you can be sure of: If *you* act as if it's awful to use a text with large print while everyone else has a regular book, your classmates will think it's awful, too. If you decide that you want all the help you can get in the seeing department and go with telescopic lenses or whatever, and you act as if that's a perfectly logical thing for you to do, then it will be easier to deal with the other kids. They will get their clues to how to treat you by how *you* treat yourself! Easier said than done, of course.

How Blind Is Blind?

How bad does your vision have to be before you are blind? How do you know if you are blind anyway? You are "legally blind" if the vision in your better eye is 20/200 or less or if your visual field subtends an angle no greater than 20 degrees. In other words, a legally blind person can see less (even with glasses) at a distance of 20 feet than a person with normal vision can see at 200 feet or has a field of vision that is limited to a narrow angle. Although most people don't know it, the legally blind person is likely to have some vision with a certain degree of light perception and motion perception; a very small number of people are totally blind.

Limited vision, also called subnormal vision or partial sightedness, has been defined as visual acuity ranging from 20/70 to 20/200 with glasses. But that doesn't mean much. For example, Sally and Pete have very similar levels of visual acuity, and they can actually differ in how useful their vision is—that is, they may differ in visual efficiency. Sally may be able to read regular printed matter by holding reading material close to her eyes, Pete may require a powerful magnifier, and still another person may use large-print materials or braille. A certain environmental condition such as lighting might aid Sally to see fairly well, while that same degree of lighting might be detrimental to Peter. So the term "limited vision" doesn't tell us much. It does tell us that a person's vision cannot be fully corrected with glasses. It does not tell us the extent to which that person is disabled.

In most school and work situations, the senses of touch and hearing and the use of technical aids permit many of you to function so successfully that your blindness is not a handicap. You can take notes while studying or attending classes or meetings, or you can use the tape recorder, braille stylus and slate, braillewriter, or memory.

Because senses other than vision can be successfully used in learning, because you can get curriculum materials and special devices for high school work, because it's quite easy for blind kids to be in school, it is not surprising that blind students are able to do very well in schoolwork and go into almost any career. In other words, your academic work is unlimited. Merilyn, a Harvard Law School student, is an example. From New Jersey she attended public school and now lives in a dormitory room which she calls "equipment city." Blind from birth, Merilyn says that the number and size of lawbooks are impossible to order in braille, so she has her 900-page legal tomes dictated on minute grooves of magnetic ribbon. The tapes are borrowed from Recording for the Blind. She also uses volunteer readers, braille, for her eight to ten hours a day of homework. Not only is she an example of a student who can get to the top in school, but she is also an example of a woman who has accepted her blindness and uses every technical assistance she can get to achieve her goals.

Most of you can get all the brailled materials, records, cassettes, and tapes you need from national and local libraries and service agencies. Other materials can be forwarded to these agencies for braille transcription and recording. When there isn't time to transcribe materials, many students use sighted readers.

Other devices which provide for independence in daily living, school, and career are: signature guides; technical instruments, such as carpenters' levels, micrometers, calipers, and protractors with brailled or notched markings or electronic sound feedback devices; the Stereotoner, which transforms letters into tone patterns; the Optacon, which transforms printed words into tactile images that can be felt with the fingertips; and the braille computer terminal.

Getting Around

Many of you will feel the way Chet Avery felt when he lost his sight at sixteen and first returned home from the rehab center at nineteen:

> "When I went home, I really needed to be connected to the world. I went out with my cane every single night and practiced walking on the street. I went up the middle of the road, waving my cane all over the place, stumbling up and down the curbs, bumping into people, scraping my shinbones, and falling on my face, but I had a terrific drive to be connected with the world."

He *did* get very connected with the world. As mentioned earlier, he is now in Washington directing the Office of Handicapped Concerns for the United States Office of Education.

Getting around on your own makes you feel good. Don't let overprotective adults talk you into needing a sighted guide every time you change classes or take public transportation. Take your time getting experience moving around, but always be thinking how you can do it on your own, rather than how you can get someone to go with you. Get someone to teach you how to take buses and taxis for places you go to all the time. Get an orientation of your school, and take the guides' help while they teach you where everything is, but make it clear that you are working on getting around on your own.

Visual 35

Helping Your Teachers

A lot of teachers will not have had many students who are blind in their class before. Most teachers will know very little about your special needs. One of the ways you can help your teacher teach you is to clue him or her in on your visual needs. You can give your teachers references in which they can learn more about materials they can use with you in their classroom. If you assume that they know almost nothing (except stereotypes, which are no help to you), then you will be best off. Be very clear on ways they can reach you and make you feel as if you're in an environment where you can learn. Here is a list of things they may not be aware of; if you would be more comfortable giving them something to read, just hand your teachers this book.

1. Ask your teachers always to call you by name before they start talking to you, so that you will be ready to listen.
2. Make sure your teachers are aware of your body position when they are giving you directions so that you are sure of "left" and "right."
3. If you are partially sighted, ask them to have your seat as close to the natural light as possible and to notice lighting and shadows on your desk.
4. Ask the teachers to let you move around the room as you need to in order to see demonstrations, the blackboard, and films.
5. If you need rest periods, be sure the teachers are clear about how much time you need before you get exhausted and can't see a thing.
6. Suggest the teachers use records and tapes as much as possible, repeat aloud what is written on the board, and spell new technical words.
7. Ask the teachers to let you be free about using special aids and devices and recording equipment in the classroom. You may need an easel or special reading table or stand for the braille and large-print materials. Be sure

your teachers are aware of the hassle you sometimes get from the other kids when you use these aids.

8. Ask the teachers for help in getting good note-taking skills. Even though you use a recorder, note taking is an essential skill for a student.

9. If the teachers change the classroom or laboratory, make it clear that you need to be told about any and *all* changes in furniture and equipment. Also ask to be told when something that isn't usually there is in the aisles.

10. Ask your teachers to help you organize your work area, especially in a lab course, where you may need a drawer or box for small hand tools or equipment.

11. Ask the teachers to give you plenty of time to touch all the equipment being described.

12. Tell your teachers that the main resource for educational materials in large type, braille, and records is: The American Printing House for the Blind, P.O. Box 6085, 1839 Frankfort Avenue, Louisville, Kentucky 40206. Your teachers can send for a free list of publications and instructional aids for the blind in the classroom.

13. Make sure your teachers know that the reading rates for braille and large print are slower than those for regular print. They should be aware that in high school, blind students read an average rate of about 65 to 75 words per minute in braille, compared to 250 words per minute for sighted students, so the regular assignment takes you a lot longer! *You* aren't slow, but the system which you can read is. I'd be sure the teachers know that (just before assignments are given). Large print is a little faster, and recordings made for the blind are read at about 175 words per minute.

Read page 242 for more materials about blindness.

5 | Hearing

"I am hard-of-hearing. It took me a long time to accept that fact. I have just as much chance of changing it as going on a trip through the Milky Way in a spaceship ... or so I tell myself. From time to time I start dreaming and think that maybe the same technology that did send men to the moon can repair the damage to my auditory nerves because being hard-of-hearing is not much fun. I dream that they will find a way to make sounds clear and understandable, so I won't have to try so hard and still miss so much.

"The biggest problem is that of friendships. Poor communication (for whatever reasons) places strains on human relationships. Whether lack of understanding results from closed minds or closed ears, it causes trouble. The result is unsatisfying relationships, poor working climates, and unhappy people.

"The effects of deafness are both subtle and deep. Since there is no outward indication of a hearing loss, one is generally unaware that the condition exists, and when a person does have contact with someone who has the handicap, it is difficult to understand concretely the effect of not being able to hear has on the individual's functioning. Often people say to me after I tell them I am hard-of-hearing that it does not seem to affect me. But they make their comment just on the basis of their experience of talking with me individually; they don't realize that there is more to the exchange of ideas than two people talking. It also includes using the phone, sitting around a table in the coffee shop, watching TV or a movie, going to a lecture, or listening to the radio. I miss out to some extent on all these.

"Often people I'm with turn their backs on me while talking or commit another no-no for lip-readers, like talking with pipes in their mouths and placing their hands against their jaws or lips while continuing to talk. But there is one group of people who don't do these things; they are the hard-of-hearing and deaf. If the hearing-impaired talk to each other, we make sure that all understand. We have lived through common experiences of loneliness in a crowd, as well as the frustration of misunderstanding, and are therefore bound together in a search for comfort and escape from stress. We simply and beautifully understand. The acceptance and companionship I find are wonderful. In working with people, they will have to know how to deal with me, and I must tell them. That is not easy to do as it requires me to reveal myself to others and, even more frightening . . . to myself."

Bob Bourke, a college student

How Deaf Is Deaf?

A deaf person is so hard-of-hearing that she or he must rely on vision for communication. How you communicate will depend on when you become deaf. If it was at birth or before learning language and speech, of course, it's very hard to learn to communicate both by speaking and by writing. It's also hard to understand others when they write and speak. For those of you who already learned to speak and write, you will have an edge on your deaf classmates because you have some basic ideas about sound and language. Joanne, hard-of-hearing since birth, was mainstreamed in ninth grade. Before that she went to a school for the deaf. She describes how it was better for her because she had some hearing:

> "My old school put too much stress on speech and language development. Other academic courses, like history and geography, were emphasized only enough to make the school look good. I was a prize pupil there because I was able to speak more clearly than most students. Visitors to the school were brought into my class and were impressed by the kids who could hear somewhat. The really deaf kids were completely ignored. . . . I felt very close to two teachers who were sensitive to the needs of the kids. They both had deaf relatives and could communicate easily with me."

A person who is hard-of-hearing (the condition is sometimes called partial hearing loss) varies so much in what he or she can hear that it's hard to describe what it's like. Wally has difficulty hearing faint speech or sounds from a distance, and he has almost no problems in oral and written communication. Marie, also called hard-of-hearing, has a severe hearing loss; she has problems in understanding speech, even with a hearing aid, and has difficulty in articulation. Sometimes the problem may involve a loss of sensitivity of hearing, the person can hear sound only if it is of a certain loudness or pitch, and some people can't hear because of a loss of ability to tell the difference between certain sounds.

Not Quite Deaf

The deaf student often becomes isolated, and the marginal status student (not quite deaf) is often put in the wrong group or not diagnosed for years. Many parents and teachers are not aware of your hearing loss, or if they are, they don't understand its implications. They set up unrealistic high expectations for your education. On the other hand, some of your parents and teachers will have exaggereated your hearing differences so much that they will underestimate what you can do. They may put you into a much lower class than you can handle or into a special education group when you could be in with the hearing just as well.

Joanne felt that she wasted her time in school because the teachers treated everybody alike:

> "I spent the first ten years at school feeling frustrated about the education I was receiving. I was always ahead of the other deaf children because of my being severely hard-of-hearing instead of completely deaf, but I was held back because the teachers made no distinction between my disability and that of other deaf kids. Consequently I lost a lot of valuable time in school."

Besides other people's expectations of you, they often don't have a good idea of what the conditions are when you can hear and when you cannot hear. Many people are sure to think you are faking it half the time when you don't respond, as all parents think about their children when they don't come back with a response as fast as they expect them to. Often, when you are tired from listening, your behavior is taken as disobedience, whereas it's really just plain irritation from being worn out.

It's bad enough to be deaf, but many people think that deaf people are retarded. They think that you lack intelligence because of your speech and language difficulties. Many people are not aware that when you were a child, you were not able to hear the language you are expected to speak. You will want to let others know that research shows that people who are deaf have the same intelligence, manual dexterity, and motor skills that everyone else in the population has. That means that some of you will have a lot of everything and some of you will have less. Just like the rest of the world.

Getting Through

Both the deaf student and the hard-of-hearing use speaking, written language, some form of sign language, or a combination of the oral and manual communication systems developed for the deaf to get through to others.

For those of you who use the oral method, which stresses the development of speech, you know how tough it was to learn the use of lipreading (speechreading) and writing—especially if you were deaf from birth or before you remember hearing language. It may seem to others that lipreading wouldn't be too bad to learn until the rest of us realize that only 30 percent of spoken English is visible on the lips and about 50 percent of English sounds look alike on the lips! Some of you do learn to speak, but as you know, along with how hard it is to say, it's also hard to be understood. The person not used to hearing you speak is put off by hearing something unusual, making it even more difficult for them to understand because they are anxious and can't listen in a clear way.

Most of you probably use some kind of hand communication, including sign language, finger spelling, and Seeing Essential English (SEE). Those of you with a hearing loss may not have yet looked into alternative ways of getting through to others. Here are some of the things you should know about different ways to communicate: Sign language is not based on the structure and grammar of English but rather is concept-based. Where the sign is placed is important in sign language. In other words, the same gesture may have a different meaning depending on where it is located in relationship to your body. There are idioms in sign, as there are in any language. Verbs, tenses, adjectives, and articles used in English are not always used in signing; for example, "I feel," "I felt," and "I have felt" may be expressed by using the same sign. So a person who is really good in sign language may still have trouble with grammar in spoken and written English and on tests in school, for example.

Finger spelling is different from sign language because it is a system of hand signs which represent all twenty-six letters of the alphabet. The English word is spelled out by the use of these motions. Finger spelling is usually used along with signing, especially to express names, places, and technical words for which there are no signs.

Some of you will have been taught Seeing Essential English (SEE). For those of you who don't know this system, SEE involves signs which correspond to the phonetics of English words. Certain signs which indicate such factors as tense, plurals, and person are used.

Another sign system is siglish. It is actually English in which the student uses the signs of sign language but puts them together according to the rules of English grammar and proper English structure.

Using a combination of communication systems is sometimes called total communication. It's an approach which teaches students to use a number of different systems, both oral and manual—speaking, writing, signing, finger spelling, and lipreading in combinations which are most comfortable for them. You use whichever combination works best for you as you try to get through to others.

Getting Through in the Classroom

The system you use will depend a lot on your educational background and the philosophy of the school or place that first taught you to communicate, the extent of deafness you have, the age of your hearing loss, your personal preferences, the achievements you have made, and the skills you have developed. Most of you who are deaf do use manual forms of communication, and most of you and your teachers have learned that lipreading is a hard way to go.

For the student who is hard-of-hearing, the classroom situation varies according to the age at which hearing was lost and the severity of the loss when language was learned. It depends a lot on the extent to which the use of a hearing aid corrects the loss. If the hearing aid is right for the type of hearing loss, and you have had training in how to use it, some of you can do very well with it. However, most of us without a hearing loss don't realize that not all people with a hearing loss can benefit from the use of a hearing aid. A hearing aid seems like such a natural way to solve the problem that many teenagers end up with hearing aids, even though the problem they have isn't helped that much by them. The professional thinks she or he has solved your problem, but you may still have it! Another problem for students with a loss of hearing is that they haven't all been trained to use the hearing that they do have. Special training can help you identify and recognize speech and nonverbal sounds and distinguish among sounds better. And your classroom work also depends on your lipreading ability, but as you well know, at best it's a hard way to learn.

The Teacher Can Help

Because catching on to what is going on in the classroom is tough, you will want all the advantages you can get. If you lip-read, be sure that you sit near the front of the class and that the lighting is good. You can explain to your teacher that he should speak normally and not exaggerate his lip movements and should face the class, and ask him to write new words and technical words on the blackboard.

Some of you will have an interpreter in the classroom who will relay statements through manual communication. You can make it clear that it's important for you to have the interpreter stand near the teacher so that you can see both of them at the same time. If you are really assertive, ask the interpreter to get new technical words from the teacher before the class, so you'll know what's coming with new signs for new words.

Your speech may be very difficult to understand, especially if the teacher has never heard you or other students who are deaf speak before and especially if she has had no experience communicating with deaf students in general. On top of your speech being difficult to get, the anxiety of listening to speech which one can't understand makes the teacher embarrassed and even harder for her to understand you. Of course, it's not just teachers who need to hear and understand what you have to say, but school is a place where you have a lot to gain and a lot to lose by not being understood. Edna S. Levine has written books about deaf students, and she suggests that you write a note to your teacher and ask him to just listen to you read without interrupting you so that he can get a chance to become used to your particular tones and rhythm of your speech. Better yet, tell the teacher what you are going to read, something he knows, like the national anthem or the Lord's Prayer, or read aloud a book that you use in school, something the teacher knows very well. Having a known verbal text to refer to helps the teacher synchronize the sounds heard with the words they stand for. During this time the teacher does not have to strain for exact understanding but should rather open his ears to your general speech pattern until it finally sets into something recognized.

You must make it clear to your teacher or have a special education teacher in your school explain that the construction of sign language is not the same as the construction of the English language. If you mainly use sign language, your teacher cannot expect you to use the grammar and structure of English. It will be important for the teacher to know this, so he doesn't think that you lack intelligence because you sign, "Movie yesterday go," while he is used to nondeaf students saying, "I went to the movies yesterday."

If you use lipreading in class and your teacher isn't getting through to you, ask her to use another word or phrase rather than to keep repeating the one causing the difficulty. If things get too bad, go ahead and write a note. The writing of simple messages can be an effective way to get over a misunderstanding and back on to known territory.

Some Complications

Most of what you know is learned not in the formal school setting, but informally through daily communication with your parents, family, and friends and through the media. If you were deaf when you were born, or became deaf soon after, you lost out on the benefit of these very basic sources of information about your world. Lacking hearing, the tool for monitoring your own speech and the speech of others, you could not spontaneously learn the language used in the hearing world around you. Reading skills may provide a visual tool for gaining information about your environment, but the development of your reading skills is often delayed because of the difficulties involved in learning the basics of reading your language.

If you were born into a family that uses sign language, you are lucky because you were provided with a way to exchange with your parents and brothers and sisters the information and feelings that the nondeaf express verbally. But most of you have been brought up in families that did not have sign language skills and, even worse, may not have wanted to learn a manual communication alternative because they didn't want to admit that their families were "different." The result of your family's not finding an alternative to speaking and of too little emphasis on helping you express yourself is that it's easy for you to become isolated. Without the skills for making known your understanding, reaction, and emotions about what is happening around you, you stand alone. If your parents are overprotecting and overpermissive, if they deny your disability, and if you feel isolated from everyday knowledge of things, then you really have problems getting through to others and having others get through to you! This means that by the time you are in high school you have missed out on ordinary questions about sex and friends and what to do when, how to look when, or what to say when. Here you are a great big kid. Everyone else seems to *know* these things you missed out on. How can you—as a teenager—ever ask these crucial questions??

A Way Out

Whether you need a way out of isolation or out of unrealistic or false expectations, you'll find it best through a friend, someone you trust. It doesn't have to be a friend of your own age;

the main part is to have it be a person you trust, someone you can sit down with, take your time with, write a note to if that's the best way to get through on a sensitive subject, someone who will listen while you say, "Here I am, I know this and this and that, and I can't believe it; but I don't know this and this and that. And what bothers me most is that I have missed out on so much stuff the other kids know I don't even know where to start to ask what it is I want to know. Things I missed hearing, or I heard wrong, or I heard, but that didn't make any sense. Now tell me, what's the story about . . . ? What have I missed in . . . ?" Maybe you could get a volunteer college student to help you fill in the gaps you are concerned about. Whoever it is, don't try to catch up on fifteen or seventeen years of missing out in a couple of hours. It will be tiring! Take an hour's session or so at a time. Have fun with it. Try not to worry about what you've missed; you are going in exactly the right direction now to catch up. It could be something as ordinary as what the World Series is really about, and who is in which league, or the origin of Easter or Yom Kippur, or as complex as teenage sexuality. For the sexuality part, you can start with the chapter and references in this book. Read them together with your friend. They will be a good springboard for your further questions and discussions. Friends won't judge you on what you don't know. They will feel terrific for being able to be trusted by you and for helping you on the crucial road to tuning in.

Helping Your Teachers

You aren't the only one who needs help. Your teachers are going to need lots of help since passage of the new law that students with disabilities be educated with nondisabled students as much as possible. Most of your teachers will know very little about your special needs. One of the ways you can be helpful to your teachers is to clue them in on exactly what your hearing needs for a regular classroom are. One thing you can be sure they know: the stereotype of deaf students. Assume that they know almost nothing else. You can be very clear on ways they can reach you and create an environment which will be best for you to learn. If you would be more comfortable giving them something to read rather than trying to say or sign it, just hand your teachers this book with these pages marked for them. Here is a list of things they may not be aware of:

1. A specific report on exactly what your hearing loss means to teachers and the way they teach their classes. For example, a report stating that you have a hearing loss of so many decibels in a certain frequency range will be of almost no help to most teachers. To be meaningful, a report from your doctor and speech therapist must present diagnostic information that describes the *classroom* implications of your hearing loss.

2. Ask your teachers to ask the best note takers in class to make carbon copies of their classroom notes for you.

3. If you are lip-reading, ask your teachers:
   - To provide good lighting.
   - To allow you to sit close to the front of the room.
   - Not to walk around the room and turn their backs to you.
   - To spell new words on the blackboard.
   - Not to lecture while writing on the blackboard.
   - To verbalize instructions, when demonstrating the use of equipment, before undertaking the demonstration, because you cannot watch the instructors' faces and the demonstrations at the same time.
   - To avoid smoking or covering their mouths.
   - Not to speak rapidly, exaggerate enunciation, or shout.

4. If you have an interpreter in the classroom, it will work best if, when technical vocabulary is used, the teachers confer with the interpreter before the semester begins and provide him or her with a list of technical words. This will prepare the interpreter to finger-spell the words for which there are no signs or to learn or develop signs for the words.

   Interpreters should stand close to teachers so that you

can pick up the teachers' facial expressions and gestures. It is helpful for teachers to pause briefly after using new words or proper nouns, so that interpreters can finger-spell them. Teachers should verbally explain a procedure before demonstrating it.

The use of interpreters should not be limited to the classroom. If you are to be integrated as fully as possible into all school activities, they should be available for field trips, assembly programs, and certain aspects of work experience activities, such as job interviews and first-day-at-work orientation sessions.

5. The same equipment used by nonhearing students can be modified:
   - A red light installed next to the switch indicating when the machine is in operation.
   - Bells connected to a light that turns on when the bell rings—this adaptation is applicable to typewriters, class bells, timers, fire alarms, and emergency stop procedures.
   - A teletype machine serves as an intermediary for telephone communication in Connecticut. Call (203) 236-6266 for more information.

6. For some of you, the following classroom procedures would help. If these apply to you, ask your teachers to:
   - Close windows when there is loud traffic outside or close classroom doors when there is noise in the hall.
   - Use visual aids (charts, overhead transparencies, slides, captioned films) to reinforce basic concepts in their teaching.
   - Emphasize demonstrations and hands-on experiences rather than verbal explanations, especially in laboratory courses.
   - Keep required bookwork in laboratory courses, such as art, home economics, and industrial education, to a minimum. Begin with concrete examples. Work from the concrete to the abstract.
   - Prepare glossaries of technical terms essential for the

mastery of a particular course; definitions should be written at a reading level suitable for you.

- Consider reading level when selecting instructional materials.
- Develop some simple signs with you. This helps communication in courses such as art, home economics, and industrial education, for which the services of a full-time interpreter are not available and may not be considered necessary.
- Give you an outline of the lesson before the class or write it on the board at the beginning of the class; this will help you follow the classwork.
- Give you a script when a cassette tape or record is used in class.

See page 243 for more materials about loss of hearing.

6 | Diabetes

What your teachers should know is that diabetic coma, a serious complication resulting from uncontrolled diabetes, does not come on suddenly and should not be a major concern of the school. What should be a major concern of your teachers is that they be informed that you have diabetes and that they understand the fundamentals of the disease and its care, especially as the care relates to you and your specific needs in school.

One of the hard things about having diabetes is that you don't *look* sick. And when you don't look sick, it's easy for others to deny that you are. One high school senior feels this way about it:

> "I have diabetes. I think one of the things that is the hardest about it for me is that I don't look sick, so the type of invalidation I get is: 'Wow, I never would have guessed it. You look so healthy!' I don't need to hear that. I'd like to talk about some of the things that get me down. One thing is not being able to eat sugar; you find out very quickly that about eighty percent of all prepared foods have sugar added to them; things, like beans, that you wouldn't expect to have sugar added have sugar. You

can't get life insurance. Life expectancies are not that much different for other people anymore, but you still can't get life insurance except at very high prices."

How to Explain It

When people ask, "What is diabetes anyway?" this may help: "A person's pancreas produces insulin. My pancreas doesn't produce enough insulin to use the sugar and starches I eat properly. The sugars and starches that I eat are not converted into energy or stored for future use, as they are in you, if you are nondiabetic. My major concern is to maintain a balance among diet, insulin, and exercise. I supplement my body insulin with injections of insulin and by following a prescribed diet and a regular routine of daily activity. In that way I control the condition so that sugars and starches taken into my body will be properly used." I know, it seems like a simple minded explanation to you. But the people who aren't even used to the words "diabetes" and "insulin" and aren't that tuned in to health things need a simple explanation.

Where Are Your Limits?

For most of you, if you follow your diet, take insulin, and regulate your exercise, you can do anything in school that nondiabetic students can do. Kids with diabetes play sports—as long as they have eaten and slept enough and don't suddenly overdo. In other words, you have to keep in shape—even more than other athletes. The problem for teenagers usually isn't that they can or cannot do certain activities. You may feel out of it because you have to make sure you get enough sleep, take insulin, regulate your activity, and avoid foods that your friends are eating. For some of you, this attention to diet and sleep comes off as making you different in a way that you don't want to be different. So it's your choice. You can be in control of your health with no limits on your activities, or you can act like the other kids—eat junk food, not sleep enough—and pay the price of cutting down on your sports or activities. The nondiabetic can get away with lousy food and sleeping habits while they are teenagers, but you really can't.

What Are Your Future Limits?

When you are thinking about your career plans, here's what the American Diabetes Association has to say: People with diabetes who can be treated with diet alone, or with diet and an oral blood-sugar-lowering agent, have no employment restrictions and can pursue both hazardous and nonhazardous jobs. One exception is that people requiring oral agents cannot be commercial pilots. People who do require diet and insulin should not pursue potentially hazardous jobs such as working on scaffolding or near heavy moving machinery, nor will they qualify for driving commercial vehicles engaged in interstate or foreign commerce. People with diabetes *are* capable of performing heavy manual labor. Jobs with erratic working hours are best avoided. Where there is some doubt about the advisability of a certain school activity or career goal, you should consult with your doctor.

Helping Your Teachers

Most of your teachers will know very little about your special needs as a student with diabetes. One way you can help them is to clue them in on exactly what your special needs are. Knowing will help your teachers get rid of the stereotypes they have of people with diabetes (and even teachers act on stereotypes). The more information they have about you, the more easily they can create a classroom environment in which you can best learn. If you feel that your teachers would like to learn more about diabetes from a book, then just hand them this book, and show these pages.

1. Your teachers should know that if you undertake more strenuous activity than is usual, haven't eaten enough, or have an imbalance of insulin, the amount of sugar in your blood may become too low, and an insulin reaction may begin to develop. The symptoms may be light-headedness, faintness, hunger, trembling, sweating, blurred vision, tingling sensation, irritability, confusion, mood change without apparent cause, drowsiness, headache, nausea, or loss of consciousness. School personnel should be alert to the warning signs of such reactions, and ideally you will be encouraged by the school to recognize and report them. The information card prepared by the Diabetes Association of Greater Chicago, "What School Personnel Should Know About the Student with Diabetes," says that at the first indication of any warning signs, the following treatment should be administered:

   "Give sugar immediately in one of the following forms:
   a. Sugar—five small cubes, two packets, or two teaspoons.
   b. Fruit juice—one-half to two-thirds cup.
   c. Carbonated beverage (not diet or sugarless pop)—six ounces.
   d. Candy—one-fourth to one-third candy bar. The student experiencing a reaction may need coaxing to eat. If improvement does not occur within fifteen to twenty minutes, repeat the feeding. If the child does not improve after administration of the second feeding containing the sugar, the parents or physician should be called. When the child improves, he or she should be given a small feeding of half a sandwich and a glass of milk. He should then resume normal school activities, and the parents should be advised of the incident."

2. The school nurse should provide a private place where you can administer your injections and a refrigerator to store the insulin. Ask your school nurse to give each of your teachers a copy of the information card above.

3. Scheduling in school should be worked out according to your daily routine; for example, it is best not to schedule physical education just before lunch or to be assigned a late lunch.

See page 244 for more materials about diabetes.

7 | Muscular Dystrophy

You may have one of the muscular dystrophy types of disease which started when you were under six or which has just started. Being in school can be quite different for you from what it is for other teens who have muscular dystrophy, depending on how severe it is right now and how you have learned to cope with the idea of having it. Your condition may be progressing rapidly or slowly, or you may not know your exact condition because you haven't discussed it with your parents or your doctor.

Some of you will have very minimal disability right now, and others will have severe disability. As time goes on, you may not be able to count on your body. What you *can* count on is your mind. Mental deficiency is not a part of the muscular dystrophy condition. Even though your physical condition is ever-changing, whether it is slow or fast, you can always count on a growing mind and a career that uses your head.

Physical Dependence

One of your current problems, while you are still in school and not yet at work, is being as physically independent as you are able to be. Just getting to school is usually a hassle. A tenth grader says:

"No matter how many times I have been picked up for school by a special driver, my head whirls with: Will I get in the van O.K.? Will I get dropped? Will I get to school early enough? Will I be let off at the right door? Will someone be there to open the door? Will the snow make the ramp too slippery? Can I carry all my books and lunch without dropping them? Will anyone speak to me?"

When your teachers hear that you have muscular dystrophy, they may want to do everything possible *for* you rather than let you do it yourself. As discouraging as some days and some situations are, you know that it feels good to do as much as you can for yourself. Ask for and get all the adapted aids that you can get, including a "grabber," a long, wooden, scissors-shaped device with a magnet on the end for picking things up. If there is a local chapter of the Muscular Dystrophy Association in your city, go there to find out what aids it has especially for teenagers in school. Ask the people there what will happen next, so you can be thinking about how you will handle more disability at a later time. If you can see things coming, it will help you cope with them when they actually get to you. If there isn't a chapter in your city, write to your state chapter or to the Muscular Dystrophy Association for the aids it has for teenagers in school. Don't wait for your parents and teachers or therapist to suggest everything; take the initiative yourself. They may not be sure how much you really want to help yourself.

If you are a student who has little physical independence, you can make it clear that even though you can't do physical things on your own, you can still make decisions on your own. Don't let everyone else decide for you what courses you can take or what you are going to read or see. You can develop your decision-making skills as one of the skills you are good at regardless of the state of your physical condition.

Career Possibilities

Concentrate on careers that will permit you to depend on your *mind* because you can be sure of it. Taking business and business management courses, in order to have a business of your own, is one way that students with disabilities have found workable careers. Your own business can permit you to put in the kinds of hours you are able to work and can allow you to adapt everything in the business to what you can physically do and need. Be sure to get the business courses that are necessary while you are still in school. If business doesn't interest you, then, of course, you shouldn't consider it a good place to be regardless of the opportunity. Look at all your career possibilities with your particular disease and its consequences for change as you decide where you want to go. If you are still in high school and planning to go to college, you don't have to worry about what career you'll end up in. What you have to think about now is how well you can do in high school subjects. Get an understanding of what you like and how well you can learn. Read "Charting Your Course" (special section) and "Educational and Career Decisions, Strategies, and Goals" (Chapter 18) in this book for some ideas about how to plan your education.

While you are still in school, try to learn as many recreational skills as you can. The more interests you have now, the more resources you will have to draw on when you're out of school. Play sports as much as you can, but also get into recreational interests that don't demand physical fitness, so that you can keep up your games, cards, or music listening even when your physical condition is regressing.

Helping Your Teachers

The main thing to keep in mind as you work out educational and career decisions with your teachers and counselors is to try to get them to see you now as a teenager with the same needs of independence that all teens have. Bill, a high school senior, finds this a hard thing to do. He says:

"I think the biggest problem is not being seen for myself but for my handicap. And then having teachers and other people think things you do are wonderful when, in fact, they have nothing to do with your handicap at all and are things that everyone else does as a matter of course."

Even though you may not be as physically independent as the other kids, you still have the independence needs of all kids. You are often thinking about being with your friends, about sex, about times away from your parents, about what you can do to make money. Talking about these issues can be a help. Be straightforward with the people at school as you express where you are and what you expect from them in getting what you want. The more clearly you know what you want, the more likely others can help you get it.

See page 244 for more information about muscular dystrophy.

8 | Cerebral Palsy

Cerebral palsy is so many things to so many people, including both the disabled and the nondisabled, that it's hard to know where to begin. Every time you ask professionals about it or to describe it, they say it's not uniform, and it varies so much that they can't describe it! We can say that cerebral palsy is a neuro-muscular disease that may range in degree of severity from affecting only one limb to rendering all four extremities as well as neck and back muscles nonfunctional so that the person has to use a wheelchair. Everyone will agree that a lack of motor control is caused by an insufficient supply of oxygen to the brain usually at or near birth. That lack of motor control can also come out as facial grimacing and drooling, difficulty in fine skilled movements of the hand, and problems in chewing and speech articulation. Besides that, many of you will have visual and hearing disabilities, and seizures are often present. If you are in school, some of you will know that you have perceptual disorders, mental retardation, or behavior disorders that complicate your lack of motor skills. Your physical condition can be described by five major factors: the type of disordered move-ment (for example, spasticity, dyskinesia); the parts of the body that are involved (for example, one half of the body or one limb); the degree of severity; the state of muscle tone; and associate dysfunctions which are present, such as sensory (vision, hearing, smell), convulsive, intellectual, perceptual, learning, and emotional.

Chances are that if you are mainstreamed, or in a combination of having special teachers and being mainstreamed, you have limitations in movement and speech articulation, but you do not have the associated disorders that would make school too much of a hassle to be there.

Helping Your Teachers

Your teachers should be able to get information about special typewriters you may need from the special education department at your school. Some of the other things that can make the classroom more acceptable for you is for your teachers to:

1. Give you a duplicate set of textbooks or other supplies, one to be stored in the classroom and the other kept at home.
2. Be familiar with the many special devices (oversized pencil or special pencil holder, easel to hold books, page turner for books, special typewriter plate) that can assist you to compensate for lack of manipulative ability.
3. Allow you to type tests, homework, and any extensive written work required during the class period.
4. Arrange note-taking services so that a classmate makes a carbon copy of classroom lecture notes for you.
5. Know, if you have hand problems, that it takes you longer to finish the task than it takes the other kids.
6. Give you a chance to demonstrate a procedure in lab courses. If you have to repeat it a couple of extra times, ask the teachers to remember that it takes you longer, but you'll get the point with a little extra practice.
7. Let you go early from class to give you enough time to get to your next class—especially when the halls are less crowded.

Take a Chance!

When you are in school, you wonder what your chances for coping are. School is important because it's your road to a career, whereby you can make money and live more independently than when you don't make money. The competition between you and other students may seem impossible. Winifred Strunk, a social worker at the Nassau BOCES Cerebral Palsy School in Roosevelt, New York, says that it's hard for cerebral-palsied youth to test the reality of their experiences. She says they have often been overprotected by their parents and schools. Many of you haven't had a chance to participate in activities that most kids are in, and you lack the opportunities to test out your friendship skills and explore new interests.

Strunk stresses that risk taking is an important part of life. She says that if you make yourself even more dependent on others than you need to be and if you need to be the center of attention, no one will want you around. She urges you to take a chance and try things on your own, even though the first few people aren't that enthusiastic about having you around. She wants you to take a chance and come out of your isolation—a chance for some excitement and happiness along with the rejections and hurt that everyone, especially teenagers, gets. In other words, as you peel away your layers of fear and anxiety about how others will treat you, you will find *both* pleasure and pain. But many people think the new pleasure is worth the pain that sometimes goes with it. One thing we all know when we are trying to bring about change: To get out more, be with people, test our skills with others to see what happens, we need friends—a support group, people to talk to about what's going on and how awful or how wonderful it was to talk to someone new today (even though you had to repeat yourself the first four times before she or he got it). The support group can be your family, one person in your family, a college student volunteer, another disabled teenager, or anyone you trust. But one thing is certain: Everyone in this world needs a friend to talk about the risks they are taking in their lives.

People who work in rehabilitation with cerebral-palsied youth say that unrealistic attitudes about school and career are a problem with them. And most often it's an unrealistic overestimation of the kinds of programs they can get through and jobs they can get. College guidance isn't that good. Many times teenagers with extremely limited hand use have graduated from accounting programs, for example, and can't find jobs. They lack—and always will lack—the necessary hand speed for the work. One way to check out your career plan is to ask your school counselor for the test scores, academic marks and evaluations, and personal skills that people have in a career that interests you, so that you can get an idea of where you stand. Pay attention to the information. Realize that if you are somewhere close, it would be a realistic choice. That doesn't mean you can select jobs only where other young people "just like you" have been before. But it does mean that if rehab people say that cerebral-palsied students usually overestimate their career possibilities, you should consider this fact in your planning.

Reality Testing

Summertime, your Christmas holiday, or a year off after high school is an ideal time for students to test in a work situation what they learned in the classroom. Students who are disabled are in a better place for future planning and for references in future job hunting if they have on-the-job experience. Read more about work experience in the educational goals chapter (Chapter 18) in this book.

Four Factors for Planning Your Career

The career future for cerebral-palsied teens is very dependent on four factors. The first is the use of hands and speech. Be sure to be assessed in a way that your hand use and speech are clearly defined for those guiding you in your career goals. In addition to evaluation and assessment, recognize that your skills and limitations may change. Physical and occupational therapies change and expand your skills and therefore widen your choices. As you gain academic skills and work experience, you may be motivated for further therapy. Added skills through therapy count a lot in your career possibilities.

Besides skills changing, you will want to be sure of the aids, equipment modifications, and procedural adaptations that are available to you for your hand and speech disabilities. You must consider not your disability alone, but your potential for therapy and aids. Therapy and aids can remove a lot of the handicapping barriers for you, and you will want to get all the help you can get to do that.

Your perceptual capacity is the next area of concern for career planning. When you are making career plans with counselors, be sure that they have an insight into your particular areas of perception from psychological test data which measure your ability to discriminate in terms of form, color, objects, pictures, likenesses, and differences. As you can understand, there is a direct relationship between your perception capacity and the tasks needed to be performed on a job.

And finally, your appearance is a major factor in career possibilities. Besides out-and-out discrimination against people who may walk differently from others, drool, have facial grimaces and involuntary movements is also the fear that these will upset your potential co-workers and customers. Your best assertive strategy in the case of your appearance is to be ready for it. When you interview for college admissions or part-time, summer, or holiday jobs, be sure to know how you come off to others (other than your family and schoolmates, who are used to being with you), so that you can expect the reaction you may get. In fact, the best strategy is for *you* to mention first whatever about your appearance sets others off-balance. Don't let it go unspoken. If you sense it's difficult for the other person, try to be straightforward about it. In many cases you will be the first young person with CP applying for a job, and what the employer understands about other disabled employees can be learned from you. If the job you are seeking is one you are qualified for, don't be apologetic about your condition. If the only difficulty in terms of employment is your appearance, then you have a civil right to that job. Be strong and confident about that right, and know that discrimination because of physical appearance is a discrimination that happens every day, from not hiring women who are the fastest typists in the world because they are fat to not hiring you because you drool. But because it's done every day doesn't mean people have a right to do it. The more you feel that you have a right to a job, the more confident you will come off in your interview that you should have it.

There are a few other factors that students with cerebral palsy have to consider in their educational and career planning. One is that they must be responsible for teaching others more about their disability. For example, a school or employer should know that your age is not a good indication of where you are, compared to a nondisabled student. Rehabilitation people have found that from the reference point of age, cerebral-palsied teenagers come off in school and with friends and family two or three years younger than other teenagers. Don't let them compare you on the basis of age.

Many of you spend a lot of time with professionals in the medical world. The difficulty with always being with a professional, a parent, or an adult is that you begin to think that everyone else is an expert. In other words, you are seldom with equals. After a long enough time of this you begin to believe that you are *not* an equal, and you let everyone else decide for you because professionals and parents have a way of acting as if they always know what's best. The point is that in spite of their good intentions, it's still important for you to take responsibility for your own development and growth. Experts can't accept your disability for you. You have to accept your own disability and learn to be responsible for what you are going to do about it.

Another factor to consider is your speech. When people are having trouble understanding what you are saying, try to repeat it a few times. If they still don't get it, say the same thing in different words. If things get too bad, spell it, or write it out.

When you're with your family or classmates who don't have a speech disability, don't let them always speak for you or interpret to others what you are trying to say. Ask the other person to be patient, and look for another way to get through.

See page 245 for more information.

9 | Spinal Cord Injuries

Everyone has losses in life. Some of us can even see some of these losses coming: death of a parent; loss of a love; divorce; breaking off of a love affair. But the loss of a healthy body has no warning in most traumatic spinal cord injuries. It's a *shock* —out of the blue. It's hard to take a shock like that, hard to cope, hard to adjust, hard to start all over again with another self-image that may have little to do with the one that was suddenly smashed in a car, sports, or work accident.

One thing that helps is to know that it takes time to get used to the idea of the injury and going through life with it. The best doctors, therapists, the most understanding parents and friends can't hurry along the healing process of your heart from such a loss.

It just seems unreal that one day you can be playing sports, talking about educational and career plans, thinking about your relationship with your boyfriend or girlfriend, and the next day you have to change all these plans because of your injury. Some of you may be paraplegics with a loss of movement and feeling in the lower part of your body and lower extremities. Others may be quadriplegics with a partial or total paralysis of all four extremities, and still others may have had a neck injury resulting in a loss of feeling and voluntary movement in everything below the injury. To go from a strong healthy person to the extreme dependency of a person who cannot walk, has no control of bowel and bladder, and relies upon the constant care of others is tough, especially for a teenager.

In her novel *On the Move* Harriet May Savitz describes how Bennie feels about this:

> He'd take care of himself. He didn't want to feel like a load of freight, delivered to someone else's living room. Paraplegics were used to that but it had always been an inside fear to him, ever since he had been shipped from the alley to a hospital, then shipped to the rehab center. He had watched fellow patients who didn't have anyone who cared shipped to homes for incurables, and others shipped themselves to workshop shelters as though they were lifeless, meaningless, worn-out machines on their way to the junkyard. Inside those bodies, lights were burning, bright lights called minds, but nobody around saw them. He wouldn't be shipped. He would take care of himself. . . . So now it was just he and the car. Bennie slid over behind the steering wheel, folded his wheelchair, and put it in the back seat of the car.
>
> He put on his gloves, turned the key, and let the car warm up.
>
> Where to Bennie, he asked himelf. How come you know so many people and you still don't know . . . where to?

Coping and Healing

One thing we know about these injuries is that at this time there is no way of repairing the damage to your spinal cord. Another thing we know on the positive side: Neither paraplegia nor quadriplegia causes any loss of intellectual functioning. In other words, your head is not going to give out on you. You can develop and grow in your thinking capacity in relation to how well you learn to cope with your accident.

How you get over your accident and start on the road to recovery—recovering your feelings of worth, coping with your disability, and figuring out where you go from here—depends a lot on how you coped with any problems and difficulties before you had your accident. It makes sense to realize that if you were a coper before, you will be now. If coping with change and things not going your way has always been tough for you, it will be now, too.

Even though you can cope in the long run, your short-term reaction will be similar to that of anyone who suffers a terrific loss. When you suffer a loss, the first reaction is shock. You just can't believe that the thing happened to *you*. After the shock there are three stages of recovery. The key word here is "recovery." Denial and disbelief are the first stage of recovery, and it can be a slow phase. Next after the denial come anger and depression and, finally, understanding and acceptance.

The degree of severity has nothing to do with the degree of denial or disbelief. What does the second stage feel like? It hurts! It feels painful. You feel depressed and sad. With this second stage come feelings of being helpless, fearful, empty, irritable, angry, guilty, and restless. In *On the Move*, Carrie expresses the second stage like this:

A sudden fear crept through her whole being. Give up. She knew the feeling. She had felt it at the top of the hill . . . when she had spilled into the mud. She had felt it now and then, like a pointing finger, even before, when happiness seemed all around her, but none for her and her alone.

Who am I? she used to ask the wallpaper when she lay in bed at night. Where am I? What will I be?

The questions had overwhelmed her then. And frightened her so that she crept back into the safe cocoon of family and friends. But family wouldn't be there forever. And friends would come and go. She, Carrie, would be there . . . always.

When you get to the anger and depression stage of healing, you will have a mourning or grief period in which all kinds of fears take over. You just can't get into physical and occupational therapy and expect good results until your grief time is over. It's good to know that this is all part of the healing process. Going through anger and depression and pain for the loss of your fit body and what that means to you is something you have to do. If you don't go through it now, you will later. Let your feelings take over. Be angry. Go with the pain. Don't act as if you "shouldn't" hurt with this new physical image you have to be working out. It does hurt, and on some days it seems impossible. On those days you figure you're the last one this injury should haved happened to. You are the last one who can handle it well.

The length of time in each stage and the intensity of the denial, anger, and acceptance are different for each person. With the loss or death of a spouse, for example, it may take a year of denial before anger sets in and two years of anger before understanding begins. With you, it may take a month or two for each of these things. You can't predict healing time. It helps to know that you *will* get better. In the nature of healing, there is a beginning, a middle, and an end. You will heal because nature is on your side. You will survive. And you will learn that it's OK to be a paraplegic or a quadriplegic.

Once it's OK for you, you will be ready to start letting others help you help yourself. You will be in yet another stage of recovery: the understanding and acceptance stage. Although many people *never* accept their injury, those who come close to acceptance make a faster healing and recovery. When you are on the way toward acceptance, you will be ready to find out what aids and devices will help, aids to help you function independently. You will be ready to see what the future holds for you and to think about your career plans. But don't expect too much too soon when planning your future. As Skip from *On the Move* says:

At seventeen, I thought I knew where I was going. Today, I honestly can say I don't know where I'm going and I don't care. Do I think of college? . . . Sometimes. Do I think of the future? Sometimes. But most of the time, I think about that mine, and my leg, and everyone who said, "Skip, you're now ready for the outside world," except I'm not sure I am. Not yet.

Helping Your Parents

For many reasons, most parents have a very hard time letting you go. You will really have to be aware of the built-in comforts of home that will keep you there, away from learning to cope for yourself, taking risks with friends and physical situations in your wheelchair, and trying to get into schools and jobs you need.

Parents are in shock about your injury, too. They are often angry at themselves, feel guilty, and try to overcome these feelings by keeping you close at home. Often their first move to help you is to bring everything to you. Carrie in *On the Move* talks about home when she describes why she gave up wanting to go to work in an office:

> Besides, there seemed to be no real reason to go out. Everything had been brought in so conveniently. There was plenty to do in the house, food to eat, people to see and to talk to, and slowly the office dream had faded and the sewing machine, so handily there, had taken its place.

When Carrie first started going out on her own, she was hurt that her parents weren't more enthusiastic about her life away from them. You have probably wondered why your parents haven't given you more support to go off on your own. Maybe you have often felt the way Carrie felt when her parents wouldn't go to the wheelchair basketball games that were such an important part of her life away from home:

She tried not to think of what her parents were feeling. The look in their eyes was one of fright and doubt. They still had not attended any of the basketball games. Glen had told her this wasn't unusual. Many parents of paraplegics in families similar to Carrie's, where the one in the wheelchair has been protected too much and exposed too little, refuse to accept the fact that there could be a life outside the house. It posed problems that the parents couldn't face. Carrie couldn't get over that. There was a problem that her parents couldn't face, but that she could.

As long as you are comfortable doing what you are doing and being where you are, of course you won't make a move. Carrie felt she had everything she needed until one day:

She sat there for a long moment, looking at the three people closest to her in the whole world. Suddenly she didn't feel close to them at all. She felt trapped . . . inside the circle that they formed standing around her.

Your awareness of your parents' need to protect you will help as you make your moves to get out of your home and on your own. Talking about things away from home that concern you may be the biggest help you can give them right now. You may not be able to wait until your parents are ready for your move. You may have to go right ahead and just hope that they will catch up with you later. Most parents do.

Helping Your Teachers

If your teachers don't know about it, be sure they get any help they can about your career possibilities from the local branch or the national headquarters of the National Paraplegia Foundation. Some Veterans Administration hospitals offer group counseling for teens with spinal cord injuries; check there, too.

Work with your counselor on setting realistic goals for employment, education, adaptation to home and wheelchair living.

Ask the counselor to get as much information about self-help devices, so that you will be knowledgeable about the range of career possibilities that can be adapted for you.

Be sure your counselor is clear that spinal cord-injured students *do* have careers in their future just as they have friends, sex, and marriage because they expect to be in on both love and money in their life.

As Marilyn Golden of Houston, Texas, says:

> The attitude I want to inspire in people toward my handicap is twofold. It sounds contradictory but is not. First, you need to have a real appreciation of how hard things are for me. Second, you need an understanding of how bad my life is not—i.e., I am alone, live independently, support myself, camp out, have sex, travel alone, and am usually quite happy. I do the things you do; I am as like you as the next able-bodied person. I may look a little different; that's all. Are you going to let that get in the way?

See page 245 for more material about spinal cord injuries.

10 | Epilepsy

As most of you already know, no one is more stigmatized than people with epilepsy. If you are one of the few in school who is not completely seizure-free, you know, too, that you have to deal with the threat of a seizure. Besides the fear of complete loss of control, there is the worry about the response of everyone around watching.

Of all the fears people have, not knowing when and where something awful is going to happen is the greatest. Seizures can be awful when they are neither predictable nor constant. When you can't predict your own behavior or when people around you can't predict your behavior, fear and stigmatism take place.

Most of you in school will be on medication, and you will be completely controlled. In fact, unless you tell others, there is no way they would even know you have epilepsy. Many of you in school will have good control. That means that it's unlikely you will ever have a seizure in school, but it is possible. The possibility is your number one worry. A second worry is whether to tell others about it.

Biofeedback

Have you heard about biofeedback? It's a popular health concept used these days especially for control of pain or weight. It's a process by which people can learn to self-regulate certain aspects of their bodily processes. One of the ways biofeedback is being used with epilepsy is to learn more about the emotional factors that start seizures. By having you listen to a series of tapes showing emotionally charged situations—that is, situations that make you anxious—researchers have been able to identify the type of emotional situation that triggers a seizure. Treatment then consists of having you watch videotapes of yourself and discussing these situations with your family and a therapist. A process develops in which you learn to self-regulate certain aspects of bodily processes, resulting in fewer seizures. This idea is in the experimental stages, but people working in biofeedback certainly believe in the possibility of your getting help from it.

Out of the Closet

If your epilepsy is well controlled and doesn't have anything to do with a friend or situation, there is no reason to tell about it. If, however, you make a point never to tell *anyone*—your best friend (although best friends often change in high school and confidences are sometimes broken as your best friend becomes someone else's best friend tomorrow), your teachers, your coach, the person who is interviewing you for a job—then there is the problem that you can be in a physically dangerous situation. Worse yet, if you are not telling anyone because you are ashamed of your condition or, more likely, because you are ashamed of how others react or treat you after a seizure, then you have some things to consider:

1. Do I accept my epilepsy?
2. If I don't even say the word "epilepsy," how can I learn to accept it?

You have to find out as much about your seizures as you can, ask questions, read, and start thinking about seizures in day-to-day terms: How long do they really last, one minute, five, ten? How do I really act; do I fall down, just stare, walk around? Then you have to say to yourself, "Yes, these things do happen, I do have epilepsy, and this may not change." This is crucial to an accepting attitude about yourself. Once you accept your condition and you are able to share it with at least one other person, then whether others know or not becomes less important (and you can learn to take them on one at a time).

It's hard for you to know how your epilepsy is going to be taken by others until they know about it. When you find that people don't react as negatively as you feared, that fact will be a help to you. Of course, it doesn't always work that way! They may act worse than you expected. Talking about having epilepsy is much easier if you can talk to someone else who has it. Looking for someone else who has epilepsy to talk with will be worth the effort because once you can share your worries and the "worst that can happen" stories with someone who really understands how it feels, it will be easier to share with others.

What Do You Tell Them Anyway?

How do you explain to a close friend who doesn't know it that you have epilepsy? What do you tell a school counselor, an employer, a college admissions officer? First of all, tell them that it isn't a disease and it isn't contagious. Epilepsy is a symptom of an intermittent imbalance of electrical activity of the brain. This imbalance causes seizures that cause a temporary alteration of the conscious state and a loss of muscular control. Whenever it's over, the normal activity of the brain cells is restored.

Besides the right medication, enough rest and no booze help in this control. What this means to you is that the way to be more like the other kids is *not* to follow their no-sleep all-night parties, ignoring your medication and feeling free to experiment with drinking. The way to fit in is to control your epilepsy the best you know how. That will enable you to do the activities and work that kids your age are doing.

Teaching Others

There always has to be a definite decision on your part whether you want to protect yourself against discrimination (and of course, many people *do* discriminate against you) or whether you will be one of the ones who decide to educate everyone by saying, "Hey! Look at me. I'm a person with epilepsy and I'm OK! You know me and accept me and see me do well in school and sports. I'm a person who has lots of friends. I'm a person who needs medication to control my epilepsy. Like people with diabetes who need insulin, and some parents who need tranquilizers, and some students with asthma who need lung expanders, and some teachers who need caffeine to wake up, and other adults who need a drug or alcohol to calm them down so they can sleep, I need my drug to survive, too. Even better than most drugs—mine are prescribed!"

If you decide to educate the world, are you expected to do it alone? By no means! Read the disabilities rights chapter (Chapter 12) to learn more about making the personal political—in other words, teaching others about epilepsy has to do with all the people who have epilepsy, not just you. Read about coping with your disability (Chapter 3) in this book to get some ideas about how everyone needs a support group, friends, someone to talk over all the things that happen to one—especially because of all the different reactions to seizures.

One group ready to help you is the Epilepsy Foundation of America, 1828 L Street, NW, Washington, D.C. 20036. Write to find out if there is a local chapter near you. If there is no chapter, ask for the names and addresses for people with epilepsy near you. The EFA sponsors a school alert program to help everyone in school better understand and accept students with epilepsy. Maybe your school would sponsor such a program. In addition, there are public information programs on television designed to educate the public about this grossly misunderstood condition.

School and Career Planning

Epilepsy in itself is not the only school and career problem that you have. A big problem is talking about your epilepsy. If you just can't talk to a school counselor, try talking to a rehabilitation counselor. If you are a student with epilepsy or are looking for work and are lucky enough to live in Atlanta, Boston, Minneapolis, Cleveland, Portland, Oregon, or San Antonio, where there is a Training and Placement Services Project (TAPS) sponsored by the Epilepsy Foundation of America, you can get the group support you need while you are looking for employment. Even if you don't live in one of these cities, many other cities are doing similar work because TAPS has proved so successful. Check with your local or state Epilepsy Foundation to see if the vocational rehabilitation center near you is doing something similar, especially for students with epilepsy.

If you are not getting any special help planning your career, here are some of the things you will want to cover with the counselor who is working with you about your education or career decisions:

1. Be sure you are clear about the extent to which your seizures are controlled.
2. If your seizures are not completely controlled, be certain about when they occur. If they occur while you are sleeping or soon after you awaken, they would have very little effect on educational and career choices.
3. Be definite about the type of seizure you have.
4. Be specific about how you act after a seizure. If you require a period of rest or are confused and have to be supervised, your school and career plans would be affected by your particular reaction.
5. If you are already thinking about a particular career, are there any licensing restrictions concerning epilepsy?
6. Are you clear about tension and anxiety as they relate to seizures?
7. Do you have to avoid any particular physical work condi-

tions, such as poor ventilation, extreme temperatures, flashing lights, or loud noises?
8. Do you have any side effects from your anticonvulsant medication?
9. Are you eligible for a driver's license in the state where you want to work?

Besides being open with your counselor about these points, you have to confront the ever-present question of whether you should disclose your epilepsy condition to a potential employer. It's hard to know what to do because it's harder to get a job if you say you have epilepsy. On the other hand, research has found that those who did not disclose the fact that they had epilepsy had more seizures at work and were fired when a seizure occurred because the employer didn't know. Some feel that the anxiety about being discovered precipitated the seizure at work. But no matter what, it's a tough question, and it certainly depends on the extent to which your seizures are controlled by medication and on how well you can talk about your seizures in work-related terms. Telling an employer also depends on the support group you have while you are looking for a job. It's your decision, and it will probably change as you change jobs and confidences; your first interview for a job won't have to be at all like later ones.

If you do decide to say you have epilepsy, it will help your employer or college admissions officer to know the general facts about epilepsy and employment. During your interview be sure to let the interviewer know that:

1. About two million adults in America today have epilepsy —that's two people out of every hundred.
2. About 80 percent of all people with epilepsy are able to work with no complications from the disability.
3. United States Department of Labor studies show that people with epilepsy have slightly better safety records than others.

4. Studies show that workers with epilepsy do not take more time off the job than others.
5. Studies show no difference in productivity between those with epilepsy and others.

Find Someone

If there is anything that people who work with the disabled have learned, it's that no matter what your disability, you can't stand alone and get very far. The first step for you to take to get beyond your disability is to find someone to talk with about your epilepsy. Try to find someone who has it, too. And talk about it. Talk and talk and talk. Finding someone to talk with may not be easy because others may feel just as you do and don't want to say that they have epilepsy or any special problems with it. After you make that effort and do find someone to talk with, it's all uphill from that moment on. You may go slowly uphill at times, and you may stand still every once in a while. But talking with another person who has the same feelings and carries the same stigma and fear of having a seizure at school or work makes all the difference. Try it, and you'll see.

See page 247 for more material about epilepsy.

11 | Getting Tested for Physical Disabilities

Test scores by themselves don't mean anything. They help only if whoever is testing can translate the test results into treatment, training, or teaching strategies designed specially for you. Even then, educators have to pay more attention to your potential than to what you have achieved or where you are now.

As it stands now, testing for most physically disabled students does more harm than good. And because a lot of people who work with the disabled know this is true, the new law for getting every child into public education very carefully states that you and your parents have something to say about: (1) if and when you will be tested; (2) how the test results will be used; and (3) what kinds of tests can be used in the first place. As a teenager you will want to be in on all this test talk and to get your parents to help you with your ideas, adding some adult clout to your opinion.

Tests Are Scary

Douglas D. Dillenbeck, an executive at the College Board, writes about testing for all high school students in his chapter on testing in Joyce Mitchell's book *Free to Choose: Decision Making for Young Men:*

> When the teacher tells the class there will be a test tomorrow, everyone moans and groans and carries on as if it were the end of the world. Some students really mean it, tests worry them. They're afraid they won't do well, or they may even fail. If they fail the teacher may criticize, other students may laugh (or sympathize, which is even worse!), and their parents may be angry or disappointed. It's no fun to have other people finding out about your faults or weaknesses. If that's the main thing you think about when someone mentions tests, you probably worry about them too.

If all students have something to worry about when they take tests, then you have even more to worry about because most of the tests you take discriminate against disabled students. Your disability and where you go to school—in special classes, a residential school, or a mainstreamed setting—have a lot to do with your test scores. At best, tests can be scary to all students, and at worst, they can place you in the wrong educational group.

For example, a disability can affect your developmental experiences, both sensory-motor and social in nature. When used with students who are physically different, many commonly used intelligence, achievement, and aptitude tests are more often a measure of school and home experiences than they are of the factors the test has been designed to measure. The fact is that your developmental experiences are different from those students upon whom tests have been standardized, and that makes the results for you very different from what they would be if your experiences were just like those of a nondisabled student. In other words, the closer you are to the students of the standardization population in life experiences, the higher the test will be in authentic results for you. So when you and your parents agree to go with the results of a test, you should think first about how your early-childhood experiences compare with those of students without a disability. When you and your parents have a chance to say which tests you will take and for what reasons, here are some of the things you will want to be sure are going on when you are tested.

Selecting the Test

Whatever the tests are that your teachers or other professionals are planning to give you, check to see if they have taken into account your potential limitations. To what extent does the test contain items in which visualization, manipulation of objects, receptive and expressive communication abilities, and language skills are key factors? Here are some examples of how a physical disability may negatively affect your test sources:

1. Your disability may impose a "language" barrier. If you have a severe hearing loss, tests which require verbal facility will reflect your language deficiencies rather than the factors intended to be measured.
2. Your disability may interfere with the perception of the test problems or materials. If you are blind, you cannot see the performance test items, for example, and if you are deaf, you cannot hear items presented orally.
3. Your disability may interfere with the speed with which you can read the test or respond to items, thus making timed tests inappropriate.
4. If you have little or no use of your hands, you may be unable to manipulate or handle the test materials.
5. You may not be able to make the response required for indicating test answers. An inability to use a pencil, for example, may prevent you from marking responses on answer sheets, or a speech defect may keep you from responding verbally.
6. If you have certain health or physical impairments, you may be placed on antispasmodic, anxiety-reducing, or

anticonvulsant medication. Many such drugs have direct, noticeable effects on the central nervous system, which can easily interfere with testing and affect the results.

What Can You Do about It?

You and your parents can check to be sure that:

1. You are taking the best tests and getting good test procedures which can compensate in part for these disadvantages.
2. In selecting the test(s), the examiner should match the test to your disability so that there will be minimum physical interference. For example, the verbal scales of the WISC (Wechsler Intelligence Scale for Children) and the WAIS (Wechsler Adult Intelligence Scale) are considered appropriate for disabled people with unimpaired language development but are inappropriate for deaf people with impaired language development; the WISC and WAIS performance scales provide a more accurate assessment of the deaf individual's intelligence than do the verbal scales.
3. It is essential to know the language level of personality, vocational aptitude, and vocational interest tests. Often the reading level of students with disabilities is such (approximately eighth grade or higher) that the tests are unsuitable for students, whatever their disability, if they are poor readers.

Even after an appropriate test has been selected, adaptations in test format or test administration may be required. Examples of adaptations are:

1. The use of a braille or orally presented version of a test if you are blind.

2. Presenting of instructions for performance tests by total communication (e.g., voice plus signs or finger spelling) rather than via voice alone if you have hearing differences.
3. The use of an amanuensis if you are unable to write.
4. The omission of certain test items which are beyond your *physical* capability.
5. Modifications of time limitations to compensate for physical liabilities (e.g., even if you are a proficient braille or large-print reader, you cannot read as fast as your sighted peers; manipulation of objects will necessarily be slower if you have manual differences).
6. Modifications of test materials (e.g., if you have manual involvement and you cannot pick up small blocks, you may be able to handle large ones).

The purpose of these adaptations is to equalize, insofar as possible, test *conditions* for nondisabled and disabled students.

In many cases, even with modifications, test conditions for the disabled are not equal. For example, tests administered orally may place you at a disadvantage if you are blind because you are expected to hold accurately in mind four to five multiple-choice responses while you choose among them. And group testing is almost impossible if you are trying to compensate for a sensory impairment or motor disability. Results from group tests do not accurately reflect your ability, and who wants to take a test when the best you can do doesn't even show? Sometimes you will be OK in a small group for testing—but only *if* the test selected is right for each of you in the group being tested and if the group is no more than ten students, all requiring similar adaptations of the testing procedures, and if the examiner is experienced in testing physically different students, and, lastly, if the tests that are going to be used have been carefully chosen to be nondiscriminatory toward your specific physical disability.

Teacher Tests

Most tests that you will take in school are tests that your teacher makes up, and they have to do with the material you are learning for that particular class. Teacher tests can be a daily quiz on last night's homework, a weekly test, a midterm, or a final examination. In grading these tests, the teacher usually compares you only with the other students in your class.

Standardized Tests

In most public schools, around the third grade, students start getting several standardized tests each year. A standardized test is one that has already been tried out on thousands of other students to be sure that the questions are clear and that the tests are testing what they are supposed to be measuring. Usually standardized tests are long, with more than a hundred questions, but most are short-answer questions. These tests are often printed in booklets with a score sheet for each student. The trouble with standardized tests for you is that usually the thousands and thousands of students who were tested to find out what is average and what is clear do not have many students with physical differences in the group. That means that your test results will be compared to the school and life experiences of nondisabled students.

Intelligence Tests

The most common test given to all students is the intelligence test. This is one test you and your parents really have to watch out for. A group intelligence test that is used in school to classify you or place you can really do you in. The problem is that the measurement of intelligence is based on the following assumptions: The subjects to be tested have lived in similar environments, they have had similar interests, and they have had equal opportunities to explore these interests. These assumptions are simply not true for many disabled students. When you were an infant and a young child, physical differences may have restricted your ability and opportunity to move freely about and to explore your environment. This restriction limits the number and quality of experiences to which you were exposed. There is more and more evidence that school development is dependent on and related to the extent to which children have been exposed to a stimulating environment in their early years.

Another disadvantage of intelligence tests standardized on nondisabled populations is that they often require knowledge that most people acquire *informally* from their environment by means of vision, hearing, mobility, and use of the upper extremities. Unless you were specifically shown or told about certain aspects of your environment, you are not likely to acquire knowledge about it.

Here are four intelligence tests often used for students with physical disabilities: *Wechsler Intelligence Scale for Children* (WISC) Form R—ages fifteen and under (the verbal IQ is a good predictor of school progress for the visually impaired; arithmetic score may be low because math is not easily translatable into braille); *Wechsler Adult Intelligence Scale* (WAIS) Revision of Form I—ages sixteen and over (performance scale is considered one of the most accurate instruments for assessing the intelligence of deaf students; it includes picture completion, picture arrangement, block design, object assembly, coding, or mazes); *The Leiter International Performance Scale*—ages fourteen to eighteen (yields lower IQ scores than some others because the mean is 95 rather than 100; it consists of sixty-eight nonlanguage tasks); *The Peabody Picture Vocabulary Test* (PPVT)— designed specifically for cerebral-palsied and speech-impaired students, ages two to eighteen (the lack of fine detail in the picture minimizes confusion; students must choose one of four pictures as a "definition" for a word; the sets of pictures get harder; this test is untimed and requires no special training).

Interest Tests

Another common test, especially in junior high school and high school, is the interest test. Aside from purely "mechanical" difficulties—for example, inability to understand the language used or to see or manipulate test items—there are other problems that limit the use of these tests:

1. An overly restrictive school and home environment may have robbed you of the opportunity to develop your innate potential in a variety of areas. Thus, if you never had the opportunity to help your parents around the house or yard or to participate in shop courses or science laboratories at school, you cannot realistically be expected to have developed career-related mechanical or scientific skills.
2. Because of differences in vision, hearing, or mobility, you may have had limited exposure to, and thus limited awareness of, the world of work. Obviously you will not be interested in an activity or occupation about which you know absolutely nothing.
3. Responses on interest inventories may not reflect your true interests but rather what you believe a person with your disability *can* do.

Here are two common interests tests: In the *Kuder Occupational Interest Survey,* considered too highly verbal for many deaf students, students must be able to read at at least sixth-grade level. It is often used with blind students and may be given orally, in braille, or by tape recording. Braille answer sheets are available. The *PRG Interest Inventory for the Blind* was developed to overcome students' tendencies to answer on the basis of what they can or cannot do, rather than on their true interests. The inventory is based on jobs done and hobbies chosen by blind people. It can be administered orally or by tape recording.

Achievement Tests

Achievement and aptitude tests are the most common tests taken in high school and also the ones that you take for college entrance. If care has been given to the right test and good procedures for you, achievement tests may give you a reliable measure of your *current* functioning in an area. They are not a reliable indication, however, of what you *could* achieve in a given area if you had special instruction suited to your disability. Achievement and ability are *not* the same thing. If you have been absent from school a lot because of illness or rehabilitation, or if you have had poor instructional materials and teachers, there is no way you can test well in school achievement.

If you are planning to go to college, some of the achievement tests that you will take in high school include these:

1. *Preliminary Scholastic Aptitude Test/National Merit Scholarship Qualifying Test (PSAT/NMSQT).* This test is given every October in most high schools, mainly for juniors, although anyone who wants to can take it. It's like the College Board Scholastic Aptitude Test (SAT) that hundreds of colleges require, so it gives you a chance to see what the SAT is like and how well you can do on it. It takes two hours, but there is an extended time for students with physical differences, and you get two scores—a verbal score to show how good you are with words and language and a mathematical score to show how well you handle numbers and quantities. You can compare your PSAT/NMSQT scores with the SAT scores of applicants and freshmen at the colleges that require the SAT. They're published in a directory, *The College Handbook,* which all high schools have for their students to use. If you take the PSAT/NMSQT in your junior year, you will also be considered for the scholarship programs administered by the National Merit Scholarship Corporation.

2. *Scholastic Aptitude Test (SAT).* This is one of the admissions tests of the College Entrance Examination Board, required by about a thousand colleges of applicants for admission. It is given at test centers all over the United States and in other countries around the world on five Saturday mornings every year. Your own school may be a test center, or you may have to travel to the nearest test center at some other school or a college. The test takes

three hours, but there is a time extension for disabled students, and you get a verbal score and a mathematical score, like the PSAT/NMSQT scores. Your school gets them, too, so it can help you with your plans for college. And your scores are also sent to the college or colleges that you ask to have receive them. You can have them forwarded to colleges later if you don't know where you want them sent at the time you register for the test. You should take the SAT in the spring or summer of your junior year in order to get the most benefit from it. That way you get your scores early enough to use them when you're deciding what college or colleges to apply to. Also, if they happen to be lower than you think they should be, you still have time to take the SAT again and try for higher scores. If you don't take it in your junior year, though, you can take it in the fall or winter of your senior year, and that's early enough for most colleges.

The American College Testing Program (ACT) and the College Board test (SAT) are highly verbal and may not be an accurate reflection of the deaf student's potential. These tests are available in braille and large type or can be given orally for the blind. Answers may be typed. Tests can be administered with flexible time limits if the special registration form is used.

3. *College Board Achievement Tests.* These are the other admissions tests of the College Entrance Examination Board, required by several hundred colleges. They are one-hour tests in fourteen high school subjects, and as a rule you would take only two or three of them, depending on what was required by the college or colleges you were applying to. Some colleges give you a choice, and you pick the ones in your best subjects. The achievement tests are also given at College Board test centers on certain Saturdays. Usually you wouldn't take any achievement tests before the spring of your junior year or winter of your senior year, but you might want to take one as early as the spring of your sophomore year if you were

taking a subject that year—say, biology—that you would not take any more of in high school and you thought you might have use for a good test score in this subject.

Visually disabled students may take the College Board Achievement Tests at their own speed. Students may use a reader or amanuensis. The American College Testing Program (ACT) is available in braille, large type, and cassette.

4. *American College Testing Assessment Program (ACT).* This is an admission test of the American College Testing Program required by many colleges for applicants of admission. It is given at test centers throughout the United States and in several foreign countries on five Saturdays during the year. It takes about four hours, and you get scores in English, mathematics, social studies, and natural sciences.

5. *Advanced Placement Examinations.* These examinations in college freshman courses are offered by the College Entrance Examination Board and given by high schools to students who have taken special college-level courses in high school or learned the equivalent knowledge in some other way. Colleges may use your grades in these examinations to let you skip the corresponding freshman courses in college and even, in some cases, to give you credit toward your college degree. In some colleges, a student who has received satisfactory grades on three or four of these examinations may enter as a sophomore and complete his or her undergraduate program in only three years instead of the usual four years. The examinations take a half day each and are given during one school week each May.

6. *College-Level Examinations.* This is a program of examinations in college subjects, administered during the third week of each month at test centers throughout the United States and at military bases overseas. Although originally developed to serve adults who needed a way to show colleges or employers that they had learned the

equivalent of certain college courses in their work experience, by independent study, or by some other means, College-Level Examinations are being used by colleges more and more as a basis for granting college credit to incoming freshmen. If you have special knowledge of some subject that is commonly taught in colleges for credit, you might want to look into the possibility of taking the appropriate College-Level Examination and getting college credit for it.

Personality Tests

Most high schools do not give personality tests to most students. Sometimes educators think that students with physical differences should have personality tests to decide if they should be mainstreamed. Because of all kinds of disagreements about test modifications, all the possible physical differences of students and the varied attitudes about the disabled on the part of the tester, I can't imagine any reason why you or your parents would ever agree to your taking a personality test or having the results of a personality test on your record. Why test when observations of everyday situations can determine what the school wants to know? If the school wants to know your methods of solving a problem, reaction to failure, persistence in spite of incoordinate movements, desire for moral support from teachers, and use of hands and speech, its staff can watch you in class and discuss these coping skills with you.

Testing Considerations for Specific Disabilities

IF YOU ARE DEAF

The content and instructions of most tests are highly verbal. That means that these tests may measure language deficiencies more than they evaluate things they say they are for, such as intelligence, achievement, or aptitude. Hard-of-hearing students vary according to whether they learned language before or after they became hard-of-hearing or to how much they can actually hear, so that there is no general way to test students who are hard-of-hearing. Make sure that whoever is giving you the test and whoever is using the test results know for sure that your difficulties in speech, language, and conceptual difficulties result from your inability to acquire language through hearing. Period. Many a deaf child is put into a special class for mentally retarded students because of this problem. There will be many reasons for you to decide when and if you will take what test. Here are some guidelines that can help you decide. Share these guidelines with your teacher, especially if you are mainstreamed and your teacher has not had special training in testing the deaf.

1. If your hearing loss is less than 15 decibels in the speech range, take the regular group tests, sitting in the front of the classroom near the teacher.
2. If your hearing loss is 75 decibels or more in the speech range, all the tests you take should be special tests especially for the deaf.
3. If you are in the middle group with a loss between 20 and 70 decibels, many people don't realize how hard-of-hearing you really are. You can fake a lot of hearing, and at testing time you can do yourself in. You appear to hear and have the language skills, and the test results come off low because you really don't have the language skills you seem to have. You will have to decide for yourself how much you want to appear nondeaf. You have to decide if you will let others know that you are really missing all that verbal stuff going on around you and ask them to accept you that way. In that case, you will have to ask them to say it again—LOUDER!

If you are being tested, most teachers will want to know what will help you relax so that you can do your best in a testing situation. Your teacher will usually be glad to get your input about testing conditions that are best for you. Here are some conditions that will work best:

1. The teacher must use the mode of communication that you prefer, be it a particular type of manual communication, pantomiming, speechreading, or writing. An interpreter is seldom effective.
2. Several practice items should be given to be sure you understand the testing procedure.
3. You should be given the easiest or less involved tests first so that your anxiety is minimized. If both performance and verbal tests are to be given, it is advisable to give the performance tasks first because they may produce less anxiety.
4. You should be tested in small blocks of time rather than in long concentrated periods. This helps ease the strain and fatigue that may occur as you try to cope with a variety of communication difficulties during the testing process.
5. Tests should be administered individually rather than in groups unless there are small groups with similar disabilities and similar preferred modes of communication.
6. The room should be as quiet and well lit as possible.
7. The teacher should be facing you so that the lips or hands are not shadowed. Your teacher should know that more than half the sounds in the English language are not visible on the lips or, if they are, appear identical to other sounds, so it must not be assumed that you can see or understand everything.

IF YOU ARE BLIND

If you have little useful vision, your results on an intelligence test designed for sighted students will measure your visual differences rather than what the school is after—your intelligence. If you: (1) can hardly see a test page; (2) can handle only large objects; (3) can read ink print efficiently only if it's in large type or if you use a magnifier or special visual aid, then you need special tests—those used and developed for the blind. What your teacher should know is that *you* are the best resource for deciding what kind of test should be used. Not all of you are that good at braille. Depending on your educational background and your use of low-vision aids, some of you will prefer braille, others will choose large type, and still others, regular ink print.

Other alternatives for testing include using tapes or orally reading the material. Keep in mind that when someone is reading the test for you, you have to remember a number of multiple-choice alternatives while you choose among them.

If you are going to be tested, your teacher will want some clues from you to help you relax and do your best. Some testing conditions that you will want to check out are:

1. You must have good lighting—enough of it, no glare or flickers.
2. You decide if you need low-vision aids.
3. Visual or auditory distractions in the testing room should be eliminated.
4. You should be tested in short blocks of time rather than in long concentrated periods. You may become more readily fatigued than the sighted students.
5. Adjustments of time limits may be required with tests standardized on a sighted population. Even the most efficient visually different reader seldom can achieve the reading speed of other kids. This applies to reading any medium, be it braille, large print, or regular ink print read with the assistance of low-vision aids.
6. You should be tested on an individual or small-group basis with no more than ten subjects. Even if you are taking the same test as the other students, adjustments in time limits are almost always required, and this makes it impossible to administer a test to you in a large-group situation.
7. The teacher should tell you all the information about the test and testing situation that a sighted person would pick up visually.
8. In performance types of tasks the teacher should describe the objects being used and let you touch them.

Some of you won't need any testing modifications at all. The extent to which any of you needs to have testing modified depends on the age at which you became disabled, the severity of the disability, the particular types of physical differences you have, the extent you have been exposed to life experiences which count in a test, the degree to which you have been rehabilitated to compensate for your physical differences, and the effects of your medication.

You will want to be straight with your teachers about the medication you are taking because it should be noted for test scores. For example, medications taken for epilepsy may make you tire more quickly than the other students; if you are diabetic, you may be more alert at one time of the day than at another; if you have a cardiac condition, you may tire very quickly under testing conditions.

Share these examples of types of test adaptations for disabled students with your teacher. Start with this list, but add any of your own that are important to you, too.

1. Adjustments in time limits may be needed. When regular time limits are used, students with severe speech defects (on oral tests) or impairments of the upper extremities (on written or performance tasks) will be at a disadvantage because of their often slow and laborious performance.

2. Adjustments in the manner of *recording* answers may be required on written tests. In some instances you may have no use of either hand. In other cases you may have some use of one hand but may have difficulty in marking the answer space correctly. This is especially true for machine-scored tests in which precision in marking the proper space is absolutely essential. Possible solutions include:
   • Use of an amanuensis to record answers.

- Specially designed answer sheets such as a larger-than-normal response spaces to accommodate people with poor writing skills.
3. Adjustments that may be needed if you have upper- or lower-extremity physical differences. Some ideas:
   - A lapboard which fits over your wheelchair will facilitate work which requires near-point vision or manipulation of objects by hand.
   - Large objects on performance tasks can be substituted for small objects, or a matchstick or similar object can be glued to the object to make it easier to pick up.
   - You can sometimes tell the examiner what to do on the test instead of drawing or manipulating an object yourself.
4. Possible adaptations of orally administered tests if you have normal hearing but no usable speech include these:
   - Response by blinking, pointing, grunting, or head shaking can at times be substituted for the spoken word.
   - A response can be pantomimed if the content of the answer is quite clear.
   - Some test items can be modified to a multiple-choice form. You can then respond by pointing to or otherwise indicating the correct answer. Tests involving arithmetic problems, general information questions, and naming objects from memory can frequently be administered in this manner.
5. Some of you with neurological differences may have a high level of distractibility. Environmental changes that can help improve this problem include:
   - Lower levels of lighting.
   - Short periods of test administration to allow for fatigue.
   - The wearing of earphones to muffle sounds while memory and attention are being tested.

Tests Are One Measure

As you learn more about tests in this chapter, you will learn that test scores cannot be your only basis for a good decision. Tests give you one piece of information about yourself—not the whole picture. Still, that bit of information about you may be counted by counselors or by recruiters for jobs, school, and colleges differently from the way it is for your nondisabled peers. You can use test results if they work for you. If other information you have seems to contradict the test score—for instance, if you get a low score in history and you always do very well in history—chances are that the test score is wrong. Douglas Dillenbeck in his chapter about tests for teenagers says:

If you think about tests with a healthy skepticism and as only one of many possible measurements, you will see that there's less reason than you may have realized to be nervous or fearful when you take a test. Tests aren't mystical. They can't come up with an answer about you or your ability that isn't there. The more aware you are of your academic abilities and interests the less surprise a test score will be to you. Being very disappointed or overjoyed when you find out your test scores should be about like the way you react to a grade in a term paper or book report. They are all a part of your evaluation.

Think of tests as information along with your marks, teacher comments, and your own evaluation and interest in a subject. Information that can help you make sound educational and career decisions. Information that will permit you to choose appropriate plans for your future.

If tests don't help, and if you think tests are unfair for you, then by all means don't agree to use them for your evaluation! Use other things, like observation, marks, teachers' evaluations. You are in on your educational program, and your opinion is important. What you think—even about tests—counts!

III | Beyond Your Disability

12 | Fight Handicapism: The Disability Rights Movement

Handicapism. How do you spell it? What is it? Handicapism means the attitudes and practices that lead to unequal and unjust treatment of people with disabilities. The word "handicap" comes from the time when people who were disabled had no choice but to beg in the streets, cap in hand. Handicapism means that the nondisabled are just a little more privileged—a little bit "better" than the disabled. You can see handicapism at work in children's books, in the unemployment rate of the disabled, and in the nonaccessibility of the disabled to buildings and events. You can read about it in *Handicapping America* by Frank Bowe (see page 108). A handicapist society is a society that values the nondisabled and the nondisabled stereotype more than it values the disabled. It means that regardless of the qualifications, a nondisabled person will be selected for the job, scholarship, or college or will be elected to office only on the basis of being nondisabled. It means that everyone else can act as if she is just a little bit better when with the disabled. It means that nondisabled spouses feel they have the right, on the basis of their being nondisabled, to make the final decisions. It means that the nondisabled expect their wives and husbands and people at work who are disabled to adjust to their way as best they can. . . . Handicapism, like sexism and racism, is present throughout our society. It is reflected in our schools and jobs and books and magazines and movies and unemployment rates. In a handicapist world, both the disabled and the nondisabled value the nondisabled more.

Most of you have heard of sexism and racism—discriminating against groups of people on the basis of their being female or nonwhite. Some of you have heard of ageism—discriminating against old people. Discrimination makes the news most often when a law is passed to protect the rights of people; often the law is about the education and employment rights of people regardless of sex, color, sexual preference, or age. For example, when Section 504 of the Rehabilitation Act was passed, the awareness of our country's bias against people with disabilities was greatly increased. For the first time, many people thought about discrimination against people with disabilities in employment.

The organization of groups to fight for the compliance of new laws helps to increase the awareness of the public about discrimination. Just as the civil rights and women's rights movements brought nonwhite and women's issues into the limelight, activists from these groups, plus disabled groups and the Vietnam veterans' groups, organized the disability rights movement. These organizations made everyone much more aware of handicapism and how to get rid of it.

Organization: The Disability Rights Movement

The disability rights movement aims at restructuring society to accommodate the needs of the disabled and to affirm their equality with other people. It started among people with disabilities who were fed up with having to adjust to life in a society that ignores and insults the existence of the disabled.

Like the civil rights movement and the women's movement, it began with specific issues.

In 1969 in Berkeley, California, a group of disabled people started a wheelchair repair operation and other desperately needed services for themselves. This led to the creation of the Center for Independent Living (CIL), a large organization which offers many services to people with disabilities living in the Berkeley area. The center is administered by disabled people, and most of its employees are disabled. There are many other CIL groups in other parts of California. The CIL now offers job counseling, welfare advocacy, housing and attendant referrals, and repair of wheelchairs, and it publishes *The Independent*, a newsletter for people with disabilities.

At about the same time the CIL was started, a young woman in Brooklyn, New York, was rejected from a teaching job because she was disabled. She sued the city of New York, the case was settled out of court, and she got her job back. The publicity the suit received gave her the idea to organize Disabled in Action (DIA) to fight similar battles for other people with disabilities. Besides New York, DIAs now exist in Philadelphia, New Jersey, Baltimore, and Syracuse.

Next, the disabled Vietnam War veterans and antiwar movement people joined forces with the CIL and DIA and helped develop the philosophy, techniques, and strategies necessary to organize a dynamic disability rights movement.

The passage of the civil rights section (Section 504) of the Rehabilitation Act and the education law (PL 94-142), along with the federal decision for the low-floor, wide-door, ramped bus called TRANSBUS, added to the growth and success of the movement. You can read more about how these laws can be meaningful to you and work for you in "It's the Law" (Chapter 17) in this book.

People with disabilities have learned, as women and blacks have learned, that in order to make changes in the world, organization is crucial. An individual does not have the political clout and power that are needed to pass laws, to get people to spend money, or to get people to change their priorities for spending money. All civil rights movements are concerned with changing the world. Blaming the victim (women, blacks, the old, or the disabled for being different) and blaming yourself for not trying harder are not going to make things better. Joining other people with disabilities and working together to bring about change *do* change the world. Joining others also helps your own attitude about what you can do if you do organize. Minority groups know that you can't wait for people's attitudes to change before you get equal opportunity. Organization, action, and changing of attitudes all have to go on at the same time.

Action: Disabled Women's Rights

In the land of "Miss America," where cars are sold by ads of perfectly formed women in sexy outfits, a physically disabled woman doesn't exactly feel as if she belongs. Women with disabilities have a double set of injustices to cope with, and nonwhite women can be said to have a triple whammy.

The implications of sexism for women with disabilities, just like that for their nondisabled sisters, are especially clear in career development. Women are not offered equal opportunity for programs and education. The Rehabilitation Services Administration of the United States Department of Health, Education, and Welfare reports the following information on women and men rehabilitated by state rehabilitation agencies in 1976: 1.) more disabled men than women receive vocational and on-the-job training from state rehabilitation agencies; 2.) 93.7 percent of men were rehabilitated into wage-earning occupations while only 68.5 percent of the women were; 3.) the average weekly earnings of men were significantly higher than women's wages at the end of rehabilitation training; 4.) in addition, men were employed in a wider range of occupations while most women were clustered in service and clerical fields.

Activists for disabled women from the Disabled Women's Coalition of Berkeley have organized to share their experiences and to express their struggle for self-discovery that "We are women. We are disabled. We are strong." Write for their book *What Happens After School? A Study of Disabled Women and Education.* Send $3.50 to: Women's Educational Equity Communications Network, Far West Laboratory, 1855 Folsom Street, San Francisco, California 94103.

Action: Compliance

One of the major activities for the disability rights movement is to work for enforcement of the employment and education laws that have already been passed. A law may say that there can no longer be discrimination in education. But unfortunately for everyone, passing a law isn't all there is to it. Unless someone pushes for compliance to the law (that means making people obey the law), employers and educators can go right on with their sexism or racism or handicapism as usual. Someone has to say, "Hey! Wait a minute. It's against the law not to hire me on the basis of my disability." Or, "It's against the law to mainstream me in that classroom without making accommodations for my physical differences." In order to get compliance (enforcing the law), someone has to organize a group with enough power so that educators and employers will have to listen. And if that group has the law of the land on its side—as you do—it (and you) will (and do) win. In other words, compliance to the law requires organization. The disability rights movement gives high priority to enforcement of the civil rights law for people with disabilities.

Action: Representation

In addition to enforcing laws, the movement is asking for the disabled to be the ones who create and control the policies of the agencies which are supposed to benefit them. For example, the DIA (Disabled in Action) demonstrated against the United Cerebral Palsy policy makers to convince the group to hire more people with disabilities, especially in the professional jobs, and to place more people with disabilities on its board of directors. The DIA felt that if public agencies were organized to help the disabled, the disabled should be a lot better represented in these policy and professional groups than they have been until now. Another example of not being represented: A group of 2,000 educators at a recent national conference for career education and the disabled met with only a handful of disabled participants. Once again the nondisabled were making educational plans and policies with very few people with disabilities there to represent them. The disability rights group is working toward turning that kind of planning around to get its own representation into the meetings, on the boards, and into planning for action for itself.

Action: Language

When I was discussing the chapter about epilepsy in this book with a professional worker for the Epilepsy Foundation for America, I used the word "epileptic." I was quickly corrected to "a person with epilepsy." In other words, while "epileptic" sounds as if that's all there is, "a person with epilepsy" sounds like someone who can get beyond his or her disability. One of the things we learned in the women's movement is that the person in the minority group is the one who has the right to name the language. Often men will say to women, "What difference does it make to be called a girl instead of a woman?" Or "What difference does it make to say, 'a student . . . he,' 'a dentist . . . he,' 'a therapist . . . he'?" What we want to say here is: If it makes a difference to the person most directly involved, then it makes a difference!

As a group the disability rights movement does not use the word "handicapped" because it feels it has a paternalistic sound, with emphasis on helping and overprotecting the disabled. Joan Tollifson, a disability rights activist, says: " 'Disabled' needs to be our word for ourselves and does not have all those paternalistic associations. For these reasons, I would encourage the use of the term 'disabled.' " She goes on to say,

"The word 'cripple' is very definitely a hate word, although amongst disabled people, we often use the term 'crip' to describe ourselves." Leslie Milk, the executive director of Mainstream, Inc., an organization established to assist the mainstreaming of people with disabilities primarily in employment, says that Mainstream uses both the terms "disabled" and "handicapped." It believes that people have a right to be called whatever they wish. It also understands that "handicapped" is the only term recognized by the law. Mainstream works in the field of legal compliance assistance. However, Milk goes on to say that it never talks about "our handicapped," "people who suffer from diseases," "victims of polio and epilepsy," or "those confined to wheelchairs." These expressions define dependence, not disability.

Many of the disability rights activists do use the word "handicapism" to describe stereotypes and institutional oppression.

What Can You Do about Handicapism?

Get together a group of other disabled students and as many of their parents as you can to take one or more of the following actions:

1. Get the cooperation of librarians in helping children understand unfair portrayal of disabled persons in books and the media by means of special displays, discussions at story hour, screenings of antihandicapism audiovisual materials and films.
2. Ask for your school's mainstreaming policy. Get the federal guidelines from the American Coalition of Citizens with Disabilities (see page 108). Plan actions when necessary to secure compliance.
3. Find out about programs which have been developed toward the consciousness raising and training of teachers and other school personnel to meet the needs of disabled

students. Collect information about successful school programs in other towns, and share it with parents, teachers, and community groups.

4. Investigate state and federal policies for the finding of accessible transportation, equipment, medical care, and attendants for disabled people. Support local and national disability rights groups in their attempts to insure the finding of adequate services.

More Information for Disability Rights

Read!

1. "Handicapism," *The Bulletin,* Vol. 8, No. 6 (1977). Council on Interracial Books for Children, 1841 Broadway, New York, New York 10023. $2.
2. *The Independent,* a quarterly magazine by and about people with disabilities. Free to members of Center for Independent Living (CIL), 2539 Telegraph Ave., Berkeley, California 94704.
3. *The Closer Look Report,* a periodical, free of charge, published by Closer Look, Box 1492, Washington, D.C. 20013.
4. *Handicapping America.* Frank Bowe. American Coalition of Citizens with Disabilities, 1200 Fifteenth Street, NW, Washington, D.C. 20005. $10.95.
5. *What Happens After School? A Study of Disabled Women and Education.* Women's Educational Equity Communications Network, 1855 Folsom Street, San Francisco, California 94103. $3.50.

Write!

1. American Coalition of Citizens with Disabilities, 1200 Fifteenth Street, NW, Washington, D.C. 20005. An organization representing seventy disability rights and

advocacy groups. Publishes a monthly newsletter, *The Coalition.*
2. Mainstream, Inc. A national nonprofit organization that offers programs and services to increase awareness of affirmative action for the handicapped and to help with the mainstreaming process. 1200 Fifteenth Street, NW, Washington, D.C. 20005. Publishes *In the Mainstream.*
3. Council on Exceptional Children, 1920 Association Drive, Reston, Virginia 22091.
4. Federation of Children with Special Needs, 120 Boylston Street, Room 338, Boston, Massachusetts 02116.

Join!

1. Center for Independent Living, 2539 Telegraph Avenue, Berkeley, California 94704. A nonprofit organization run for and primarily by disabled people. A nonresidential program providing services which enable severely disabled people to live independently in the community. Publishes *The Independent.*
2. Disabled in Action of Metropolitan New York, 175 Willoughby Street, Apartment 11-H, Brooklyn, New York 11201. Publishes a newsletter, *Advocate.*
3. Disabled in Action of Pennsylvania, 1319 McKinley Street, Philadelphia, Pennsylvania 19111. Concerned mostly with architectural and attitudinal barriers of physically disabled.
4. Disabled in Action of New Jersey, P.O. Box 243, Paramus, New Jersey 07652.
5. Disabled in Action of Syracuse, 243 Roosevelt Avenue, Syracuse, New York 13210. Concerned primarily with social services and independent living.

13 | Getting Around

A power wheelchair, power lift, power steering, and power brakes and windows, plus adaptive equipment, make driving a reality for you.

Getting around on your own by bus, car, cab, train, plane, and ship is the key to integration in our society, the key to mainstreaming. Getting around makes possible employment, education, recreation, dating, ball games, movies, parties, school, church, medical and dental care. We live in a very mobile society. You've got to be in on mobility to be in on society.

Teenagers can't wait to get their driving permits and licenses. And many parents can't wait until they do because it's the best negotiating tool a parent has: "You can't use the car unless . . . you do your homework, cut the grass, write a birthday card, come in on time, ask your cousin to go, too," and on and on. The family car is about the strongest power a parent holds; besides, the kids can do all those picking-up errands, including picking you up!

Every disabled teenager is as eager to drive and learn to take public transportation on his or her own as any nondisabled kid is. It's important. Mobility puts you on your own in ways that you should be.

No matter what your physical differences are, you will want

to get maximum mobility skills possible for you. The first place to learn about getting around is by using public transportation.

Public Transportation

Many of you will have had little or no experience using buses, cabs, trains, and planes. If you are physically capable of using public transportation, start now with getting the skills you need to feel comfortable doing this. Maybe you have always gone on the bus with someone else; try going alone. Stretch yourself, and keep trying until you feel good about doing it. Public transportation for the physically disabled is tough. So many people aren't aware of the barriers you face. Famed concert violinist Itzhak Perlman, stricken with polio at four years of age, is very aware of these problems, and he tells what it's like for a well-known musician to get around with public transportation. As he describes it, no matter how famous you get, no matter where you are going—to a television studio or to a classroom—the problem is still *how to get from here to there.* No matter how high you have climbed in your career, you still have to cope with the same obstacles that face most disabled people. "A step is still a step; a curb is still a curb; a flight of stairs is still a flight of stairs." The garbage elevator still stinks whether it takes you up in a low-income housing project or up in the Ritz. Perlman says that like most disabled people, "I am always more or less anxious about how I am going to get where I am going during the allotted travel time." He cites a recent federal survey that reports that more than 7 million people can't use public transportation because of permanent disabilities. That number does not even include the thousands of other people with temporary problems, like broken legs and so on, as a result of accidents.

Getting Around for the Blind

If you are visually disabled, you can learn mobility skills and orientation from special instruction for the blind. Mobility and orientation instruction is essential if you are new to a school. If it isn't offered, ask the counselor or special education teacher for help with orientation. Orientation means becoming aware of the existing situation; it doesn't mean using someone else's arm. If there isn't a special course for mobility, then ask the counselor to contact the local vocational rehabilitation office or community rehabilitation agency. Try to get it to give you an orientation of the community you live in, not only of the school.

If you start the school year out with a sighted guide, do just that: Start the year. After a while you should be able to go it alone. Going it alone is the foundation of your independence.

Driver Education

No matter what your disability, try driver education. Many physically disabled people—including those who are quadriplegic, paraplegic, hearing-impaired, and visually impaired and those with epilepsy (with controlled seizures)—are capable of learning to drive and are eligible for licenses. Excluding you from instruction in this area imposes an unnecessary barrier to independent living, social opportunities, and occupational choices.

Many of you will require only minor modifications in your driver education course, such as individual (rather than small-group) road training or classroom materials at a particular reading level. Those of you who are severely disabled may need cars with adapted equipment or specialized screening and instruction. The department of motor vehicles in each state should be contacted for information on licensing and on special screening and driver education programs which may be offered to physically disabled residents of the state.

Many state departments of education have special programs for disabled students in driver education. The state of Vermont, for example, has developed a screening process for disabled students. Any student fifteen years old or over can be referred to the driver education program to be screened for the possibility of learning to drive. The referral can be made by your school counselor, parents, or *you.* The Vermont department of education believes IT IS THE RIGHT OF EVERY DISABLED PERSON TO BE CONSIDERED FOR A LICENSE. For those of you who are severely disabled, enough so that your parents or the school think you cannot drive, convince your parents that you need a careful screening to decide if driver training should be attempted. If the screening doesn't result in a recommendation that you take driver training, you can repeat it at a later time. What you have to do is to get to the screening. Let the driver educator for disabled students decide whether you can take driver training or not; don't decide not to get driver training on the basis of what you or your parents or teachers think without the screening. Your parents and teachers really don't have the information about all the adaptations that can be made. The driver educators will evaluate the type of adaptive equipment needed, if a special vehicle is required or if a modification of a standard one is OK. For example, even Edward Roberts, director of the California rehabilitation department, drives, and he is paralyzed from the neck down. And in Illinois, three blind teenagers have just been mainstreamed into driver education. The blind students have become full members of the driving class, although they are not being taught to drive on streets and highways. Their textbooks and tests were revised in braille, and they did get to drive on the driving range during individual instruction periods. The blind students were also taught the mechanics of driving and how to take care of a car. The point to be made here is that you will get a better chance at learning to drive if you let the state department of education in on helping you evaluate your disability.

HOW MANY ARE SCREENED?

The majority of you with special needs do *not* require screening but may need some modification in methods and timing. Or you may need to work alone with a driver educator rather than in the usual small group for road training.

HOW MUCH DOES IT COST?

All disabled students are eligible for the statewide per pupil cost allotted for driver education. Many state departments have special funds from the federal government for added costs needed by some students for screening, special training methods, individual training, and added roadwork. Driver education departments often have adaptive equipment on loan for training. Check with your state department of driver education to find out what the special costs and equipment available are for you.

DRIVER EDUCATION MATERIALS

1. *The Handicapped Driver's Guide,* by John DeLellis. This is an annotated listing of resources, including: manufacturers and distributors of adaptive equipment, driver training programs, and training programs for driver education teachers serving disabled persons. Write to your local American Automobile Association club for ordering information.
2. *Tips on Car Care and Safety for Deaf Drivers.* Section I discusses ways hard-of-hearing and deaf drivers can visually and tactually detect when a car is not operating properly. Section II, intended for the young deaf driver in a driver education course, discusses safe driving tips. Write to United States Department of Transportation, National Highway Traffic Safety Administration, Washington, D.C. 20590.
3. *Vermont's Program of Individualized Driver Education for the Handicapped.* This describes a model program of screening and driver education for physically disabled persons. Write to the Vermont State Department of Education, Driver Education for the Handicapped, Montpelier, Vermont 05602.

More Information about Getting Around

One way to get started getting around is to read some of the access guides written especially for the physically disabled. Many public transportation systems have special guides and programs to help you gain access to them. Look over the list of United States Access Guides on page 247 for some basic travel sources. Send for the ones that will be a help to you.

14 | Friends

One of the rewards of the disability rights movement can be friendship. Disabled people's solidarity, reaching out to help others who are disabled, sounds so easy and natural. But many disabled kids haven't learned to value a disabled person's ideas, opinions, or friendships. They haven't accepted that it's OK to be disabled and, therefore, it would be OK to have other disabled kids for friends. A lot of people who are disabled see the nondisabled as much more interesting, stimulating, intelligent, and well informed than they are. The heroes of high school, the big money-makers, and the decision and policy makers belong mostly to the nondisabled. Looking at the world in this light, the disabled often get the false idea that if they identify with other disabled kids, they are losers. And who wants a loser for a friend? One of the reasons why you don't feel OK is that discrimination against the disabled can make many of you feel like a nobody. A nobody would rather be friends with a somebody.

If students are outstanding or different in any way, they get teased, ridiculed, or just left alone. No one is sure enough of himself or herself to risk being friends with and seen with kids who look or act "different." A social psychologist studied the social interaction between disabled and nondisabled kids at a camp and found that if given a choice in seating, not only did nondisabled children avoid those with disabilities, but whenever possible they chose to sit with the most perfect physical specimens in the entire group. Americans glorify physical perfection in women and athletic ability in men. Children, of course, follow that example.

With the help of the disability rights movement (see Chapter 12), many disabled people of all ages are learning, for the first time, that they really are interesting, bright, creative, innovating, and fun to be with. And they are learning it from each other. They are learning that they are somebodies. Somebodies have and are friends.

Ann, who is blind, remembers being a friend of other kids with disabilities in school:

> "I remember interacting in school with other kids who were disabled, kids who had clubfoot or were severely bowlegged. We were all the butt of everyone's ridicule and exclusion. There was a camaraderie among us because we were mutually hurt. I suppose that's had an influence on my life."

Blaming the Disability

All of us need all the help we can get toward building friendship skills. Sometimes you might feel that if only you didn't have this disability, life would be easy; people would automatically want to be your friend. You have only to look around you at the kids without disabilities and at adults to realize that keeping good friends is hard for everyone. If you use your disability as an excuse for not having friends, you won't put in the necessary time and effort to develop your friendship skills.

If you blame the disability, then you won't go all out to make friends because you won't feel worthy enough to *be* a friend. Not feeling worthy to initiate activities with others can come from being worried about your looks. Most teenagers feel that they are too fat or too thin, they have too many pimples, their hair is too straight or too curly, their noses are too long or too crooked, their ears stick out, or they are too short or much too tall. Besides looks, many high school students don't feel good enough to start friendships because they didn't make the team or the one-act play, or they made the team, but really goofed in the game, or made the play, but were complete failures as actors.

Because everyone finds it hard to make and keep friends doesn't make it any easier for you. When you look around at the adults you know, you will see that there are an awful lot of people out there who never learned! And it's true: It *is* harder to make friends if you are disabled because as the kid says, "We don't want freaks, wallflowers, or brains for friends!" That means if you are to have friends, you have to work harder at it.

Teenage Friendship

Here are two different articles on friendship written especially for teenagers—not only for disabled teenagers but for any teenager. The point of your reading this is for you to know that *all* teenagers are worried about how to make friends. They all want friends and are afraid that they can't pull it off. In her chapter about friendship in Mitchell's *Other Choices for Becoming a Woman,* Margaret Mead says that high school is a good time to learn to be a friend and to be with friends:

> High school friendships will make you readier to explore the world. Whether the high school years are very enjoyable or a steady grind, they are the years when you are learning to form your life style, deciding how you want to relate to other people, boys and girls, older people like teachers and coaches and counselors, younger kids, groups of people in which you may find that you are good at leading or better at carrying out other people's plans, or that you always know the words if somebody else can just carry the tune. It's the time when you find out whether you are at your best in the early morning (whether it's writing a theme or taking an early-morning swim) or at night—after everyone else is in bed.

High school is a time for making friends. Of course, some students make friends much earlier and keep their kindergarten friends all their lives, but often childhood friends are just the children who lived next door, or the children of your mother and father's friends, not your own choice. And in elementary school there isn't as much choice to make. High school widens out—there are more people to choose among, and more kinds of people. The basic thing about friendship is that it is a matter of choice. Parents, brothers and sisters, aunts and uncles, nephews and nieces, and later, sons and daughters, are just there, for you to love or put up with, be thankful for, or give up on. But friends are the kind of compensation that life offers for all the lack of choice a family offers. In a family you may wish you were the oldest, or the only child, or the youngest, or a twin; but wishing won't do you any good. But when you pick a friend you can pick someone who is a little older and more mature, or a little younger, who will turn to you for help and advice, or someone just like yourself who will understand exactly how you feel about everything. You can pick someone who is always cheery and optimistic, or someone who puts a brake on your own impulsive optimism. And the other side of the picture is that the person who you pick as one of your friends has a choice too. In a family you may adore your older sister and want to spend a lot of time with her, but she may be burdened with the knowledge that, after all, she didn't pick you. But friends choose each other, try each other out, don't have to go too fast at first, don't have to promise to have lunch together every day from now to eternity. And each step can be delicious, finding out that you went to the same summer resort when you were six, that you both like to eat pickled walnuts, that neither of you catches poison ivy, that both of you secretly hope to be lawyers.

And you can make friends with the opposite sex, boys or girls you don't date and don't want to date. But if you do things together—put on plays, edit the school paper, go on a trip—you can explore each other's minds and find out how girls and boys have learned to think about things in different ways than the way you have learned to think. Many girls don't have any brothers, and many boys don't have any sisters. Yet in today's world men and women are going to have to work together, with sometimes one and sometimes the other in a higher position. If you learn to be friends with each other in high school, you can get on with them better in the working world.

Learning to be friends with people different from you is what psychologist Harold N. Boris writes about in his chapter on friendship in Mitchell's *Free to Choose: Decision Making for Young Men:*

People who are curious about others have a greater variety of friends, which are not confined to boys with boys, girls with girls, jocks with jocks, intellectuals with intellectuals. Boys and girls can be good friends without going together, and people interested in cars can be friends with people interested in chess. Nor is it essential to have friends in the same age bracket. Older people and younger have developed substantial friendships. While they may disagree about all sorts of things, from sex to politics, the disagreements can widen each other's world as each person struggles to make himself or herself known.

Friendship has been called an art. The art of it, however, does not begin with others, but with yourself. Friends who care for you help you to care for yourself through respect and acceptance. But to depend on others to do this for you usually means that you won't take risks. As a child you depended on the love and opinions of your parents. Then, you began to turn to your friends. This freed you from being a papa's boy or a mama's boy and helped you to be yourself. However, it is also possible for people to go from dependence on parents directly into dependence on friends. Only the people have changed. The dependence hasn't.

Since the art of friendship comes first from learning how to be alone with yourself, to stand loneliness without feeling useless, worthless, afraid, or too sad, you are now freer to choose your friends. You can say "yes" and you can say "no." You can be yourself. Being able to be yourself means you allow other people to be themselves, and indeed are interested in their being so. You can be dependent and independent at the same time. Sometimes you can lean and sometimes you can be supportive. Sometimes you will seek encouragement and sometimes you will give it. This exchange is called interdependence. And interdependence takes time. Usually you get together around something—a game, an activity, an event. Gradually you learn to enjoy being with people with whom you feel safe because they like you and are like you. Later you may seek people who are different from you but who like you. Finally you can come to like people who are different from you and who don't yet like you. But this is the toughest of all: to learn to like someone who doesn't think you are all that great.

Happiness is one of the rewards of friendship. Happiness comes when we have learned to choose without being too choosy, to join in without losing our individuality, to take strength from commonality but to cherish differences. In short, to enjoy a range of people without trying to become exactly like them or to convert them into becoming exactly like us.

Everyone Needs Them

As hard as it may be to make friends, there is no other way to go. We aren't talking about friends to be used for something: for sex, or for getting a job, for getting into college, or into a special summer program. We are talking about plain old friends: *the people you share yourself with,* the people that share their life with you. The ones you talk and talk and talk and talk and talk with, about your joys and your worries, your depressions and your highs, your concerns and your purpose in life: Why am I disabled? How come you aren't? How can I get my overprotective parents off my back? How can I ever invite a friend to my house? Friends are the people you share your views with about people, religion, politics, relatives, parents, teachers, clergy, little kids, brothers and sisters: all the things you think about and are alive about. There may be things in life you can do without, but friends are not one of them.

High School Friends

There is hardly a tougher time to make and keep friends than in junior and senior high school. The oncoming sexual and emotional tensions and the tensions of doing the work in high school sometimes make the whole world seem impossible. In high school and college, there is a focus on making it: getting the grades, getting on the team, getting in the play, and being accepted by your classmates. One of the difficulties is that everyone keeps changing. You can come home from school one day and tell your parents about a new friend and go to school the next day and find yourself entirely excluded from the company of your new friend with no explanation! You can be a perfect physical specimen and come up with no friends on Valentine's Day, when all the other kids except you receive valentines from their classmates.

You are expected to initiate relationships, but you also have to be ready to deal with rejection from your tries at friendships. In some ways you want to reach out for friends, but in other ways you want to hold back, so you won't be disappointed.

Are You a Good Friend?

Let's say we all agree that friends are important. And we all agree that friendships are hard to come by, especially for a disabled student in a public high school. One of the ways to think about how you are going to make friends is to evaluate what kind of friend you are. Here are some questions that will get you started thinking about the kind of friend you are, rather than what kind of friend you want.

1. In general, what kinds of friends do you have?
   a. Disabled?
   b. Nondisabled?
   c. Popular people—the stars of high school?
   d. Kids a lot like you, with whom you feel especially comfortable?
   e. All kinds?
2. You're kind of tired of someone who used to be a friend. Would you:
   a. Gradually but tactfully stop seeing him?
   b. Keep seeing him, but only with others whom you like?
   c. Pick a fight with him in order to make a break?
3. A group you're with begins to criticize and talk down a friend of yours who isn't there. Would you:
   a. Join in the criticism but in a humorous way?
   b. Defend the friend?
   c. Not say anything until they changed the subject?
4. You've made plans to go somewhere with another disabled friend, but a popular senior who is nondisabled asks you to go somewhere at the same time. Would you:
   a. Say you're sorry but plan to go another time?
   b. Ask the nondisabled friend to join you and your disabled friend?
   c. Go with the popular kid and make some excuse for standing up your disabled friend?
5. You're friendly with a student your parents don't like, but they haven't said you couldn't be with her. Would you:
   a. Stop being friends?

b. Continue to be friends by not telling your parents?

c. Bring the friend home with you, hoping your parents will get to know and like her?

6. A student who is disliked by your friends has begun to be friendly with you. You kind of like him. Would you:

a. Become his friend and try to get the others to accept him too?

b. Reject him politely because you don't want to make things difficult with the rest of your friends?

c. See him once in a while when no one else is around?

7. One of your best friends borrows money and never pays you back. Would you:

a. Discuss it with her?

b. Ignore the problem because you don't want to upset the friend?

c. Find some clever, roundabout way to make the friend change her ways?

8. Two friends you like really hate each other. Would you:

a. Choose one to be friends with and drop the other one?

b. Keep seeing them both but never mention one to the other?

c. See both and try to patch things up between them?

9. A friend has made a remark that hurts your feelings. Would you:

a. Get angry and tell the friend off?

b. Show no reaction?

c. Sulk or give the friend the silent treatment?

10. A student you don't care for could be very useful to you on some project at school. Would you:

a. Be friendly in order to get his help?

b. Ask his help but not try to become friends to get it?

c. Have nothing to do with the student?

If you are in a class, several of you could take different choices and discuss each point of view. Go over each situation, and think of the way you would react. Maybe you would make up your own response like that of an eighth grader who answered,

"I wouldn't make any of those choices!" If you are reading this alone, write out your answers, and give the questions to a friend for her or his answers, and talk about your responses together.

Friendship Skills

Being a good friend is learned and developed. We are not born friends; everyone has to learn the skills. One of the easiest places to begin is to have friends as much like you as possible. Once you learn how to have friends like yourself, you will be more confident about having friends different from you: the opposite sex; nondisabled; a different ethnic or racial or age-group from yours.

If your parents are the kind who don't want you with other disabled kids because they think the other kids are much worse than you are and it makes you look or act worse, just be patient with them. Try to explain that for you, a disabled teenager has a lot more understanding and sharing of another disabled teenager's school and daily life than anyone else.

The reason that it's easier to have friends just like you is that you will share a lot of the same doubts and worries as your friend. If she, like you, is blind, has epilepsy, or has a spinal injury, you will experience in common how the other kids in school look at you as a person and possible friend, how your parents and other relatives treat you, what your chances are for independence and making money, what your limitations are for sports, or jobs, or mobility. In addition, if you are in the same school and have the same teachers, you have all that in common. If you both are teenagers, it will be much easier to understand and to listen and to talk with each other.

Friends take time. And patience and concentration. Friendships have to be nurtured and helped to grow. Letters or notes and phone calls make up a good part of that time. You have to listen and also to express yourself to develop friendship. Friendship doesn't evolve just because you are in the same grade and school and because you both are blind or deaf. As well as the situation's being the same for both of you, there has to be an attraction and mutual beginnings of respect. Both people have to take the initiative in contacting the other; both have to take turns supporting and comforting when things are heavy. Both have to encourage and celebrate with each other. Learning to take turns for the other person's needs is the basic skill in being a friend. Some of you will find it more difficult than others to get out and make new friends. Many of you don't have many opportunities to meet new people. Some of you may be too anxious and come on too strong, giving the other person the impression that you have really got to have him or her for a friend. Of course, the other person will be scared away, will be turned off by your too-eager approach to friendship.

Making Friends with Yourself

As eager as you may be to have a friend and to look for others to be with, it's surprising how important it is to be friends with yourself. Others get their clues to how to think of you and regard your disability by what *you* think of yourself and how you look at your disability. If you see yourself as a basket case or a drag on the school and society, it will be impossible for others to see you in a positive image.

Lots of teenagers ask, "How do I start liking myself? How can I like myself when I'm so different (taller, shorter, fatter, thinner, terrible teeth, skin, ears) from the other kids?" One of the best plans is to take just one thing that you accept in yourself and cash in on that. Take your brains, musical talent, humor, beautiful hair, height, strong arms, good voice, great eyes, sunny disposition, or the friendly way you come on with other people. Concentrate and give yourself credit for the one thing. Let everything else go, think of yourself as only this one good thing, and then go on to another good thing. Give yourself credit for the next thing you like about yourself. In other words, if you find one or two worthwhile things about yourself, you may be able to stop worrying about the things that you don't like. You may be able to see beyond your physical disability and accept yourself for your abilities.

Meeting Others

Lots of disabled teens just about die of loneliness. And it often comes off as being bored. If you act as if you are usually bored, you can be sure that others will find you boring to be with. You really have to take the initiative and not let this happen to you. If you can find some community agency or programs that work with other disabled teenagers, contact them to learn what they do for teenage groups. Get into as many situations as you can find with other disabled teenagers; find as many programs and activities as you can. If you can't get out to other places, get your parents to have some kind of recreation at your home: a Ping-Pong table, pool, badminton net, or whatever you can do for recreation to invite other neighborhood kids in. The biggest help your family can be for you, if you can't get out, is to get other kids in.

See the sports chapter (Chapter 15) in this book for ideas about what you and your friends can do. If you are like some disabled teenagers, who don't get out much, you overdose yourself with the plug-in drug—TV. Then you are left out of the friendship skills, the people skills, and the active interests that new friends bring with them.

One of the wonderful by-products of friendship is learning new interests and recreational activities together. All the things you learn to do now, with friends, will be resources for you to draw on all the rest of your life. The interests that you and your friends develop can include cards, sports, backpacking, reading science fiction, collecting and refinishing antiques, watching the stock market, or canoeing. These activities will be interests and recreational skills forever. As Margaret Mead said, "High school is for learning about how to get and keep friends. Now is the time to learn to make all kinds of friends and enjoy all kinds of activities with them." Find a friend. Be a friend.

15 | Sports

Skip wheeled over to the center of the court, rubbing his shoulders. His fingers, raw and bleeding from the other wheelchairs that had tried to block him, felt the thud of the ball as it was passed to him. He held on tightly and looked around. Two bounces and a roll on the wheels . . . he moved slowly . . . bouncing twice, maneuvering his wheelchair back and forth around in a circle, feeling the smack of steel as the other wheelchairs tried to block his way, looking for the opening. Over to the side, he saw Mac with his hand held high, his red hair shining like a lantern.

"It's yours," Skip yelled and passed the ball over the reaching hands that tried to block his view.

The sound of leather could be heard around the gym and the crowd went wild as the ball flew into the net. The score was tied again. (From *On the Move* by Harriet May Savitz.)

It *feels good* to focus one's whole self in sports, to get free from being pulled in a dozen different directions, says Dr. Natalie M. Shepard in her chapter "Discovery Through Sports" in Mitchell's *Decision Making for Young People.* For the short period of the game experience there is no fragmentation, no divided attention. You can experience being a whole person. Human beings *need* to exercise their bodies, need to use their human capacities for movement and expenditure of energy, need to experience the exhilaration of complete concentration, of being all together!

What are sports anyway? They are really many things to many people. For some they are the same as games and mean any activity—even run and tag. For others they mean only the "major" sports. And then there is water skiing, skydiving, jogging, and backpacking. And skiing, snowshoeing, swimming, boating, tennis, and golf. Must sports be competitive, or can they include fishing and camping?

In the first place, sports include physical exertion, and sports mean activity. In the second place, sports are a clearly defined task set apart from the ordinary. Rules to which all agree are established. If you don't agree to the game, you don't play. Sports prescribe exactly what one may or may not do and how one shall behave. The essential question, the challenge, the impelling fascination is how well can the person do what is prescribed. Within one's limitations how well can one perform?

Disabled students can have the same fascination and challenge from sports as nondisabled kids have. As long as you measure yourself against your particular limits and test to see how well you can perform, you will get the thrill of achievement and confidence in sports. Debbie, born with cerebral palsy, is active in wheelchair sports. She tells what sports do for her:

> "I like sports, and in the summer I like to rest. I played on the Catholic school volleyball team, which was good for me because there wasn't much running around involved. I became interested in sports in fifth grade. I liked to watch my brothers play football. In junior high school I started playing wheelchair sports. The only time I had ever been in a wheelchair was in the hospital. I thought that was the only place they belonged. My sister

and I started racing through the hospital hallways. I really liked it because I could never move that fast before. Sports have helped me to gain confidence in myself. Confidence was something I had lost a long time before."

Watching a skier come down the Nose Dive expert trail at Stowe, Vermont, on one leg, with adaptive small skis on his poles, is as thrilling as watching any skier coping with a tough environment with grace and speed. Watching the deaf play basketball using nonverbal communications signs and signals to get the team together is as exciting as watching any team that plays together to win. Being part of a winning swimming meet and watching the fastest young woman on the team, who is blind, feel the excitement of winning for her team are no different from the excitement of watching her sighted sisters in a swim meet.

The sports world contrasts sharply with the ordinary, everyday world. Life is so complex that we always have to divide our attention. But the sports world presents a single job on which all of one's being can be focused.

As you play sports, you develop skills, and your body is conditioned to the peak of your physical capabilities. For many of you, these capabilities may change as your disability changes. You can keep in touch with where you are when you work to develop physical fitness. In sports, the final purpose of all the preparation of getting into shape is found when tests of risk taking and adventure are designed to reveal the self-knowledge of your own outer limits. The whole purpose is to test the limits of your endurance—not another's, but your own. When you are there, on the team, climbing a mountain, wheeling a marathon, swimming the laps, the person you wrestle with is yourself, your own fear, your own courage, your own strength. Every personal resource is utilized in sports, until you stand naked before your own self-knowing.

And when the exhilaration and the excitement of the game are over, we leave the sports world for the everyday world. We go back to our cultural divisions of age, physical abilities, economics, and color and creed, but whenever we meet or remember, we "belong" together for that one thing we did, the one period we played together. We talk about it ceaselessly; we recall point by point, incident by incident, and moment by moment the fun we had, the failure when we didn't quite make it, the joy of achievement when we did. Belonging is one of the most fundamental of human needs, and the sports world offers each person the opportunity to join. You bring yourself and offer what you have.

Action!

Here are some sports and games, from the world of sports. You will have to modify some of them; you will have to put together and organize most of them. Go through the list, and pick three or four activities that you have never played before. Get your family and friends in on them, too. Try out your first selections, and see how they go. Another time try a few more new ones. Take your favorite sports and games to a group that you belong to; teach the members the rules and how to do it. Invite some kids in for a sports party, and have the activities all set up for a night of action. Sports and games take you beyond your disabilities. No matter how severe your disability, there will be *some* activities here that feel good for you. Give sports a try. It's fun!

GAMES

Activity: BALL TOSS

Materials: String ball, newspaper ball, balloon, regular ball, or beanbag.

Description: Object of activity is for two or more individuals to toss and catch the ball without allowing it to drop to the floor. Start with score of 15. Deduct 1 point from player who lets ball drop to floor. Game ends when one player has lost all 15 points. Winner is other player.

Modifications: For those with poor arms and hands, a balloon would allow more time to catch. A balloon or newspaper ball eliminates fear of being hit. For the nonambulatory, a string ball or beanbag allows you to be more self-reliant; simply encircle ball with tape, and attach tape to string; this may then be attached to wheelchair or suspended from ceiling for catching and striking. For those with visual handicap or blind, audioball or balloon with bell inserted will help; bounce and catch sounds give auditory clues for localizing ball.

Activity: BARREL BALL TOSS

Materials: Rubber ball or balloon or newspaper or yarn ball; 50-gallon barrel (heavy cardboard), cast off or cheaply purchaseable from some industrial firms. Face painted on board fastened to one open end with hole for mouth large enough to allow basketball to go through. Place board from bottom of mouth hole to rear barrel opening, to allow ball to roll out the back. Bricks, one for each side of barrel, will prevent rolling, but any other method may be substituted.

Description: Rules can be preset depending on whether one or more players may be used for practice; with two to four playing on two sides with set number for getting ball through hole on first trial or whatever players want.

Modifications: Target may be painted on large or small carton; used on chair or table to elevate or be used by wheelchair user, or on floor.

Activity: PITCH BACK (one or two PLAYERS)

Materials: Duck, nylon netting, or any durable fabric which can be tucked tightly to a simple three-by-four-foot frame with easel for standing target marked on frame (three to five areas with numbers for scoring from 1 to 3 or 1 to 5; circles, squares, or whatever, but big enough to permit some leeway for a five-inch-square beanbag). Four rubber balls about four inches in diameter, or five-inch square beanbags filled with polyester, cotton, cloth, shredded foam, or beans. Line marked with masking tape for player.

Description: Player throws at target to get highest score with five throws. Whether playing alone or with team member, game is the same. Winner has highest score for three, five-throw parts.

Modifications: No target on net if you have a severe motor problem and no allowing opponent to practice. Reduce number of targets or distance from net if needed. Can be played on floor or from wheelchair with easel on table. Targets for player with partial vision should be yellow and white. A metronome or clicking oven timer, placed behind target, will help a blind student locate the target if done in a quiet room. Bells sewed to target will tell if target was hit; opponent must score in the exact target area.

Activity: TARGET TENNIS

Materials: Target screen on one side of appliance-size carton, two to five ten-inch-diameter holes for targets. Taped court ten feet in length with center division to service two people. Rackets. Rubber balls (small), tennis.

Description: Object of the game is for the player to strike the ball with the racket so that it will bounce on the floor and go through one of the open spaces. After player scores a point, she or he is allowed a bonus serve. If ball hits target screen and rebounds, opponent takes turn.

Modifications: Those with muscle weakness might use underhand stroke and hit the ball through hole on the bounce or in the air. Game might be changed to target ball and individuals would simply try to throw a ball or beanbag. Hole may need to be enlarged.

Handle of racket will have to be adjusted to your grasp, and racket length and weight to strength of your arm movement.

Activity: TARGET THROW

Materials: Be creative! Any interesting-looking target—a clown with a hole for a mouth, a target with alphabet letters, even outline of big face. Wastebasket, carton, large can. Beanbags, paper wads, or rubber ball.

Description: The object of the game would vary with the target. With the clown it might be to hit it or to put beanbag through the mouth. With the letters, you might get four bean-bags and see who can spell the first four-letter word. Tick-tack-toe could be played with different colors of beanbags and some-one to keep track of plays on paper target.

Modifications: Size of target might be enlarged, and distance from target shortened, for those with little arm movement and strength. Ability to grasp must be considered in choosing items to be thrown.

If you have a visual handicap, use a white or yellow target, and for those totally blind, use a metronome above or behind target to assist in location. Perhaps use of a target (tin) which would resound when hit would be good for feedback.

Use a string ball (purchasable) or attach string to beanbag if you are a nonwalker to retrieve independently.

INDIVIDUAL SPORTS

Activity: BALLOON BADMINTON

Materials: Badminton rackets or wire coat hangers pulled into racket-head shape and covered with nylon stocking pulled taut over wire and taped at base. Balloon. Hula-Hoop sus-pended from ceiling or rope strung across room.

Description: Two people, one on each side of hoop or string, hit balloon back and forth through hoop or over string. Point scored by server when he succeeds in doing this by passing opponent's return. One point per score; extra serve for scoring; winner the first to get score of 15.

Modifications: Height of hoop and distance of hoop from players can be adjusted if you have limited arm motion of reach or are restricted to chair (regular or wheelchair). Light and short racket can be handled easily; grip adjusted to grasp and strength. For visually handicapped, eliminate hoop for string, and insert ball or bean in balloon prior to inflation so player can locate balloon from sound in order to hit it.

Activity: BICYCLING

Materials: Bicycle (tandem, exercise, or standing, standard with training wheels).

Description: Much exercise, and even mild competition via simple races, make this fun. For nonwalker it enhances mobility.

Modifications: Cycle selected should be based on your function, balance, strength. Tricycle favored over bicycle if you have limited leg function and sitting balance; should be sturdy with wide base of support to prevent tipping. Plywood backrest, to stabilize balance if needed, should be fastened to seat and be as high as user's shoulders. Pedal holders, made of tape strips, leather straps, or Velcro, will assist in holding feet on pedals if you have poor control of legs. Padding in middle of handlebars if you have unsteady balance.

Activity: BOWLING

Materials: Ball—regulation weighted ball; plastic or rubber ball; newspaper crumpled, shaped, and covered with tape; or ball with elastic fastened to rubber ball for retrieval by nonwalker. Ten pins—regulation ones; plastic pins; milk cartons; bleach bottles; thread spools glued in tower of two, three, or more. Alley—taped (masking) or painted.

Description: Object is to roll ball down lane and knock down all ten pins at once. A game consists of ten frames, and each player rolls ball twice per frame. Winner has highest score at end of ten frames.

Modifications: Size of alley may be adjusted. The weight of the ball and type of delivery may be adjusted. Player in wheelchair rolls from chair, which needs to be carefully braked before starting. Limited strength, preventing lifting and carrying, indicates use of a pusher similar to shuffleboard cue, allowing bowler to grasp handle with one hand to push the ball. If unable to use arms and hands, could push ball with feet. For visually impaired, use of string will outline alley with other player telling how many pins were knocked down.

Activity: CROQUET

Materials: Playing surface may be tabletop (large or small), floor or lawn. Balls—newspaper balls covered with masking tape; yarn balls; wooden or plastic. Mallets—homemade, small or standard. Wickets—open-ended *large* cans held in place with Plasticine; wires bent to form an arch and anchored in Plasticine; or standard wickets.

Description: Winner is first to send ball through each wicket both up- and downcourt in order shown by numbers. Each player has one turn unless ball goes through wicket when second turn is allowed. If opponent's ball is knocked out of place, opponent has to start from where ball rests.

Modifications: Number of wickets may be decreased or placement changed if needed for play. Mallet adjusted by grip, weight, and length as needed for grasp, reach, and strength. For crutch user, game played standing up and leaning on one crutch for support; mallet taped to other crutch. Tabletop croquet with small board and yarn balls for those with limited movement. Indoor-outdoor carpet sample will offer resistance and make indoor game more challenging. Wickets could be anchored to short pile rug with masking tape.

Activity: PING-PONG

Materials: Ping-Pong paddle (grip built up or cut down dependent upon user). Ping-Pong balls with or without attached fish line for easy retrieval for nonwalkers. Portable plywood board (one-third of standard plywood sheet, four feet by eight feet by half inch). Two-inch "net" made of plywood, stood on edge; string; and cardboard. (Without plywood floor could be marked with tape; "net" made of sturdy cardboard.)

Description: Object of game is to hit ball over the net so it cannot be returned by opponent. One point is scored for server if ball cannot be returned, and server gets another serve. First to get 15 points wins.

Modifications: Use on table, floor, classroom, gymnasium. If wheelchair is used, shorten board and tape to wheelchair arms.

If blind student is playing, noises should be eliminated so ball can be located by sound.

Activity: SHUFFLEBOARD

Materials: Colored disks—two colors and four of each color; use bottle caps, painted or with colored paper glued in center; or checkers. Diagrammed court done with masking tape on table, or board with siderails with open end toward board to prevent spills.

Description: Object of game is to push disks with hand to scoring area in attempt to score more points than opponent. If done individually, aim for improved score.

Modifications: Use tabletop or board rather than floor or sidewalk court. Size may be standard six feet ten inches by eighteen inches or shorter depending on balance, strength, and stretching ability. Visually handicapped need to feel entire court before starting; sighted partner tells when blind player's disk has landed and keeps score for both. Headgear with wand to push disks if impossible to use by hand; thicker disks and floor court if feet have to be used.

Activity: TABLE TETHERBALL

Materials: Ping-Pong paddles or small board tapered to make handle. Rubber ball, size of golf ball, fastened to string. Tetherball board and pole.

Description: Two players. Server starts game. Object is to hit ball to wrap entire length of string around pole to prevent opponent from hitting the ball. Score point for each time this is done, and player who scores gets another serve. Game is 15 points or whatever players decide upon *ahead.*

Modifications: Paddle grip built up or cut down if needed. Ball may be lighter (wiffleball) or larger if impossible to hit small rubber ball. Hand may be used rather than paddle. Velcro strip around hand to hold paddle if needed. Tiny bell, fastened to string above the ball, helpful to visually impaired; also board must be large and heavy enough not to tip when ball is struck hard.

TEAM SPORTS

Activity: BALLOON VOLLEYBALL

Materials: Heavy-duty large balloons. String or cord to attach to wall on two ends, posts, or chairs for "net."

Description: Each team has equal number of players. Object is to hit or toss the ball across the net and have it hit floor without being touched by opposing team. Server can hit three times to get it over; any number of team members may help to get the balloon over. Point scored by team which gets balloon onto opponent's floor side without being hit. Preset number determines score, which determines winner.

Modifications: Court may be smaller if there is nonambulatory player or player with limited arm movements. String height should be set to allow some success. Those with poor arms could sit and use feet, head, shoulders to hit the balloon. For totally blind a small bell could be placed in balloon before inflation in order to allow student to locate balloon by sound. Lightness of balloon allows extra time for movement.

Activity: TARGET BASEBALL

Materials: Miniature playing court (see drawing) on cork surface, ceiling tile, wall board for darts, plywood or wall for suction darts or beanbags. Eight darts—regular, suction, beanbags (suction or beanbags safer).

Description: Players divided into two teams (or just two players). Each player is given eight darts and allowed to throw until a score or "out" is made. Team to get highest score, once all team players have had turn, is the winner.

Modifications: Court may be modified in size or distance from players. Object to be thrown will depend on movement potential of arm and hand grasp. If unable to throw, draw a pattern on paper, tape to table, and allow players to push checkers or bottle caps. Rules may be simplified. Light string tied to suction dart or beanbag will allow nonwalking player to recover own darts or beanbags by reeling them in after plays.

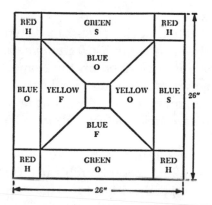

BASEBALL
Key: H—Home run
S—Strike
O—Out
F—Foul Ball

RED H	GREEN S	RED H	
BLUE O	BLUE O		
BLUE O	YELLOW F	YELLOW O / BLUE S	26"
	BLUE F		
RED H	GREEN O	RED H	

Activity: MORE COMPLICATED TARGET BASEBALL
Materials: Same as for simple Target Baseball

RED S	GREEN O	RED T
BLUE H	BLUE B	BLUE F
	YELLOW F / YELLOW S	
RED F	BLUE O	RED H
WHITE ST	GREEN T	WHITE ST

Key: B—Ball
F—Foul
H—Home run
S—Single
D—Double
T—Triple
O—Out
ST—Strike

SWIMMING

Activity: SWIMMING

Materials: Swimming pool area, preferably one with shallow area allowing you to stand with head out of water. Stairs allow you to enter and exit easily. However, you could be lowered into water with one assistant.

Modifications: Contact nearby motels in your town or city. They are usually very accommodating about your needs and allowing you to have lessons in their pools. You *must* be accompanied by qualified water safety instructor or senior lifesaver.

Activity: DOG PADDLE

Materials: Silva egg, flotation device (egg-shaped styrofoam device with attached belt)—*this is not a lifesaving device.*

Description: This stroke is performed on the stomach and moves one forward in the water. With head held out of water, and arms kept underwater, move alternately in dog fashion (as if digging for a bone). Legs are kicked alternately from hip with slight knee bend.

Modifications: If you have difficulty with the breathing pattern, the dog paddle stroke eliminates this problem. If you have limited movement in legs or paralysis, kicking is not necessary. Simply use arms. Initially the use of silva egg will allow you to concentrate on arm stroke and eliminates worry of maintaining position on top of water. The arm stroke is especially good if you have limited arm movement because you don't need to recover stroke out of water. If arm involvement is too great, the best all-around stroke for you might be one on the back, eliminating breathing problem and incorporating use of legs only.

Activity: RESTING PLATFORM

Materials: Boxlike structure or table which could be weighted down in shallow area. Wooden table or box must be sanded and varnished (would eventually warp). Fifty-gallon metal drum, painted, could also be used. Resting platform could be weighted down with cinder blocks.

Description: If you have limited or no use of your legs to swim, such a structure would allow you to rest rather than have you scull using your arms. Sculling (treading water without use of arms) should definitely be learned regardless of availability of resting platform.

Activity: AMERICAN CRAWL

Materials: Flippers (fins). Silva egg or handmade device using a square or rectangle piece of styrofoam with cloth belt. Hand paddles made from Plexiglas (purchased at hardware store), shaped like hand—tapered at end, wide as palm tied at wrist and around palm.

Description: This stroke is done on the stomach and moves you forward through the water. Stroke requires overarm recovery and a kick initiated at the hip with slight knee bend. For proper mechanical analysis refer to Counsilman's *Science of Swimming* and the Red Cross Water Safety Instruction teaching manual.

Modifications: If you have limited motion in legs, you may use fins, which will assist in giving more powerful kick. If you have no movement in legs, it is possible to perform this stroke with arms only. Hand paddles may be used if you have limited movement in arms and hands. Silva eggs, or modifications of them, will allow you to concentrate on stroke performance in beginning and not concern yourself about staying above water.

Remember:

1. Whatever your disability, everyone can play *something.*
2. It feels good to get strong through sports.
3. Start now to find *your* place in sports.

For more information, see page 265.

16 | Life Survival Skills

Independence means that you have the skills to do a lot of things for yourself. It also means that you can do some things better than others. And it means that you can call on others to help you do the things you can't do, and feel good about it, because you know you've got skills and time and energy that others can call on you for.

Here are some life survival skills, the basic necessities for daily living. Start a notebook, and copy this list. In your notebook check off the things you can do (or at least those you know how to do although you may not have tried them yet—"I think I can"), things you really are comfortable doing (you have tried it—"Sure!"), and the things that you are so good at that you didn't realize it was a skill ("Nothing to it!").

I think I can   Sure!   Nothing to it!

> Cook an egg
> Replace a wall switch
> Order advance theater tickets
> Borrow a library book
> Call a friend to go out
> Replace a faucet gasket
> Read a calendar

Sew on a button
Use a pocket calculator
Make coffee
Write a check
Get lunch for six people
Order my meal in a restaurant
Vote in a voting machine
Read a newspaper classified ad
Call long distance
Paint furniture
Feed a baby
Type
Read a thermometer
Write a business letter
Change my bed
Use public transportation
Hang a picture
Change a fuse
Patch a bicycle tire
Furnish my apartment
Cook dinner for my family
Get emergency medical help
Replace an electrical plug
Build a ladder
Paint my room
Write a book report
Call collect
Apply for credit
Sharpen a knife
Send a telegram
Read a book
Wash my hair
Read a map
Buy the family's groceries for a week
Install a dimmer switch
Do the family laundry
Use a dictionary

Figure the tip at a restaurant
Use the Yellow Pages
Cut my hair
Fill the lawn mower with gas
Bake a cake
Replace a windowpane
Mow the lawn
Learn a foreign language
Shampoo a carpet
Change a baby's diaper
Study for a test
Replace a fluorescent light bulb
Buy my clothes
Apartment hunt
Drive a car
Learn algebra
Open a bank account
Plunge a toilet
Make tea
Build a bookcase
Replace a flush ball in the toilet
Start a fire
Buy from a mail-order catalogue
Wash windows
Change a light bulb
Operate a coin-laundry machine
Change a flat tire
Shorten or lengthen my jeans

Go over the life survival list, and note all the things you have never tried. Sure, lots of them are easy, and you can do them even if you haven't tried them, but go ahead and do each of them once, just to see if it's just the way you thought it would be. Next, notice the things you have done once or twice and are comfortable doing. How about the things you have never tried? How about skills that aren't on the list? What skills do you notice other kids have that you don't? Think about the things in your home that someone does for you and you haven't tried.

Skills Are Your Independence

Life survival or personal management skills are crucial to you if you are ever to live independently. Nothing will separate you from your classmates faster than being out of it on life survival skills, skills that nondisabled teenagers will have learned by just being around, skills that some of you may not have learned because someone else always does them at home, while you were at the rehab clinic or school or sitting there watching someone else do them. If your clothes and hair and makeup are different from your classmates', you can be sure that your lack of grooming skills will handicap you well beyond what your physical disability is doing to you.

If you have never learned to use public transportation, cook, pack your lunch, sew on a button, shop, order and tip at a restaurant, use the Yellow Pages, type, do your own laundry, write a business letter, buy things, understand something about credit, ask a friend out, get advance tickets for the theater, or change a fuse, then life is going to be a lot more isolated than it needs to be for you.

Since most of you are in school, chances are that you do have self-care and clothing know-how. And probably most of you know that the level of survival skills for most disabled teenagers can be improved. You don't have to be good at everything, but you *do* need a minimal competency in all areas of personal management before you can really plan to live independently.

A few of you will feel that you know how to do the things you need to know—until you get mainstreamed. Then you may be rudely awakened to the fact that it was OK for a disabled adolescent to be where you are in a special school or class, but it is *not* OK for a mainstreamed student to be where you are. Ask your parents and brothers and sisters to help you on the things you notice you need to learn. Figure out the times you feel out of it and the times you won't go somewhere with a group because you don't know what "a la carte" on the menu means or you don't know how to get another bus home. Turn the negative experiences you have at school around so that they become learning experiences. Write down the words and actions that threw you off-balance. Find out about them so that the next time you can be prepared.

Where to Learn the Skills

Start at home with the person who does each of these things in your family. Ask your mom to let you change the fuse the next time one goes out, ask your dad to show you his popover secret the next time he cooks breakfast, ask your brother to give you some tips on studying, and ask your sister to show you how she writes a book report. They will be flattered that you think they know enough about it to ask them (or at least most of them will be). Some high schools give courses on family living and include all the skills on the checklist as part of their program. Sign up for a survival skills and family living course if you need more practice. Lots of times it's easier to learn in school than at home, where many people may be supercritical or want it done their way, instead of the way *you* like it—like an egg cooked through solid.

Some of you may have been in physical and occupational therapy when you were younger, but now that you are in school, you don't go anymore. You may want to go back for more, now that you know what you need, now that you can ask for specific skills that make sense to you. For example, you can learn cooking, grooming, and typing skills there. Therapists can help you with the modifications you might find necessary for practicing your skills.

If you live in a city, there may be community agencies that teach survival skills to the disabled. Instructors of visually, hearing, or orthopedically impaired students may teach the skills, or they may find a disabled student or adult living near you who could help.

Life Skills Center

Some schools have a life skills center where seniors in high school live in apartments or mobile homes. They live there from six to ten weeks under the supervision of adults who give instruction when it's needed. The kinds of skills experienced include food preparation, dressing and undressing, bathing, toilet, shopping, and housecleaning. The students actually decide which skills they need, and the supervisor works with them so that they can get practice in their own apartment with a few other students.

Student Survival Skills

(Read, Study, Test)

For students, life survival skills include reading, studying, and taking tests. The center of your work life right now is school. To be good at it, you must have reading skills.

Survival Skills: Reading

You can learn how to be a good reader, how to improve your reading, what to read, the importance of a good vocabulary, and how to use a reading list.

You read to learn your reactions to things that sound like you and that don't sound like you. You can learn where you stand in the range of other people's experiences on issues that concern you.

If your life includes being a student, then reading is the critical skill for you to possess—and to enjoy!

ARE YOU A GOOD READER?

A good reader reads easily and fast.
She understands what she reads.
She remembers what she reads.
She reads groups of words—thought patterns—rather than word by word.
She reads at different speeds, depending on the purpose

of her reading (test, pleasure, contrasting ideas).
He has a good vocabulary and continually adds to it.
He reads critically and questions the source and purpose
of the author. He doesn't believe "everything in print."
He reads all kinds and types of materials and books.
He loves to read.

We can all improve our reading. Most of us don't read as fast
as we could because we have been taught to read slowly in
order to get all the facts. Many students don't see any reason for
reading any faster.

A good reader knows which materials to read fast and which
will take more time. All reading shouldn't be at the same speed.
If you are taking notes to write a term paper or memorizing
dates or formulas as you read, you must read these things more
slowly. If you are reading the newspaper, a novel, or an essay,
you can read much faster and learn to skim in order to get the
main points. A good reader has learned to decide what speed
is necessary for the job.

IMPROVING YOUR READING

When you start reading, know what you are reading for: the
main idea, particular facts, pleasure, comparison of the same
subject with another author, or ideas to write something of your
own. Learn to look at the reading material: its length, the names
of the chapters, the headings used in the text, and the summary.
This information will give you an idea of the style and organization of the author. Most articles can be understood by your
reading the opening sentence to find the problem the author is
going to write about and the final paragraphs of his or her
summary. Many things you select to read won't be what you
thought they were, so don't read them through after you know
they are not what you need. Learn to browse, to explore; try a
book, and if you decide it isn't right, then choose another one.

Push yourself to read faster; practice some rapid reading
every day. Use a ruler, move it down a page at a regular rate,

and see how fast you can cover the page, trying not to move your head or to say the words in your throat. All physical motions with head and eyes and voice slow your reading rate. Look at as many words at a time as you can, and learn to give your full attention to what you are reading. Don't use your brainpower to block out a radio program when you can use it to concentrate on your reading and your understanding of what you read. Really try to develop a fast and good reading style.

DEVELOPING YOUR VOCABULARY

Developing your vocabulary is a by-product of reading. You can't learn or understand any more than your understanding and knowledge of words will permit. The larger your vocabulary, the more you can understand what you read and the more ideas you will have to express yourself in writing and speaking. Vocabulary is the most significant measurement of a student's intelligence and ability to do well in school. If schools had to use only one test to predict success in school, they would use the test that measures vocabulary.

You may have heard about many methods to improve your vocabulary, such as special courses, books, special schooling, and lists to memorize which increase your vocabulary in a week or a month. But the most logical and reliable way to build your vocabulary is to work with words as you read. This doesn't mean you interrupt your reading to look up every word you don't understand as you go along. If you can guess at the meaning of a word through the context, make a note of it, and look it up when you have finished. Nothing can make reading more boring than to stop every few paragraphs to use a dictionary.

However, figuring out the general meaning of words as you go along in your reading doesn't take the place of knowing exactly what words mean. Get into the dictionary habit. Have a plan or a system for reading that includes writing down words that you aren't sure about in a notebook or looking up a particular number of words at the end of your reading. Keep your dictionary nearby so that you can get to it without looking all over the house or going to someone else's room for it. Buy a dictionary written for high school or college students. Try to develop an interest in words, where words come from, when they are used; find the synonyms (very similar to) and the antonyms (opposite of) of words in order to learn the shades of meanings. These synonyms and antonyms are found in a thesaurus (Greek word for "treasury"). A paperback edition of *Roget's New Pocket Thesaurus* should be on your desk right next to your dictionary. A thesaurus is easy to use. It is arranged in dictionary form, and it's a must for your writing. For instance, when you are writing a book report or term paper, instead of using the word "marvelous" four times, look in your thesaurus and choose other related words or similar words for "marvelous": wonderful, fabulous, spectacular, remarkable, outstanding, prodigious, prime, splendid, superb. . . .

Reading develops vocabulary, which develops ideas, which enrich *your* life!

WHAT SHOULD YOU READ?

Most of you will have many teachers who assign all kinds of things to read so that you may never have to ask this question. Some of you, however, will have a chance to select your own reading materials from a list of assigned reading, and others of you will get no direction whatsoever for your reading.

Reading lists are only suggestions. Serving as a guide to your reading possibilities, rather than a rule about your decisions, is the intent of any reading list. The first reading list included in this chapter was written for those of you who are going to college.

The National Council of Teachers of English is a professional group of teachers of English from all over America who are concerned about what students read. It has published a list that was prepared by asking these teachers of first-year college students what they think high school students should have read before they got to college. The list is arranged alphabetically— not according to the most important books.

Some books are deleted, and new ones added to the list, as students react to what they have read and as teachers change. The best list available for the college-bound student is the *Suggested Precollege Reading* (Reading List 1) on page 267.

HOW DO YOU CHOOSE BOOKS FROM THE LIST?

Nothing is worse than selecting a book for a required reading report by just picking it from its title and knowing nothing more about it! It's making a decision on the basis of almost nothing. Again, the National Council of Teachers of English has prepared a paperback book, *Books for You,* to help high school students with their reading selections. It is well worth buying if you can't find it in your school library. It is an annotated guide to books for high school students. An annotated guide means that it gives one or two lines of description about the book. For instance, if you select Jane Austen's *Pride and Prejudice* from the Precollege List, *Books for You* describes it on page 15: "In this early nineteenth century comedy of manners, Mrs. Bennett's ambition was to find husbands, preferably wealthy, for her five daughters; but there were many crises before any of the girls reached the altar." Here is a description of Hermann Hesse's *Siddhartha:* "The search for communion and contentment within the framework of Indian mysticism is the subject of this moving, human statement first published in 1922." *Books for You* will help you to select books for required reading as well as for fun. If you can't find it at your local library, write to Washington Square Press, Simon & Schuster, 1230 Avenue of the Americas, New York, New York 10036.

For those who aren't interested in reading and who are not going on to college after high school, there is a wonderful book that will end your search for the thinnest book possible for your required English class book report; it is called *High Interest, Easy Reading.* If your library doesn't have a copy of it, write to Scholastic Magazines, Inc., 50 West Forty-fourth Street, New

York, New York 10036. Ask for the latest edition of *High Interest, Easy Reading.*

LEARN ABOUT YOU

If you read, you can learn how others your age and from other parts of the country or world think and act and how they behave in the same situations. You can learn about travel and people and animals and projects and how to build a house. And all the while you are reading you are learning about your reaction to things that sound like you, to things that don't sound like you, and you are thinking where you are in the range of the topics you read about.

You can soon learn that it's not only you who has trouble explaining your feelings to others; it's not only you who is worried about your physical differences, what will happen when you get out of high school, what to do about contraception. It's not only you who are concerned and consumed with all the things that you can't talk about or with the fact that when you do talk about them to your friends, they don't know any more than you do about them.

Reading brings to you the whole world of other people's experiences and discoveries that you will want to be in on as you are in the midst of decisions about your own world of experiences and discoveries.

See page 270 for Reading List 2 adapted from the list developed by the National Easter Seal Society about other people with physical diabilities. When you have a chance to choose your own book for a book report, maybe you'd like to report on one of those.

Survival Skills: Studying

Studying isn't natural. It may look as if it's easy for others to study because they are some kind of "study creature," but study is learned behavior, and everyone who is a good worker has learned it. The sooner you realize that studying is not something extra, the sooner you realize the need for the skill. You will then begin to get enjoyment out of the real reason for study —learning.

Many teachers, educators, and parents promote the idea that the classroom is the heart of learning. Studying then becomes doing something for the teacher or cramming for tests and examinations. In fact, the classroom situation is only your guide to what to study; your evaluation of how you do; your suggestions for new ways to look at materials such as tests, related readings, papers, and projects about the particular subject.

In order to look at studying as something that has to do with *you*, you should understand that studying is for learning. And learning is what high school is all about. It is learning what you can do academically, what you can understand, how you can relate to new materials, what you can think about.

To get anything out of studying, you must define it in such a way that it is important to you. You must set it up in your mind so that it counts. It has to have a top priority if it is going to work. If you can define your study time as your work and if you accept the fact you must work nights, it will help. There is no question about the difficulty of the hour, especially if your parents are home from their work and watching TV or playing bridge or having late cocktails and dinner while you work—but your schedule is different. You have sports and clubs and time off for activities after school, while your parents and most adults are still on their jobs. At any rate, it won't come out fair or equal with adults because high school students who study on a regular, responsible basis *do* work more than adults who have nine-to-five jobs. Your work schedule compares more readily with professional people in teaching, research, law, and medicine or with business executives who work all hours. There is no doubt that a high school student who studies three hours a night works more than the forty-hour week! And three hours a night is about average for an A or B student with five academic subjects in a competitive high school.

As you work out your study schedule and find what you can do in terms of working alone, at the library, or with homework assignments, you will be learning what you can do in college, what you can do in your career after college. All your high school experiences are teaching you about your abilities and your interests. Studying is a key place for you to learn about your self-starting ability, your motivation, your persistence, your follow-through, and your ability to stick with a problem. These traits will build. You will learn all kinds of things that you can do as well as all kinds of things you *cannot* do because of your lack of good study skills.

Your ability to study will improve as the years pass. Self-discipline is a growing ability. Good study skills grow slowly. It takes time to learn to use your mind efficiently to understand all kinds of subjects, to memorize facts, to grasp new ideas, and to see relationships between the subjects you study and you and the world. If there is no way for you and study skills, then you should know that for you, there is no way for you and college or at least a liberal arts or competitive college.

HOW CAN YOU STUDY TO LEARN?

Many things will help you study. Good teachers and interested parents who encourage you and work with you as you develop your study skills are the most help. But good teachers and interested parents are hard to find, and lucky is the student who has either! If you ask for help with your studying, from your homeroom teacher, your guidance counselor, or one of the administrators, you should be able to find someone who will encourage you so that your work will be something you look forward to.

If your family is working against you with distracting offers of other things to do and with noise in the house, you may be able to go to the local library or to study as much as possible in school or after school, in place of sports or music or clubs. Some students do all their studying before they go home because they know that conditions at home just don't help them study. They spend their time off with their families at night.

There are many books or chapters in books written about how to study, as well as lists of dos and don'ts for studying. They explain that you need a nice warm, comfortable room, good light, no radio or TV, plenty of paper and supplies, time, and concentration. And of course, the proper assignment. Many of you know that all these physical things can be in place, but after the first two or three tries of a new school year, it just doesn't work. Potato chips are added, the radio is on low, the phone rings for just one call, or a TV special is on from eight to nine that night. In other words, planning the study time and place and being there aren't the same as doing the work.

DOING THE WORK

Plan the amount of time you are going to work or study. Don't let yourself get away with reasons to change the time after you have made just one phone call or visit with a sister or brother. Figure out exactly what you want to accomplish with a specific goal for each subject: so many problems in mathematics; so many pages of history to outline; so many words to memorize in French. If you have one hour for each subject, and you start with mathematics, when the hour is up and you are only half finished, go on to the next subject. Don't use all three hours on the mathematics! Either you didn't understand the assignment, or it is too hard and the whole class won't get it either, or you aren't going to make it in math—at least not tomorrow. Go on to the French for the next hour and to the history for the third hour. If there is time left over after working on all three subjects, go back to the mathematics. *Organize* your time. Experience will help you with this, and your time will be used more effectively when you stick to allotted times. You have heard that people with the most to do get the most done—it's the same principle. If you have all day to clean the garage, you can take all day to do it, or if you have to clean it in one hour in order to go to the game, you can do it in the one hour. Don't let yourself spend all night or all day on one assignment.

Plan which assignments you will do in what order. Some students start with their favorite, in order to get going faster, and others begin with their least favorite, in order to get it over with so that they aren't too tired at the end with the worst subject left to do. After an hour at your desk, take a planned five- or ten-minute break. Get a snack or talk to someone or turn on the music and walk around and stretch.

Don't wait until a subject interests you before you plan to do the homework! Until you learn enough about it, it couldn't possibly interest you. You have to do your social studies or Latin or geometry assignments whether you like them or not. And good students *become* interested in subjects because of study.

Even though the subject doesn't interest you, the best study takes place when you know why you are studying, you care about what you are studying, and you are certain you can actually do the work. Try to understand the work for its own sake. Learn how *you* do in the subject, not how much you have to do in order to please a teacher or to get a particular grade.

MEMORIZING

No matter how modern the school you attend or no matter what the latest fashion in learning is, you can't get very far without memorizing. There is vocabulary to memorize, scientific formulas, events, names of people, authors of books, characters in literature, dates for historical periods as well as specific dates of events to learn. You can't write a good examination without memorizing specific information.

There are some helpful tips for memorizing. The most obvious is that the more you understand about what you are trying to memorize, the easier it is to remember. Learning nonsense is difficult! And many students try to memorize nonsense simply because they haven't taken the time to understand the concept in the first place.

Concentrate on what you are trying to memorize and use as many senses as possible to learn. Read the material aloud so that you can hear as well as see it. Don't spend long hours at a time on it beyond your efficiency for memorizing. Fifteen- to twenty-minute sessions with other homework in between the memorizing sessions are the most effective way to memorize for most students. Going over the memorization just before class is always a help—not to learn but to recall the poem or facts or vocabulary.

Survival Skills: Testing

You will periodically be tested on the materials you covered during the school term. If you really do understand the subject, you will be able to use your study time for review for these tests and examinations. If you have worked just enough to get by for your daily assignments, and you called that studying, then all your review time has to be spent cramming or learning the material for the first time! Cramming can work for one or two subjects, but it will never work for four or five strong subjects if you plan to do *well* in them.

A bright student *can* attend classes, cram, and learn enough to pass a test in all of his or her courses, but if academic work is something you want to develop and have grow into a meaningful activity in your life, then studying must take a priority right *now*. Read much more about testing on page 81 in this book, "Getting Tested for Physical Differences" (Chapter 11).

Survival Skills: Learning

The word "learning" or "understanding" has more to do with you than the word "homework" (which sounds as though it's for the teacher) or the word "studying" (which sounds as though you were working for the sake of the work). If you think of studying as learning or understanding new things and people and new concepts, it may help. You will want all the help you can get for this skill of studying to learn on your own, as it has to be.

WHERE CAN YOU GO FOR MORE HELP IN LEARNING?

There is no substitute for the teacher of a course to help you learn. Different subjects must be studied differently; to go to the mathematics or foreign language or history teacher is by far the most relevant help you can get. Don't be afraid to ask your teacher how to study to learn the particular subject. Most teachers will be pleased with your interest since usually teachers feel that the last interest students have is in studying to learn. For this very reason many teachers don't teach you about studying. Don't wait until you are in a crisis to ask for help, especially if it's a new subject and you aren't getting the understanding of it that you expected to have. Go to the teacher as soon as it concerns *you*. Don't wait until you are too discouraged to learn.

Educational Decisions

The sooner you take your work (learning) seriously, the sooner it will become very meaningful and worthwhile for you to be spending those three hours every night at it. You will be surprised at how interesting your work can be! Remember it is *you* who are learning and understanding. You are becoming a person who needs to know as much about your learning ability as you can in order to make the curricular, educational, vocational, and career decisions that you will have to make.

Many of you will see life survival skills as your way out—out of your parents' home and into your own college or work environment. After high school, and as a young adult, most of you will not need to be urged to learn how to live on your own. Take advantage of the survival courses taught in school and the chance to practice them at home. Learn all you can from your family and the local community agencies. These are getting-out skills, skills that will put you on your own.

IV | Independence

17 | It's the Law!

Public Law (PL) 94-142 guarantees all American children, with *no* exceptions, an education. And that's new. When the law was passed, about half of the nations' 8 million disabled children were denied the kind of education they should have, and as many as 1 million children were totally excluded from school. The ages to be served by the law are three to twenty-one by September 1980.

Basically the law provides for a free, appropriate public education for all disabled children between the ages of three and twenty-one. It is permanent legislation with no expiration date.

The law is very specific about what must take place. It is based on the idea that each student must be educated in the least restrictive environment. That means you cannot be placed in some special school or some special classroom and kept there if you could be mainstreamed with the nondisabled students part time or full time.

The law also says that in order to decide just where you should be placed, individualized education programs (IEP), must be developed for *each child* and reviewed *every year.* And even better, you and your parents have a right and will want to take the responsibility to be in on this individualized program. An IEP is an evaluation of your present education level, your annual goals, and your short-term measurable and specific services and goals. The law requires that to the maximum extent appropriate, disabled students are to be educated with the nondisabled. This usually means that if it is at all possible, you are to be mainstreamed in the public school system. But if you and your parents don't think that will work for you, *you don't have to be mainstreamed.* There must be alternative educational plans for you if you and your parents think mainstreaming would do you more harm than good. In some cases, self-contained special classes could work best for you—that is, in some cases special education could be the most effective education for your individualized education program (IEP).

The new law guarantees due process procedures. What does this legal talk mean?? It means that the school can't decide what your rights are and what your program is and put you into one kind of class or program, change you, or kick you out of school without hearing your side of it. Due process means that you and your parents have a right to say what is best for you. It means that you and your parents are experts, too—experts about you. It means that when it comes to you, you and your parents count as much as educators, therapists, and other professionals, who sometimes give you the impression that they know more about what's good for you than you do!

Very specifically, due process means that you and your parents, by law, get:

1. Notice in writing *before* any action is taken or recommendation is made that can change your program.
2. All records related to your identification, evaluation, and placement.
3. An opportunity to talk about serious complaints you and your parents have about any matters related to your education.
4. An impartial hearing when your family and the school cannot agree on what type of program will be most helpful for you.
5. Good appeals procedures. If your family is not satisfied with the results of a due process hearing, you have the

right to appeal to the state department of special education; if problems remain unresolved after all these procedures have been followed, parents have the right under law to appeal to the courts.

A New Ball Game

PL 94-142 guarantees a whole new ball game for most disabled students and their parents—with new rules that make you and your parents an equal team with school personnel. Some state and local chapters of parent organizations are helping prepare parents and students for action under this new law. If you think you should be in a different educational program from the one you are in now, find out from your state department of education how you can get a support group and other parents to help you with due process action.

Your family has lived so long with the old, discriminating attitudes toward the disabled that this change is hard to believe for a lot of parents. Many of your parents have learned to expect to be discriminated against. The law now says that discrimination must end. You can help your parents believe this law. You have the right to an educational program that fits your special needs. That means that you and your parents should settle for no less.

Learn the Law

In order to plan the best strategy to take full advantage of this new ball game, you will want to know the ground rules. What does the law say? What does it mean to you? Here are some of the key facts about PL 94-142:

1. Highest priority must be given to disabled children who are not now receiving an education and to the most severely disabled children whose education is inadequate.
2. Strong safeguards of the due process rights of parents

and students must be guaranteed by states and public schools. These safeguards must provide for the opportunity to protest educational decisions made by the school.

3. The law is strongest for mainstreaming students. It requires that children can be placed in special or separate classes only when it is impossible to mainstream them, using supplementary aids and services. In other words, you can't be dumped into a regular classroom if you can hardly see unless you are provided with special visual aids. If you can't hear, an interpreter or aids that work best for you *must* be provided.

4. Testing and evaluation must be in the primary language or mode of communication that you use. You can select braille, a recorder, a test in Spanish if you are Spanish-speaking, or whatever you use as your basic mode of communication. No educational decision can be made on the basis of one test.

5. An individualized education plan (IEP) has to be prepared for you every year. When appropriate, the child is to be included with its parent or planning team. If you are a junior or senior high school student reading this book, you can just assume it *is* appropriate for you to be in on your IEP. Be sure to be there.

6. If the best thing for you is a private school, then the government has to pay for it. The private school must meet standards set by law, and it must give you the same rights that the public school is giving you under this new law.

7. Every state in the nation has to set up an advisory board to include disabled students, teachers, and parents of disabled students. The board advises the state on things not being done and evaluates the programs you are in. Find out who is on your state board. If politics and changing the world are part of your interests, try to get on the board yourself. Otherwise, write letters to the student on the board, and let your views be known.

Another Law—The Work Law

Besides the new law on education, there is a work law that students with disabilities should know about. This law is important for you to understand when you plan your career strategies and goals.

Section 504 of the Rehabilitation Act of 1973 is the first federal civil rights law protecting the rights of the disabled. It says that "no otherwise qualified handicapped individual . . . shall, solely by reason of his handicap, be excluded from the participation in, be denied the benefits of, or be subjected to discrimination under *any program or activity receiving Federal financial assistance.*" Each federal agency has to make its own regulations to enforce this law. For example, the Department of Health, Education, and Welfare (HEW) states that no program or activity receiving HEW financial assistance can discriminate against qualified handicapped persons in the following areas:

1. Recruitment, advertising, and the processing of applications for employment.
2. Hiring, upgrading, promotion, award of tenure, demotion, transfer, layoff, termination, right of return from layoff, and rehiring.
3. Rates of pay or any other form of compensation and changes in compensation.
4. Job assignments, job classifications, organizational structures, position descriptions, lines of progression, and seniority lists.
5. Departure and return from leaves of absence, sick leave, or any other leave.
6. Fringe benefits available by virtue of employment, whether or not administered by the recipient.
7. Selection and financial support for training, including apprenticeship, professional meetings, conferences, and other related activities, and selection for leaves of absence to pursue training.

8. Employer-sponsored activities, including social or recreational programs.
9. Any other term, condition, or privilege of employment.

Nor may a recipient (employer) participate in a contractual or other relationship (e.g., with employment and referral agencies, labor unions, organizations providing or administering fringe benefits, organizations providing training and apprenticeship programs) which has the effect of subjecting the qualified disabled applicant or employee to discrimination.

The recipient is required by law to "make reasonable accommodation to the known physical or mental limitations of an otherwise qualified handicapped applicant or employee, unless the recipient can demonstrate that the accommodation would impose an undue hardship on the operation of its program." Accommodations could include:

1. Making facilities used by employees readily accessible to and usable by handicapped persons.
2. Job restructuring.
3. Part-time or modified work schedules.
4. Acquisition or modification of equipment or devices.
5. The provision of readers or interpreters.
6. Other similar actions.

When you interview for a job, you can discuss the possible need for accommodations such as those listed here so that you are prepared to talk about your needs with the employer.

In selecting among job applicants, the employer may not use an employment test or other selection criteria which screen out or tend to screen out disabled persons unless the test score is shown to be job-related for the position. Employment-related tests should assess the person's job skills and aptitudes, not the disability.

Work Law 504 calls for:

1. *Free, appropriate education for all disabled children, regardless of the nature or severity of the disability.*
2. *Positive efforts to create job opportunities so that a disability is no longer a barrier to employment.*
3. *College and postsecondary vocational education which is adapted to the needs of disabled students.*
4. *Equal treatment of people with disabilities by health, welfare, and social service agencies.*

Access

The key word in the whole work law regulation is "access." All HEW-assisted facilities must be barrier-free. If adaptations won't work, structural changes must be made within the next three years. No exceptions will be allowed.

Access also means special aids and adaptations such as interpreters for the deaf, taped tests, and brailled materials, and readers for students with visual disabilities. For a free copy of the complete regulation, write to: HEW, Office of Civil Rights, 330 Independence Avenue, SW, Room 5400, Washington, D.C. 20201.

You Can Make It Work

The best laws in our country do absolutely no good unless citizens are working for compliance—in other words, unless you push for them to be enforced. If no one says anything about your rights, about the new laws, about changing your educational program, the law won't automatically work for you. You have to initiate what you want done, and you have the law on your side to make those changes. Alice, a college student who is blind, found that she had to use the law to get her rights to tape lectures in her college classes. This is how she tells the story:

"College teachers are willing to exchange ideas and ask questions about disability, but they never get into their personal feelings. They are usually willing to make accommodations for me, like letting me tape a lecture or reading out loud what they write on the blackboard. I'm willing to meet them halfway and make my own adjustments if they're willing to make accommodations.

"I had one teacher who wouldn't let me tape his classes. I tape all my classes. I told him he was in violation of Section 504 and that I would pursue it with a college lawyer. 'I know my rights, and I use them when I need to, and if you want to discuss this further, I will arrange an appointment,' I said. He said, 'No, it's OK. You can tape it.' "

Standing up for your rights, and knowing the law, can make the difference between getting a decent education—or not. What are some of the things you can do to make these laws work for you and other teenagers who are disabled?

Get a Copy of the Law

Know as much as you can learn about the law, and get your parents in on it, too. Get a copy of the law, anyone can write for one. Write to the Superintendent of Documents, GPO, Washington, D.C. 20402, and send 45 cents for your copy of PL 94-142. Write also to the same address for your free copy of Section 504. Or just write to your Congressional representative and request a free copy of each law. Don't be afraid of the tiny print and legal talk. This law is written to help and protect you. Go beyond the unfamiliarity of the way it looks, and get right into the content and meaning for you. Get your parents to go to a workshop or parents' training session to learn the details of the law. Don't try to do it alone. Get other students and their parents with you.

Work with Other Disabled Students

When you read the disability rights chapter in this book, you learned that disabilities are not only a personal problem but also a political issue. You will have to organize to get things done, to make changes, to get what you need and want. If you are not already a member of a group of students with disabilities and their parents, join one. Get your whole family and lots of relatives in on it, too. The voices of people organized in a group with one interest are the voices that are heard. Experienced parents can help you find out how to get started. It will take plenty of united action to raise educational standards for students with disabilities, to get the funding that is your due for the programs you need, and to get rid of the barriers that prevent a climate of acceptance.

Work with Professionals

Get your teachers, therapists, and agency workers in on your organizations. Each group has its own special concerns and priorities. You must learn to listen to each other in order to unite and do the most effective job. Learn and practice how to get across your point of view, without being aggressive (standing up for your rights by putting others down) and causing anger and resentment from the professionals who are supposed to be working for you. Be assertive (standing up for your rights *without* putting others down) about your point of view, and let others be assertive about theirs. You need all the help you can get to organize for compliance to these super laws.

Speak Up

All plans written by state and local schools for special education services must be open for review and comment by students with disabilities before they are adopted. Get a group together to write to your department of education to read and review these plans. If there are needs that you feel are not being met, speak up and say so.

Be In on Planning Conferences

By law, your family must be included on the team that decides what, where, and how you are going to be educated. For many of you and your parents, it will be the first time you have had an opportunity to be equal partners with educators. You may feel that they know a lot more about it than you do. But remember, they can't possibly know more about you than you do. Express your views and if the educators talk in special education language that you don't get, ask them what they mean.

Clear Goals

Children with disabilities used to be put into special education, and that was the end of it. The new law says that whenever tests are used, parents must be in on which tests are used and how many are necessary. You can go over the results after the tests are taken. Read the testing chapter (Chapter 11) in this book to get a better understanding of tests and to get an idea of which tests are best for you. Also, according to the new education law, your parents have the right to an independent evaluation of the tests you take by a professional that they choose.

Your family can decide on which long- and short-term goals you want to set for yourself. You can be in on the exact goals of your program for the year; as you work with the team in establishing goals and priorities for each year's educational program, remember that there is no need to get less than the law calls for. Don't compromise; be sure you are clear on the evaluation that determines the goals that are set up for you this year. Be sure that you agree with the goals that are set for you. Be sure that those goals make sense to *you*. It's your law.

18 | Educational and Career Decisions, Strategies, and Goals

Edward Roberts, director of the California department of rehabilitation, is an unusual person. He is paralyzed from his neck down, draws his breath from a tube, is strapped leaning back into a wheelchair, and needs an attendant to get a drink of water. But even more unusual is the fact that he has persistently set career goals and determinedly fulfilled them.

Successful people have always known about career goals. They plan their education, their work experience, their priorities at work and home, their moves, promotions, acceptance of one job over another with an eye to whatever goals they set. As they achieve their goals and as they learn more skills and see themselves clearly, they set new goals to reach.

Disabled students tend not to make decisions and plan a strategy for fulfilling a career goal at a time when they can do most about it—schooltime. They wait for others to plan for them, they wait for the right place and the right time that anyone else suggests, and if they consider themselves lucky, they think something will come along. Many disabled students focus their attention so much on the things they cannot do that they end up with no career strategies or goals at all.

Often students follow the misjudgments given by professionals to their parents. For example, Mr. Roberts's parents were told by all the doctors and all the experts that when he contracted polio at fourteen, he would never be more than a vegetable. Lucky for him, he never believed a word of it. In high school Roberts found that everyone wanted to talk about his limitations—talk about the things he couldn't do. As a student trying to find every way possible to develop the things he could do Roberts applied to and was rejected by the California department of rehabilitation because it thought he didn't have enough potential—rejected by the very group that he now directs!

Taking Risks

Roberts remembers his greatest fears from high school days. It was a year after he went from a perfect body to the most imperfect body he could ever imagine; he was out of school that year. His greatest fears about going back to school were of being a helpless cripple—totally dependent on others—and of other students staring at him. He turned the staring fear around by deciding it wouldn't be too bad to have them look at him; after all, that's *one* way to be a celebrity. Many of you have probably noticed, too, that more students tend to *avoid* looking at you; rather than have the problem of staring, you have the problem of getting the kids even to look at you long enough to see you! Roberts began to realize that he would have to take some risks if he were to be back in school and make something of himself. Making something of himself meant to do something meaningful in life—using all the talents and abilities he has in order to take the responsibilities he is capable of taking. Soon he could see that he did have some choices. And this was a surprise to him. He learned that success builds on itself. He learned that no matter how physically different he was, or anyone was, there really are choices.

One of the activities that helped Edward Roberts most was

working with other people who also had disabilities. Helping each other was much better than always being helped. As we say in the friendship chapter of this book (Chapter 14), learning to take the risk of friendship with other disabled people is sometimes easier than chancing it with the nondisabled. It's a good place to learn the skills that friendship takes. Roberts also took the risk of learning to drive a car. And that's when everyone acted as if he were crazy! How could a person paralyzed from the neck down drive? But regardless of what his parents and relatives and teachers knew about it, the motor vehicle department specializing in driver education for the disabled knew more. It added enough adaptive devices for his car so that all he needed to do was to push buttons, and after a few mishaps he was driving!

Roberts said that until he learned to cope with his disability, his worst fear of all was: "What will happen to me when my parents die?" Because of his complete dependency on his parents, they shared the same fear.

How do you get rid of these fears? How do you learn to lessen the fears? How do you learn to cope with the disability and go on with your fears? Roberts advises students to *minimize* their disability and to *maximize* their abilities. In other words, don't concentrate on your physical differences; center, instead, on your likenesses with others.

A Right to Plan a Career

Because you are used to other people's expectations for you and because others are always looking at your limits and your disabilities, you will have to accept the conflict and anxiety that go with others' always thinking you need help. You can't change everyone else's attitudes toward you. You can't wait to make your plans and actions until other people see your possibilities and your abilities. But you can change some people. Most people learn how to react to you and how to treat you by the way you look at yourself. As you gain confidence and learn that it's

OK to have physical differences, as you act as if you have a right to be in school, to be on the job, to take people's time, to have a good time, to have access to all buildings and events, then others will begin to catch on and learn from you.

One of the main reasons why you aren't more into planning a career is that you are not expected to be. Nicci has fragile bones (osteogenesis imperfecta), and as a child she broke bones in her legs about forty times. Here is what she said was expected from the disabled:

> "I survived high school because I realized the situation that was happening. The school tried to make us feel different. It was as if they were saying: 'Don't expect too much because you're crippled. Don't expect anything for yourself after high school.' They weren't career-oriented. They never thought I would be living away from my mother. The school held the view that independent living was simply out of the question."

You are expected to go from one disability program to another, hoping that enough of them will come along to occupy your life. You are expected to sit there and take the next training or educational program designed for you rather than design your own educational strategies and goals. And worst of all, when you finish all those training or educational programs so well designed for you, very few of you will get a job placement out of them!

Unemployment and the Disabled

In an age of inflation, when unemployment figures are high for everybody, it's about time that the disabled notice how little money they make, compared to the nondisabled. Disabled workers earn about 70 percent of the earnings of the nondisabled. This means that a household with a disabled adult in it must make do with a third less income than other households.

It means that of disabled people, 36 percent live in poverty, opposed to 20 percent of the general population. And it means that the proportion of disabled people at the lowest poverty level—15 percent—was almost twice that of the general population—8 percent—in 1973.

Since you know that the disabled make less, doesn't it make sense to start planning your educational strategies now to be in on the money? When you read more and more about the disabled and unemployment, you will see the need for your own educational strategies and goals. Unemployment for everyone is bad enough, but the United States Department of Labor estimates that 58 percent of the disabled are unemployed. And even worse, in New York City it is estimated that 64 percent of those disabled New Yorkers who have a skill and can work are unemployed. Those are not people without skills we are talking about. Those are not people who want to sit at home in front of their TV and be supported by the government. Those are people with skills who want to work: disabled people; people discriminated against because of their physical appearance in a society that markets physical appearance as a way to sell. In California, an estimated 3.5 million disabled people between the ages of sixteen and sixty-four are skilled but cannot find work. You should be aware that only about one in ten of the people in so-called special workshops for the handicapped finds work after training. To top it all off, a recent study shows that only 21 percent of disabled young adults are employed or at college. The remaining 79 percent of disabled young adults are underemployed, unemployed, or institutionalized.

One of the ways for you to get on with your career plans is to get in on your educational plans. Don't let everyone else do it for you. Another way to get on with your educational stra tegies is to take the risks and decide to live with your fears. You can't wait to resolve all your fears and conflicts before you decide to take action. *No one* would ever get anywhere if he or she waited until their fears and doubts were gone before making a move.

Career Strategies and Decisions

Career strategies start with you when you are in on your individualized educational program (IEP). The law says that you can design the way you want your educational program to go. Your career decisions start right now, when you choose your school courses and majors, when you choose to work after school and in the summer, when you decide which job to take, when you decide how much education you need and where and which school you will attend.

Everything you do, every skill you learn, every interest you develop build into possible career choices. Career choices are developmental, and they involve everything you do in your life. For you to be planning your own career strategies—no matter what else you are doing toward developing your physical skills —is a realistic strategy that will help you see how it all ties together.

If you are a student in high school or college, all your curriculum choices are career decisions. If you choose algebra or general math in the ninth grade, you are opening some doors and closing others, depending on your choice. If you choose special education or mainstreaming, you are creating career options which will vary according to what you decide now. Your educational and work choices are career choices. If you choose college, the military, an apprenticeship, a federal training program, or parenthood, you are making a career decision.

Your responsibility to yourself as a student with disabilities is best fulfilled, as it is by any student, by your using school to learn as much as you can about your interests and abilities. Learn what you can do and how well you can do it. Learn also about your motivations, your ambitions, your dreams, your hopes and fears.

Mainstream or Specialize

One of the first questions to consider for your IEP is your school placement. Will you be in a special program or mainstreamed with the nondisabled students? Just because everyone is on the mainstreaming bandwagon these days doesn't mean that it will automatically be best for you. Think about it before you decide.

A student with cerebral palsy found a special school was best for him:

> "When I returned to school, I went to Cameron, a school for physically disabled kids. It was the first time I ever enjoyed school. They tested me, and I started working at my own level and began catching up on things I had missed. It was a small school, and everyone knew everyone. It was more like a family instead of a school."

Education means learning. Just because you are spending time in a program is not enough; only when learning takes place in that program can it qualify as best for you. Being present in the classroom is not enough to guarantee that you will learn or be socially accepted by the other students. Mainstreaming does you no good if you are just dumped in the classroom. You may have specific needs which require accommodation and attention. The other kids in the class may need special help in how they treat you. If you have severe communication, educational, or social problems and you choose an educational program not geared to your special needs, you are looking for *big trouble*, both educationally and emotionally. It's hard to take, to have special educational needs and not have them met and to have the other kids all think you are weird on top of that! It's too much to ask of yourself to go into any educational program without some support or skills to build friendships. It's not something to take on by yourself; you will need some help, and you will want to see it forthcoming before you risk walking into that situation. If you are pretty sure that you will be overwhelmingly rejected by the other kids in the regular school setting, you should seriously think of something else to do: either special education part time or full time or getting one or two other kids with disabilities in there with you. If, on the other hand, you find most of the following accommodations present for you, your IEP should include mainstreaming:

1. Regular school personnel are knowledgeable about, and committed to, adopting instructional services to your special needs.
2. Other students will be reasonably accepting.
3. There is at least minimal ease of accessibility to classrooms, vocational and scientific laboratories, the library, cafeteria, guidance office, and restrooms.
4. Specialized instruction will be provided as needed.
5. Special instructional materials and equipment, such as readers, note takers, tutors, and resource room instructors, will be provided as needed.
6. Guidance and counseling services will be provided by school guidance staff. These services will be supplemented as needed by specialists from the local educational agency, educational cooperative, or community agency.
7. There will be close collaboration between the school and community and state agency resources and between the regular and special education staff.

Born hard-of-hearing, one young man decided to be mainstreamed in a public school with special services after a bad experience in private school. He tells us:

"I went to a private high school for Jewish kids for one year. It provided no interpreter services and no tutoring, which were a necessity for me if I were to keep up with the hearing students. At the end of the school year I told my father not to waste his money on private tuition."

Another student tells us what it was like to be mainstreamed. She has cerebral palsy. Not walking and talking well are hard to take in high school. Still . . .

"For three years I went to a school that had a mainstreaming program. At first, none of the classes was accessible. That created a problem for me. But now there are ramps to every classroom. In my senior year I started going to regular classes full time. I liked the teachers, but sometimes the students teased me because I could not walk well. Still, I learned a lot and feel pretty satisfied about the education I got. Before mainstreaming, I didn't think I could accomplish anything. I thought I'd be sitting around all my life. I would think my problem came from being disabled, being a woman, and being black. But mainstreaming changed my life. The school encouraged us to do what we could and make the best of it."

When deciding about where you should be placed in an education program, remember your IEP is a team effort and *you* are part of the team. It's a process that is done *with* you, not *for* you. Answer the questions asked you, but remember that you can ask questions, too. You can get as much information about the program as educators get about you. You need information in order to make a good decision. Go get it!

What Are Your Placement Choices?

You can't decide what you are going to do until you know your choices. In the case of educational placement you can end up on any level from homebound to attending public school with all nondisabled students. Somewhere in between can be special instruction, part-time or full-time special classes in your local school, vocational school, or a residential school or hospital. Be sure you understand what your choices are before you are asked to choose. Adults are famous for telling how kids can't make up their minds when all along you aren't given enough information to make good decisions in the first place. Some of the kinds of information you will need, regardless of the type of placement you decide is right, are the accommodations you can get in *each* of the situations the team is thinking about for you. Here is a guide to help you make your own list of necessary accommodations. Use your notebook to copy the following ideas suggested here. When you make your list, be sure to add what other accommodations you need, not just those listed here.

IEP Accommodations

AIDS AND EQUIPMENT

Typewriters (large print, electric)
Magnifiers, optical enlargers
Laboratory and shop equipment
Tape recorders
Other

ARCHITECTURAL ACCESSIBILITY

Building access (reserved parking; gradient of sidewalk; curb cuts; ramps; threshold; hardware; doorway width)
Stories of building (elevator, stairs)

Classrooms
Laboratories and shops
Guidance offices
Cafeteria
Gymnasium and
recreation sites
} (doorway width; threshold; door hardware; height of work surfaces; knee space; aisle width; positioning and type of controls in laboratories and shops)

Rest rooms (doorway width; height of toilet; stall size; door opening outward; height of lavatory, paper towel dispenser; hardware)
Water fountains (height; placement of controls)
Elevator (height of controls; brailled floor identification; door opening time)
Other

ATTITUDINAL CLIMATE

Willingness of regular teachers to accept you
Willingness of students to accept you

CLASS SIZE

Class size that permits individualized attention

IN-SERVICE PREPARATION

Of guidance personnel and regular class teachers regarding accommodation for:
Hearing impairments
Orthopedic or neuromotor impairments
Visual impairments
Other health conditions

INSTRUCTIONAL MATERIALS

Braille
Captioned films
Large print
Tapes
Other

INSTRUCTIONAL SUPPORT SERVICES

Interpreters
Note takers
Readers
Tutors
Other

SPECIALIZED PROGRAMS AND COURSES

Adapted physical education and recreation
Braille reading
Home or hospital teachers
Independent living skills
Manual communication
Mobility training
Prevocational laboratory
Resource room
Special education classes
Subjects
Speechreading
Work experience programs
Other

SUPPORT SERVICES

Attendant for personal care
Nursing services
Parent counseling
Modified van for transportation
Other

THERAPIES

Occupational therapy
Physical therapy
Psychological counseling
Speech pathology and audiology
Other

Make up your own accommodation needs for your IEP team. Use this list for a guideline, but be specific—just for you. Educational accommodation isn't all that is needed. What about how you feel? Your attitudes about where you want to learn? Answer the following social questions in your notebook, and add them to the information your IEP teams is collecting:

1. Do you want to be in a nondisabled class setting?
2. Are you working on your coping skills for a nondisabled classroom?
3. Are you within two years of the ages of the other kids in the class?
4. Are your interests and social life interests similar to those of the other kids in the class?
5. Do your parents want you mainstreamed; will they support you, listen to you, and be OK about negative as well as positive responses you have to the class?
6. Can you understand the teachers? Can they understand you well enough for you to function successfully in class?
7. Will you be able to put your attention on the work and not on being different in the classroom or at least enough to do the work and follow directions?
8. If you use special devices, are you good enough at them to succeed in a mainstreamed class or laboratory?
9. Have you been clear about what special or remedial instruction you will need?
10. Have you made clear what kinds of skills you have? For example, here is a checklist of skills that your IEP team should be aware of. Go through this list, and add this information to your notebook. Get the list to your team as you plan your program:

Skills Checklist

SEEING

Capable of doing own reading?
Capable of reading blackboard?
Capable of seeing demonstrations?

Capable of viewing films?
Capable of viewing pictures?
Capable of sighted travel through building?
Capable of doing own diagrams?
Special adjustments?
  . . . Lighting?
  . . . Lenses?
  . . . Readers?
  . . . Guides?
  . . . Oral instruction?
  . . . Talking book?
  . . . Braille?
  . . . Large typewriter?
  . . . Heavy dark pencil?
  . . . Special orientation to building and classes?
  . . . Seating?
  . . . Other adjustments?

Communication

HEARING

In a large classroom?
Normal range of radio or tape recorder?
Interference from normal traffic noises and other extra-
neous sounds?
Functional use of hearing aid?
Attitude toward hearing aid?
Lipreading?
Special adjustments?
  . . . Seat in front of room?
  . . . Louder presentation by instructor?
  . . . More careful articulation by instructor?
  . . . More board illustration and written materials?
  . . . Special hearing devices?
  . . . Others?

SPEECH ARTICULATION

Adequate for classroom use?
Adequate for speech courses?
Adequate for occupational choice?
Use of speech board?

WRITING

Capable of writing classroom notes?
Resources for dictating notes?
Knowledge of typing?
Capable of writing on blackboard?
Special adjustments? (For example, time and light)

MANUAL COMMUNICATION

Types used?
 . . . Total Communication?
 . . . American Sign Language (ASL)?
 . . . Signed English?
 . . . Fingerspelling only?
 . . . Other?

LANGUAGE

Can the student communicate adequately in the classroom?
 . . . Through spoken language?
 . . . Through written notes?
 . . . Through manual communication?

Manipulation

Capable of self-care in building?
Capable of handling laboratory equipment safely?
Capable of writing, using pen or pencil?
Capable of handling chalk in classroom?
Capable of eating by self-feeding?
Capable of carrying own books?
Capable of turning pages?
Capable of handling coins?
Capable of steady hand movements?
Capable of speedy hand movements?
Capable of two-handed coordinated movements?
Capable of picking up gross objects?
Capable of picking up fine objects?
Capable of opening doors?
Capable of typing movements?
Capable of raising hand for instructor's attention?
Capable of manipulating papers?
Others?
Special adjustments? (For example, time, light, location
   of seat and classroom)

Mobility

Travel to and from school?
Travel on level surfaces?
Special devices used?
Walking up and down steps?
Relative speed of mobility?
Steadiness and balance?
Assistance required?
Ability to sit in and rise from chair?
Ability to walk up incline?
Ability to walk on hard smooth surface?
Ability to pass through narrow aisles and doorways?

Special aids?
 ... Special elevator service?
 ... Early dismissal?
 ... Student helper?
 ... Paid attendant?
 ... Close safety supervision?
 ... Others?

Special Health Problems

Description of condition?
Special medication and health care required?
Activity limitations?
Possible curriculum limitations?
Progressive or static?
Special adjustments? (For example, time, privacy for taking medication, and class scheduling)

COURSE SELECTION

You will have to choose your courses whether you are mainstreamed or in a special program. When you think about which courses to select in high school or college, it helps to know why you are taking the course in the first place. In other words, what is the purpose of high school or college? Is it to prepare for a job? Or eventually to make more money? Or to get into college or graduate school? These reasons are often given as the purposes of high school. The problem with selecting courses on the basis of what college or career you want is that you will change your mind. If you look at the purpose of school as the place to find out what you can do academically and how well you can do it, then course selection makes more sense. You will want to take the toughest courses you can do well in. Find out if you can do English, and how well; mathematics and science, and how well; business, foreign language, the arts, and how well you can do them. After you find out that you do well in an area, take as much depth in these subjects as you can get. Start with a program and course that interest you. As you learn more about your abilities, you can begin to make career decisions based on your courses studied.

Often your parents, counselor, or school act as if they were responsible for what you take in school. But the responsibility is really yours. You can't tell someone ten years from now that you didn't become what you wanted to be because "someone" didn't tell you about it. It is always your final decision to drop a course, to elect a new one, to try to change teachers, to take on extra work, to goof off. All the advice from all the people who are quick to give you opinions will not be a substitute for your own decisions.

Sometimes, when you are selecting a course, your counselor will tell you that it's too hard for you, that you aren't being "realistic." You, like all students, have a right to fail. If you feel strongly that you want a course and everyone says you aren't being realistic, you can say that you understand that the educator doesn't think you can do it, but you think you can, and you want a chance to fail just as other students have that opportunity. Of course, lots of people who have a chance to fail *do* fail. Getting the opportunity won't assure success.

Some schools automatically exempt disabled students from music, physical education, vocational lab courses, science lab courses, and driver education. In some cases there are good reasons for the exemption, but in many there are not. If automatic exemption happens to you, check it out, so that you don't miss out on courses where adaptations can be made for you to do the work and learn the skills.

COLLEGE CHOICE

A number of you, including those with severe impairments, will be able to go to a college successfully. In general, the college selecting process for you will be similar to that for nondisabled students. Some of you will have special needs, however.

A precollege program may be necessary to prepare you for college attendance. These programs are generally six to ten weeks long and conducted before regular enrollment (usually in the summer), and they are offered by service agencies, special schools, and colleges. Some involve residence at the college. There are various types of precollege programs available, geared toward one or more of the following:

1. Orientation to the physical environment, life-style, and health, social, academic, psychological, and housing services.
2. Improving independent living skills (orientation and mobility, housekeeping, personal care).
3. Remedying academic deficiencies.
4. Teaching academic and study skills (term paper writing and typing, research techniques, note taking, use of library, acquiring and using instructional media, listening skills for lectures and readers, how to budget time, typing).

Check with your school counselor and with the director of admissions about precollege programs for the disabled.

In addition to basic college guides, such as *The College Handbook*, available at every school and published by the College Board, the following guides may help:

Abt Associates, *College Guide for Students with Disabilities*. A comprehensive resource on architectural accessibility, support services, policies, and disabled student populations and organizations at 500 colleges and universities. Also includes information on outside sources of financial aid, services, learning aids.

A Guide to College/Career Programs for Deaf Students (revised edition).

If you are planning to go to college, check for financial assistance through your state vocational rehabilitation (VR) agency. Don't wait until the last minute; you should become a VR client during your junior year in high school in order to comply with the VR requirements for receiving financial aid. Get a counselor or someone from your high school to help initiate the procedure for you to become a VR client if you are not already one.

It's your responsibility to have learned to use the support services you will need to study and cope with living when you are away from home and in college. When you check with colleges, find out if they have the following special program and services that you need while you are there:

1. Special classes for deaf students.
2. Interpreters for deaf students in regular classes.
3. Manual communication training for deaf students.
4. Tutoring services.
5. Note-taking services.
6. Vocational development services.
7. Personal counseling services.
8. Vocational placement services.
9. Speech and hearing services.
10. Medical services.
11. Supervised housing.
12. Architectural accessibility of classes, laboratories, administrative buildings, recreational facilities, and housing.
13. Attendant services.
14. Reader services.
15. Adapted equipment, special aids and devices.
16. Precollege program to orient the student to the college, remedy academic deficiencies, and improve socialization skills, personal adjustment, and independent living skills.

Just as choosing school courses is your responsibility, so is your college selection. You can get help, but you are the one who must get the information. You are the one who must apply. You are the one who must decide where you want to go.

Some students get more information than others to help

them decide. When Larry Pisano, a recent Stanford graduate, was just about to leave the rehabilitation center, a friend from home who was a freshman at college called and asked him what he was going to do next:

"I said I'm not going off to any school for the deaf. I'm going home and finish high school. So my friend said, 'Why don't you come over for the weekend before you go back home?' So I did. He took me to a political science class, and I was absolutely turned on by that lecture. For one reason, I could understand what was going on. 'How,' I thought, 'how could a poor dumb deaf guy like me know what was going on in that lecture?' But I did! That night I was really excited when we talked and talked and talked all night about going to college. The next morning my friend took me to the admissions office. The director of admissions told me that if I understood that lecture, I ought to come to Stanford. He said, 'I'll tell you what. If you go back home to Oregon and get all As, show some leadership qualities, and take some outside activities to show that you are interested in world issues, your chances will be excellent for early admissions.

"When I stepped out of that college admissions office, I knew from then on *exactly* where I was going to go. I got off that train that day in Oregon and told my family, 'I'm going to get all As and go to Stanford.' And I did."

Like Pisano, some students know exactly where they want to go, and they go there. But most students have in mind several places that would be good choices. It will help if you know that there are many good colleges for all students. Many students transfer before they get their degree—it's not usually a permanent decision. Try to figure out the best place for now. As you learn and change, that best place may change, too. Put some planning into your college selection. Keep in mind that there probably are many places that would be "best" for you.

How about a Job?

Paid or unpaid work is a strategy to gain the practical experience you need to test your career goal.

A characteristic of some physically disabled young people is that they will have had few of the jobs and work-related experiences that nondisabled children and adolescents have had. Too often disabled students have been overprotected and sheltered. As a result, they may be immature, lacking in self-confidence, or unrealistic in their career aspirations. Some may have aspirations that are too low; others have aspirations that are too high. This lack of work experience places you at a disadvantage compared to the nondisabled students.

The skills you learn, the visibility you have on a job, the people who learn what you can do, your observation of the work system, and your testing of how you can work outside school and home are the reasons for a work situation. When you take a menial job, it can become meaningful to you if you learn the system of your company, profession, or department and notice what everyone else does. How do others relate to having a disabled employee around? How do they relate to the work you are doing? How has the company defined your job? Which staff areas provide the move in which directions to get to what jobs? Where does your boss's job lead? Do you like your boss's job? Which line of work provides the basic experience that leads to other jobs? Can a physical therapist become a hospital administrator? Can a paramedical? Do engineers or sales people get the executive positions at IBM and the telephone company?

What you get from work experience, no matter what the work is, is a chance to broaden your experience and skills in learning new jobs, a chance to gain confidence that you can learn new jobs, and a chance for employers to see your abilities in a great variety of job functions.

Transferable Skills

When you begin to notice how everything about a job counts, then your present school and work activity take on new meaning. When you understand how your new volunteer job for fund raising for the blind teaches you transferable skills, then that volunteer job counts a lot for you. Transferable skills are skills that are learned in one place but can be used in a great variety of places—skills such as goal setting, problem identification, decision making, problem solving, time management, sales, and planning. When you work at a fast-foods place in the summer or after school, you can learn what the public is like, what the company you work for is like, what it's like working with non-disabled kids, how others see you, if they trust you. You can learn all kinds of coping skills that count for more than the money you will make, and that feels good, too! Learning survival skills and how to get around are also transferable skills. Learning transferable skills is a strategy for exploring your career possibilities.

A Support Group

As carefully as you plan your career strategy, it's hard to get far without a support group. If many skilled people who want to work can't get a job, if the special workshops and training programs can't place all the disabled workers, what does this mean to you? It can mean that acquiring job skills is not the whole story. How to get a job, learning how to keep a job, and how to ask for a promotion are skills you will also need. Discrimination and unemployment of the disabled are social problems that you aren't going to solve for yourself by yourself. Making friends in high school can be a beginning for your support group, or making friends with other disabled kids whom you meet in an agency or at the rehab center is just as good. The Epilepsy Foundation of America has special programs for job training and placement (TAPS). The director of the Boston program has learned, from years of experience with many students, that the *single most helpful service* her agency can provide is a place and people who offer a support group to people with epilepsy looking for a job, a place and people for job seekers to talk it over. Read carefully when you read the friendship chapter in this book (Chapter 14) because friendships, whatever the ages of the friends, make all the difference in how much energy you will have to follow through on your educational and career strategies.

A Winning Strategy

Your educational decisions are important for you. Make them as if your life depended on them because it does. It's true that the disabled are programmed to be helped and taken care of. You don't hear often enough that meaningful work contributes to a meaningful life. A well-paid career is a good beginning toward a promising life—a life beyond your physical differences.

You can't know everything about the changing world of work and the employment situation for the disabled. But if you stick with assessing your own skills; learning transferable skills from volunteer work, paid work, school, training programs, the rehab center; getting in tune with your values and interests as they change; staying in tune with your body as your body and adaptations to your physical differences change; and sharing your career goals with friends and relatives, you will be designing a winning strategy for your career goals.

19 | Making Money Feels Good!

How much does it cost to:

Buy a car?
Buy a used car?
Take a friend to dinner?
Buy credit?
Buy a cashmere sweater?
Buy adaptive equipment for a car?
Go to a university for a year?
Smoke for a year?
Go to a private vocational school for a year?
Take a correspondence course?
Fly to New York?
Eat for a week?
Buy a year's subscription to your favorite magazine?
Take the bus to Boston?
Take Amtrak to San Francisco?
Spend the week in a national park?
Do the laundry for a month?
Heat the house for a week?
Get married?

Take a bus tour of Washington for a week?
Buy insurance for the car for a year?
Have a baby?
Pay apartment rent for a month?
Pay apartment rent for a year?
Buy clothes for the year?
Get a divorce?
Buy a pizza for eight?

Have you ever wondered how some students get so hung up concentrating on their disability and how they are going to cope that they seldom think about making money? Isn't it odd that in a culture as materialistic as America's, you don't talk more about making money? I bet that you have all kinds of things you dream of having, and they all cost money—like a power van with special equipment and the latest stereo and best housekeeping stuff in it so you could take off with all the adaptations you would need to tour the country for a few months. Or you may dream of having all the money you need for a trip to Europe with attendants to take you everywhere you want to go. Or one of your dreams might be terrific clothes, and you would need extra money to make them fit.

The only thing that can keep you from thinking about making money is that you don't need it. You figure someone else will make money for you: like your parents, the government, or your future wife or husband. Of course they might. But you can be sure it won't be as much as you will want. But then, if they come up with all the money you want (because you have decided to live on a "survival level"), you miss out on the satisfaction of earning it. Making money feels good. It feels good because it takes a certain amount of assertion and using your abilities, persistence, and skills to make it. Making money contributes to a healthy feeling of independence. And it feels good because it's yours. Because it's your money, you can decide what you are going to do with it. You can decide whether to use $8 to buy a record—and go without dinner—to save it, to drink it, to use half of it going to the movies alone, or to take someone else to the movies.

Making It

Now that you are interested in making money, the next step is how. First the bad news. Making money, for the disabled, is discouraging because the disabled make much less than the nondisabled do. For example, a disabled white male makes 60 cents compared to $1 that the nondisabled white male makes. A disabled black male makes 25 cents on the $1 that a white male makes, and a disabled black woman makes 12 cents on the $1 compared to a white male. And for some reason, the white disabled women isn't even included on the scale put out by the United States Department of Labor's *Monthly Labor Review!* This means that like many women, disabled white women are not even expected to work for money. WEECN (Women's Educational Equity Communications Network) writes that disabled women are just beginning to question their work possibilities. It has found that "parents are often uninformed, and rely on the schools for guidance; high school teachers and guidance counselors are often just as unaware of the career options available. Young women fear that they have been prepared for nothing more than returning to their parent's home or to institutions."

Making money for the severely disabled is discouraging because there are disincentives, as Frank Bowe, author of *Handicapping America,* describes it. These disincentives are the disqualifying conditions for disability insurance, Medicare payments, Supplemental Security Income (SSI), and transportation expenses. All this means that you have to have a very high-paying job in order to offset the medical and other benefits you get if you are disabled and unemployed. It's an impossible situation that the disability rights groups are working to change.

The good news is that you, unlike many other disabled students, are aware of the needs and difficulties of making money. Being aware, seeing things coming, helps people cope. So even though it's tough, if you are aware and can see what's coming while you are still in school, you can plan your educational and career strategies to beat the bad news.

At Home with Rehab

It's hard to plan career goals and talk about making money if you are spending all your time in rehabilitation, learning to use a device or aid for better efficiency. Making money may not seem important to you right now. When you combine your short-term goals of getting around and using your body most effectively with long-range career plans and the strategies to get them, your rehab and schoolwork can become more meaningful to you. If you see how you are going to use both rehab and career goals, you won't get into the either/or mentality. Rehab or career planning—both are important. Finding the balance is one way to cope.

Managing Money

Just as important as making money is learning how to manage money. How you manage your money makes the difference between getting what you want or taking you farther away from your hopes and dreams. Money management involves having a plan for where the money comes from and where it goes. Even if you are on an allowance, rather than a paycheck, you can still apply the same good money management skills to whatever your income is and start noticing where your money goes.

Shopping skills are necessary for good money management. That means buying what you plan for—not impulse buying: buying the items nearest the checkout counter put out there just for you to grab and buy at the last minute or from TV commercials. Shop at stores or from catalogues that you can trust. One free copy of a Sears' or Ward's or Penney's catalogue will give you all kinds of consumer information so that you can learn what to expect for quality for what price. Catalogues will give you the weights, different styles and qualities, and the range of items available for what you want to buy. And you can sit right at home in your kitchen, taking your time to explore the whole shopping world! You can find out about musical instruments, clothes, boots, ladders, lamps, mattresses, stereos, cameras, and even wheelchairs. Even if you don't buy from the catalogue, you're getting ideas and questions you can ask a clerk when you are shopping, making you a wise buyer. Besides that, think of the time and hassle you save, sitting at home with the catalogue rather than running all over town looking for three different tape recorders to compare in the stores.

Knowing how much you should save and how much debt you can afford are all part of good money management. Knowing how much money you should save is just as important when you are living at home and getting an allowance as when you are getting a paycheck. As a starter, Sylvia Porter, the well-known economist who writes a newspaper column, suggests you put aside 5 percent of your total monthly income for savings. She writes that a guideline on how much debt you can afford is not more than 20 percent of your yearly after-tax income. Get into the savings habit as a student, so that saving becomes automatic when you are bringing in the money.

Students Away from Home

The first year away from home takes a lot of planning for good money management. Good management will be easier if you consider your money your paycheck—regardless of where it comes from. Money deserves the kind of respect that you give a paycheck when you are working. Use a checking account so that you will have a good record of where your money goes. Besides, if it's a little hard to get at your money, it will last longer. You won't be tempted to spend it all at once, peeling off a roll of bills, as soon as you get your money for the month. When thinking about buying, always keep in mind that it's *much* easier to keep the money you have by not spending it than it is to find new money. In other words, if you spend too much, you have to go out and find new funds, and not spending it in the first place may be the easier thing to do.

How Much Does It Cost?

People who can plan and manage their money well are those who have some idea of what things cost and know how much they will need for the things they want. Use the list at the beginning of this chapter, and find out, for your locality, exactly how much each of these things costs. Get a friend to do it with you. You can split up the list, or each of you can take the whole thing and see if you come up with different answers. Use the Yellow Pages. Remember if you are figuring the cost of a pizza for eight, you have to see if it's delivered free, or if that's extra. Look in your local newspapers for apartment rentals. Look in the catalogue for clothes and in the paper for new and used cars. Use your imagination. If you can't imagine spending money for some of these particular items, make up your own list. But do find out how much a variety of things cost.

Money Changes

Knowing how much things cost and having a money management plan aren't the whole story. Inflation, good luck, good planning, bad planning and the unexpected car tuneup, dentist bills, and birthday presents can send your plans in all directions. Some major life events, like a college education, a baby, a marriage, or moving, throw everything out of kilter. But whatever it is, don't let it throw you. Try to be flexible; expect change. Go right back to the basic good money management principles of having a plan and knowing how to buy, how to get credit, and how to save, and just start again with another plan. Don't be discouraged with change and the unexpected. It happens to everybody.

Be In on It

Spending money is a matter of priorities. No one has enough of it to get everything he or she wants all the time. You can spend just so much beyond what you make. *The best part of money is making it.*

The purpose of career and life planning is to tie in meaningful work, something you are crazy about doing, with making money. If you can do that, then you will have it made!

V | Special
Section

Charting Your Course:
Life Career Skills

by Ellen J. Wallach

Do you know these people?

Bobby Clarke   Mary Tyler Moore
Tony Coelho   Itzhak Perlman
Lou Ferrigno   Stevie Wonder

These well-known people are using their talents, skills, and abilities in a variety of different career fields. And they share something in common and with you: Each has a physical disability.

Robert Earl "Bobby" Clarke: A second-round draft choice for the Philadelphia Flyers hockey team. Other teams shied away from him because of his diabetes, but he has missed only one game in four seasons—as a result of a boil on his elbow! A star forward, Mr. Clarke has won many hockey awards.

Tony Coelho: Elected in 1978 to the House of Representatives from California's Fifteenth District, Congressman Coelho has epilepsy.

Lou Ferrigno: Television's Incredible Hulk has a hearing disability. Prior to his acting career, Mr. Ferrigno was Mr. America, Mr. World, and Mr. Universe.

Mary Tyler Moore: As Mary Richards, producer of a television news show, Ms. Moore starred in her own television series for a number of years. She is diabetic.

Itzhak Perlman: One of the world's greatest violinists, Mr. Perlman developed polio at the age of four. His legs are paralyzed, and he uses braces or crutches for mobility on and off the stage.

Steveland Hardaway "Stevie" Wonder. Although born blind, Mr. Wonder has become a superstar composer, musician, and singer.

All these people have developed their strengths; they have focused on what they *can* do, not on what their disabilities prevent them from doing. These people are stars, but there are many other people, less well known, who are equally as successful at whatever careers they have chosen: mechanics and repairers, bakers, travel agents, computer programmers, secretaries, lawyers, scientists, teachers. The list goes on and on. There are physically disabled people working in almost every occupation you can think of, even President of the United States! Franklin D. Roosevelt had polio and was confined to a wheelchair when he ran for the presidency. He won and became our nation's thirty-second President. From 1933 until he died in 1945, President Roosevelt led our nation from a wheelchair.

Every human being is unique. Each of us is special. There are no two of us alike. And each of us can do some things well, some things not so well, and some things not at all. None of us can do everything well. Some of us are good at working with our hands; some of us are not. Some of us are good at memorizing information; some of us are not. Some of us are good at talking to groups of people. How are you at that? Not so good? Afraid? Can't do it? Well, join the crowd! Of 3,000 people in the United States who were asked what they were most afraid of, 1,230 said, "Speaking before a group." Each of us must find our own talents, abilities, and skills. Once you know what you can do well and what you enjoy doing, you can begin to think about which careers might make good choices for you.

See Your Abilities

One of the ways we learn about ourselves and our abilities is from the feedback we get from other people. We tend to believe what others tell us. But their views may not be accurate! Many times people are uninformed about the effects of a physical disability. This lack of information limits their understanding of what you are capable of doing. It is important to stress again that sometimes it is *our* behavior that gives others clues to how to treat us. If you are shy and therefore hesitant to discuss your disability with new people you meet, they may misinterpret your behavior. They may feel that you would be hurt if they asked you any questions or tried to be helpful. Since they don't want to offend you or hurt your feelings and really don't know how to treat you, they may choose to avoid you or to have minimal contact with you. What kinds of messages do you send to others?

Sometimes we limit ourselves, either by not knowing enough about our disability or by being unaware of aids, appliances, and services available to enable us to function more easily in the world. How much do you know about your disability? For example, if you have epilepsy, are your seizures predictable? When do they occur? Is there a warning? Do they occur without loss of consciousness? Is there falling? What is the frequency rate of your seizures? Are there outside factors that may induce your seizures? If you can't answer these questions or aren't sure of the answers, start keeping a record. The more you know about yourself, the clearer you can be about what you can and cannot do. If you learn that flashing lights induce a seizure, you need not eliminate being a switchboard operator as a possible career. Switchboards can easily be converted to provide audible signals. So begin again to evaluate what you can and cannot do. Try to put aside all that you have learned, perhaps as a result of other people's lack of knowledge and understanding of your disability or misinterpretation of your behavior. And try to increase your own understanding of your disability and the things and people who can help you. Keep an open mind; you may learn something new about yourself!

How Do You Choose?

You have probably already started thinking about your career. You may even have a few ideas about some possible choices. Have you ever wondered how other people made their career decisions? Before you continue reading this section, ask four people you know, "How did you decide on your career?" Ask your parents, your friends' parents, teachers, counselors, or other people you have contact with every day: the mail carrier, librarian, or salesperson.

Most people don't plan their careers. They find *a job* and then another job and another. Their careers just seem to "happen." I'll bet that most of the people you asked told you a story that suggests one of the following two methods:

1. The menu approach—"I need a job. Tell me what you have, and I'll tell you what I want." People who use the traditional ways to find jobs, without having any idea of what they want to do, use this technique. They see what's available through newspaper advertisements and employment agencies and then make a choice. It's just like choosing from a menu in a restaurant!

2. The wait-and-see method—"I don't really know what I want, so I'll hang loose and see what comes along." These people are gamblers, trusting their future happiness and fulfillment to luck. Maybe Uncle Oscar owns a bank, and

they'll work there; perhaps Aunt Anne is a plumber, and she'll take them into the business.

These methods have two things in common. First, they trust your future to luck and timing. Maybe you will be successful at finding a career which you will enjoy, and maybe you won't. And second, neither approach requires any awareness of what *you* want, what *you* will enjoy doing. Neither method involves any self-awareness or planning. Both methods leave you powerless, like a cloud being blown around by the winds of fortune. What are your chances of being happy with your career if you use these methods? Perhaps you should ask people not only how they decided on their careers but also if they would make the same decision again. What are the odds of finding a rewarding career if you really don't know what you want to do or where you want to do it? Your guess is as good as mine, perhaps fifty-fifty?

Whatever the odds, you can increase your chances of being satisfied with your career choice. The more you know about yourself, the easier it will be to make career decisions and the better your chances of being happy with them. Self-awareness is the key.

Can You Fly?

This section will help you to begin to think about yourself and your career. The exercises will assist you in:

1. Finding your skills, abilities, and talents.
2. Choosing which ones you most enjoy using.
3. Exploring new opportunities to develop old skills and learn new ones.
4. Learning about career possibilities which interest you.
5. Evaluating career requirements in relation to your disability and the available aids, appliances, and services available to compensate for your physical limitations.

The exercises in this section follow a logical order. They build on each other; they form a process. Begin at the beginning. Work slowly, perhaps an hour at a time. Do just one exercise each time you work on your career planning. Keep all your work together in a notebook. The exercises are not difficult, but they will take time and thought. The more thinking and effort you give to this task, the greater the reward in increased self-awareness and the surer you will be that you have made the best decision for you.

It is important to be honest with yourself. You are the only person who will see your work. Remember, don't think about the limitations of your disability in the beginning. Many people have told you that you *can't, won't be able to, shouldn't.* Take another look, and make sure of what is realistic and what is not. Don't eliminate anything. Keep your options open. You will have a chance to check out the reality of your career choices in relation to your disability later. For right now, be open to new ideas. *Anything* is possible. You don't think it is? Consider the following:

> The body of the bee is very large considering the small size of its wings. A scientist would say that the bee's wings are too small for the bee to be able to fly. Isn't it wonderful that the bee doesn't know this and spends its life flying from flower to flower!

Maybe you can't fly (I wish I could), and maybe there are other things that you can't do, but there are many things you can do. What are they?

Finding Our Skills

What can you do? What are your skills and abilities? We can determine our abilities, aptitudes, and talents by examining some of our life experiences. These abilities, aptitudes, and talents are called our transferable skills. You will find that each person seems to use the same skills over and over again in many different situations and in a variety of activities. There are some skills we use more often than others. There are some skills we may enjoy using more than others. By finding the skills we have most enjoyed using in the past, we will be better able to predict which skills we will most enjoy using in the future. We will also become aware of skills which we may wish to learn, develop, and practice further.

We often take for granted the skills which are our strongest. Perhaps it is because they seem to come naturally, effortlessly, without pain. I have a friend who has had only one year of piano lessons, yet he can play a record, listen to it once, and then put it on the stereo again and play along on the piano. I took four years of piano lessons and can just play "Happy Birthday," right hand only! He isn't impressed with his ability. I am. It is always easier to see how many "talents" our friends have. It is more difficult to find our own skills.

EXERCISE I: *Choosing a Life Experience*

The best way to find your transferable skills is to look at the experiences in your life which you consider:

1. A success.
2. An accomplishment.
3. A satisfying experience.
4. An experience you really feel good about.
5. An experience of which you are proud.

Think of one life experience which qualifies. It doesn't matter what the rest of the world thinks. In fact, you may be the only one aware of what you did! If you feel proud, if you feel it was an accomplishment, it counts! None of us has as yet won an Academy Award or been given a standing ovation in the Superdome! *You* are the only person to judge what is important and meaningful in your life. If you feel good inside, *it counts!*

Take a piece of notebook paper, and write the title of the experience you chose at the top. Think about what you did.

Write it down in the order that it happened. Write the story as though you were telling it to a young child—simply and clearly. Start at the beginning, and tell it as it happened. You don't need to write complete sentences or worry about grammar or punctuation. The important thing is to remember as much as possible about all the things you did to make the experience happen. If you don't like to write, jot down some key words of the story, and number them in the order that they happened. Or outline your story. Or tell it into a tape recorder or to a friend who can write it down for you. Again, keep asking yourself, "What did I do to make it happen?"

As an example, here is a story of which I am proud:

> My grandmother's birthday is May 1. The year that I was fifteen it was April 15 when I realized that I didn't have enough money to buy Grandma something special. I had saved only $4, but I knew that the gift would be very special to Grandma if it was something that I made for her myself. I thought a lot about it. I decided to embroider a sheet and pillowcase with a flower design from a pattern that my mother had. I went to the store and bought what I needed. The salesperson showed me how to do the needlework. Two weeks later at the party, when the presents were opened, mine was the most appreciated. Was I proud!

In our society we place a high value on modesty. We are not expected to tell everyone how wonderful we really are! Well, this is not the time for shyness and modesty. Be brave; be bold; tell the world just how terrific you are! Allow yourself the pleasure of enjoying the wonderful life experiences that you may have made happen.

As time passes, we sometimes forget all the small things that were part of an experience. If you write everything down, your mind will focus on this experience and keep recalling new things about it. Your remembrance of the experience will be more complete.

EXERCISE 2: *Finding Your Skills*

There is a skills chart, listing 100 skills, on pages 214–222. The chart will assist you in identifying which skills you used to make your experience happen. The chart will be easier to use if you photocopy each page. Also, you won't have to write in this book.

The skills are arranged by cluster title; for example, "Using My Hands," "Using My Body," "Using Words" are cluster titles. There are twelve cluster titles (lettered *A* through *L*).

Before you begin using the skills chart to analyze your story, look at the first slanted space at the top of the chart. It says, "Sample: Grandma's present." This refers to the story I have just told you. I asked myself, "What skills did I use to make this experience happen?" Then I looked at the first cluster title: "A. Using My Hands." I looked at each of the skill words. Did I use this skill? When I got to number 7, "Showing manual or finger dexterity," I decided that I had used it, so I colored in pencil the appropriate box in the sample column. Then I continued considering each skill in each cluster area. It's difficult to get the hang of it in the beginning. So be patient. You may need to review the entire skills chart two or three times for each experience. Remember, always give yourself the benefit of the doubt. If you aren't sure, color it in anyway. Most people tend to underestimate what they did when they first try using the chart.

Put the title of your experience in the slanted space above the number 1 on your photocopied skills chart. Look at cluster A, and consider each of the skill words in the cluster. Did you use this skill to make your experience happen? If so, color it *in pencil.* (Most people do a great deal of erasing in the beginning.) Continue to cluster B, then C, and so on, until you have completed the entire skills chart for your first story.

You may find other skills you used which aren't listed in the skills chart. Add them in the "Other" category at the end of the cluster when appropriate. If you need more space for listing your skills, take a piece of notebook paper, and make another page for your skills chart.

Name of Skill	Example of a situation where that skill is used	Sample: Grandma's present					Other skills I use	Skills I want to develop	Skills for my future work
A. USING MY HANDS		**1**	**2**	**3**	**4**			
1. Assembling	as with kits							
2. Constructing	as with carpentry							
3. Or building								
4. Operating tools	as with drills, mixers							
5. Or machinery	as with sewing machines							
6. Or equipment	as with trucks, station wagons							
7. Showing manual or finger dexterity	as with throwing, sewing	▓						
8. Handling with precision and/or speed	as with an assembly line	▓						
9. Fixing or repairing	as with autos or mending							
10. Other								
B. USING MY BODY								
11. Muscular coordination	as in skiing, gymnastics							
12. Being physically active	as in exercising, hiking							
13. Doing outdoor activities	as in camping, etc.							
14. Other								

From *The Quick Job-Hunting Map, Beginning Version* by Richard N. Bolles and Victoria B. Zenoff, © Copyright 1977 by Richard N. Bolles and the National Career Development Project

Name of Skill	Example of a situation where that skill is used	*Sample*	1	2	3	4		*Other skills*	*Develop*	*Future work*
C. USING WORDS										
15. Reading	as with books; with understanding									
16. Copying	as with manuscripts; skillfully									
17. Writing or communicating	as with letters; interestingly									
18. Talking or speaking	as on the telephone; interestingly	▓								
19. Teaching, training	as in front of groups; with animation									
20. Editing	as in improving a child's sentences in an essay									
21. Memory for words	as in remembering people's names, book titles									
22. Other										
D. USING MY SENSES (eyes, ears, nose, taste or touch)										
23. Observing, surveying	as in watching something with the eyes, etc.	▓								
24. Examining or inspecting	as in looking at a child's bumps, etc.									
25. Diagnosing, determining	as in deciding if food is cooked yet									
26. Showing attention to detail	as in shop, in sewing	▓								
27. Other										

Charting Your Course: Life Career Skills 215

Name of Skill	Example of a situation where that skill is used	Sample					Other skills	Develop	Future Work
E. USING NUMBERS		**1**	**2**	**3**	**4**			
28. Taking inventory	as in the pantry, shop							
29. Counting	as in a classroom, bureau drawers							
30. Calculating, computing	as in a checkbook, arithmetic							
31. Keeping financial records, bookkeeping	as with a budget							
32. Managing money	as in a checking account, bank, store							
33. Developing a budget	as for a family							
34. Number memory	as with telephone numbers							
35. Rapid manipulation of numbers	as with doing arithmetic in the head							
36. Other								
F. USING INTUITION								
37. Showing foresight	as in planning ahead, predicting consequences							
38. Quickly sizing up a person or situation accurately	getting a total view, rather than just one or two details about them							

Name of Skill	Example of a situation where that skill is used	Sample						Other Skills	Develop	Future work
39. Having insight	as to why people act the way they do		1	2	3	4				
40. Acting on gut reactions	as in making decisions, deciding to trust someone									
41. Ability to visualize third dimension	as in drawings, models, blueprints, memory for faces									
42. Other										
G. USING ANALYTICAL THINKING OR LOGIC										
43. Researching, information gathering	as in finding out where a particular street is in a strange city									
44. Analyzing, dissecting	as with the ingredients in a recipe, material									
45. Organizing, classifying	as with laundry									
46. Problem solving	as with figuring out how to get to a place									
47. Separating important from unimportant	as with complaints, or cleaning the attic									
48. Diagnosing	as in cause-and-effect relations, tracing problems to their source									
49. Systematizing, putting things in order	as in laying out tools or utensils in the order you will be using them									

Charting Your Course: Life Career Skills   217

Name of Skill	Example of a situation where that skill is used	Sample						Other skills	Develop	Future work
50. Comparing, perceiving similarities	as with different brands in the supermarket		1	2	3	4				
51. Testing, screening	as with cooking, deciding what to wear									
52. Reviewing, evaluating	as in looking at something you made, to see how you could have made it better, faster									
53. Other										
H. USING ORIGINALITY OR CREATIVITY										
54. Imaginative, imagining	as in figuring out new ways to do things, or making up stories									
55. Inventing, creating	as with processes, products, figures, words									
56. Designing, developing	as with new recipes, new gadgets									
57. Improvising, experiments	as in camping, when you've left some of the equipment home									
58. Adapting, improving	as with something that doesn't work quite right									
59. Other										

Name of Skill	Example of a situation where that skill is used	Sample	1	2	3	4			Other skills	Develop	Future work
I. USING HELPFULNESS			1	2	3	4					
60. Helping, being of service	as when someone is in need										
61. Showing sensitivity to others' feelings	as in a heated discussion, argument	▨									
62. Listening		▨									
63. Developing rapport	as with someone who is initially a stranger										
64. Conveying warmth, caring	as with someone who is upset, ill	▨									
65. Understanding	as when someone tells how they feel										
66. Drawing out people	as when someone is reluctant to talk, share										
67. Offering support	as when someone is facing a difficulty alone										
68. Demonstrating empathy	as in weeping with those who weep										
69. Representing others' wishes accurately	as when one parent tells the other what a child of theirs wants										
70. Motivating	as in getting people past hang-ups and into action										
71. Sharing credit, appreciation	as when working in teams										

Charting Your Course: Life Career Skills   219

Name of Skill	Example of a situation where that skill is used	Sample					Other skills	Develop	Future work
72. Raising others' self-esteem	as when you make someone feel better, less guilty		1	2	3	4			
73. Healing, curing	as with physical, emotional, and spiritual ailments								
74. Counseling, guiding	as when someone doesn't know what to do								
75. Other									
J. USING ARTISTIC ABILITIES									
76. Composing music									
77. Playing (a) musical instrument(s), singing									
78. Fashioning or shaping things, materials	as in handicrafts, sculpturing								
79. Dealing creatively with symbols or images	as in stained glass, jewelry								
80. Dealing creatively with spaces, shapes, or faces	as in photography, art, architectural design								
81. Dealing creatively with colors	as in painting, decorating, making clothes								

© Copyright 1977 by Richard N. Bolles and the National Career Development Project

Name of Skill	Example of a situation where that skill is used	Sample					Other skills	Develop	Future work
82. Conveying feelings and thoughts through body, face, and/or voice tone	as in acting, public speaking, teaching, dancing	1	2	3	4				
83. Conveying feelings and thoughts through drawing, paintings	as in art								
84. Using words on a very high level	as in poetry, playwriting, novels								
85. Other									
K. USING LEADERSHIP, BEING UP FRONT									
86. Beginning new tasks, ideas, projects	as in starting a group, initiating a clothing drive								
87. Taking first move in relationships	as with stranger on bus, plane, train								
88. Organizing	as with a Scout troop, a team, a game at a picnic								
89. Leading, directing others	as with a field trip, cheerleading								
90. Promoting change	as in a family, community, organization								
91. Making decisions	as in places where decisions affect others								

Charting Your Course: Life Career Skills 221

Name of Skill	Example of a situation where that skill is used	Sample				Other skills	Develop	Future work
92. Taking risks	as in sticking up for someone in a fight	1	2	3	4			
93. Getting up before a group, performing	as in demonstrating a product, lecturing, making people laugh, entertaining, public speaking							
94. Selling, promoting, negotiating, persuading	as with a product, idea, materials, in a garage sale, argument, recruiting, changing someone's mind							
95. Other								
L. USING FOLLOW-THROUGH								
96. Using what others have developed	as in working with a kit							
97. Following through on plans, instructions	as in picking up children on schedule							
98. Attending to details	as with embroidering a design on a shirt							
99. Classifying, recording, filing, retrieving	as with data, materials, letters, ideas, information							
100. Other								

Perhaps you would like to share your work with someone else: a parent, brother or sister, teacher, counselor. Sometimes it is difficult to be objective about our own accomplishments. Showing your skills chart to another person could provide a different point of view. Other people can help you make sure that your chart is complete, that you have really given yourself credit for all your skills.

EXERCISE 3: *Completing Your Skills Chart*

In order to complete your skills chart, you will need to think of three other life experiences that you are proud of or consider a success or an accomplishment. Most people have trouble thinking of three experiences immediately. You may even be thinking, "I don't have three more accomplishments in my life." Perhaps I can help by having you focus your thoughts. Think about your whole life, not just this past year. Also, think about your life in pieces:

1. School and educational experiences.
2. Volunteer experiences.
3. Leisure and hobby experiences.
4. Paid and unpaid work experiences.
5. Family and friend experiences.

School and educational experiences: Were you a member of the school band? Did you write an outstanding paper? Did you design a poster? Write for the newspaper? What clubs did you belong to? Which school projects are you proud of?

Volunteer experiences: Did you volunteer in a hospital or clinic? Did you collect money for charity? Were you ever part of a fund-raising activity? When have you helped other people?

Leisure and hobby experiences: How did you spend your free time? Do you teach Sunday school? Swim? Sew? What do you enjoy doing?

Paid and unpaid work experiences: Did you ever earn money? Selling? Baby-sitting? Making things? What about nonpaid work experiences? Did you paint your room? Decorate it? Bake a cake for a special friend? Just because no one pays you for your efforts doesn't mean it isn't work! Think about your unpaid work experiences.

Family and friend experiences: Did you do something special for someone you love, like my present for my grandmother? Did you help someone out of a jam? What special experiences have you had with your family and friends?

Don't be concerned with which category things belong in. The categories overlap. The goal is to reflect on your life and remember your satisfying experiences, the ones you are proud of.

This exercise may take a few days to complete. It's hard to remember everything at once. Write down as much as you can. Then show it to someone else. Perhaps a parent, friend, brother, or sister can refresh your memory and help you add to your list. Then leave it on your desk in your room, and glance at it each day. You will probably find that you will remember more and more as the days go by. Your mind will be working on remembering your life experiences even though you may not be consciously thinking about them. And don't worry if you can't think of experiences in each category. The categories are just to help you remember.

Try to develop a list of more than three experiences. The more you write down, the more you'll think of. The longer your list, the greater choice you'll have in selecting three for your skills chart. Again, you may not think of everything at one sitting. Leave it for a few days. Eventually you'll be surprised at how many things you've done in your life that you are proud of.

Once you feel that your list is fairly complete, you can begin to select three or more to add to your skills chart. You might choose the accomplishments of which you are most proud. You might choose four which represent different aspects of your personality: creative, physical, emotional, intellectual. Or you might decide to select one experience from different school levels. The decision is yours. There is no right or wrong. If you can't decide on three, that's OK. In fact, once you get started, you may want to add new ones and eliminate some of your original choices.

Enter the titles of your three experiences in the slanted spaces marked 2, 3, and 4 on your skills chart. Begin with your second experience, and go through the entire skills chart, coloring the box next to each skill you used to make the experience happen. Then continue to the third experience. And the fourth. Remember to add any skills in the "Other" category at the end of each cluster that you may have used but are not listed.

As you analyze each experience for the skills you used, you should begin to see patterns, skills you use over and over in different circumstances. These are your strongest transferable skills.

As we discussed earlier, modesty is considered a great attribute in our society. In order to lessen its effects, I suggest you show your skills chart to someone who may be more impartial about you than you are about yourself, perhaps a parent, a friend, a teacher, or a counselor. Let that person look over your skills chart and see if you have left anything out. Describe one or two of your experiences, and see if he or she can add any skills to your list.

EXERCISE 4: *Other Skills You Use*

Once you have completed the entire skills chart for each of your four experiences, look at the next column on the chart— "Other skills I use." Look at the skills chart, cluster by cluster, skill by skill. Are there any skills that have not been used in any of your four experiences? Consider each of these skills. Have you used them? Do you think you are good at these skills? If so, color the appropriate box for the skill in the "Other skills I use" column. This will help make your skills chart more complete. You are making sure that you are giving yourself credit for using skills that may not be represented by the experiences that you have chosen.

You might also consider evaluating more than four experiences for the skills you used. Take pieces of tracing paper, and cover the right portion of each page of the skills chart, the grid portion. You will then be able to write the titles of additional experiences in the slanted spaces on the tracing paper and to look for skills in each of these.

EXERCISE 5: *Enjoyable Skills*

Each of us have many transferable skills, but we don't enjoy using them all equally. This exercise will help you select which skills you most *enjoy* using. For example, when I purchased the supplies to make my grandmother's gift, I had to show attention to detail to buy the amount of supplies I needed. I included this skill on my skills chart. However, I do not *enjoy* showing attention to detail.

Look at your skills chart, starting with your first experience. Consider each skill which you used to make this experience happen. For this experience, did you enjoy doing it? Sometimes we will enjoy using a skill at one time and not at another. So focus on this first experience before continuing to the next. If, in fact, you enjoyed using this skill, recolor the appropriate box with a bright colored pencil or marker.

For each experience, look at each skill you used and consider it, using enjoyment as the only criterion for your coloring.

Follow this procedure for the "Other skills I use" column as well.

You now have a colorful array of boxes representing the skills you have used that you enjoy most.

EXERCISE 6: *Developing Old Skills and Learning New Ones*

You probably have a number of transferable skills which you enjoy using and would like to develop further. There are also other skills which you haven't used a great deal or at all and would like to try. Look at the next slanted space on the top of the skills chart, "Skills I want to develop." Go through your chart again, considering each skill in each cluster area. Look at the skills that you've colored, the ones you've most enjoyed using. You will probably want to get more experience using these enjoyed skills; you'll want to develop them further. Color the appropriate box in the "Skills I want to develop" column for your enjoyed skills. Also, consider the skills which you haven't had a great deal of experience using or perhaps used at all. You may not think you would enjoy using them, but you really won't know until you try them. So color in the box under the "Skills I want to develop" column for these skills, too. Don't ignore or eliminate skills because you think you can't do it. You won't know until you have had some experience trying them and practicing them. Complete this exercise for the entire skills chart.

You now have a list of skills which you would like to develop further or perhaps try out for the first time. What kinds of experiences do you need to explore in order to do this?

EXERCISE 7: *Expanding Your Skills Through New Experiences*

How can you plan new experiences to explore and develop your skills further? For a start, choose three skills which interest you from the "Skills I want to develop" column. Choose three skills from different cluster areas. Also, choose at least one of your three that you haven't had much experience using.

Take a piece of notebook paper and make a Skills Development Chart, using the illustration below as a guide:

SKILLS DEVELOPMENT CHART	
SKILL	EXPERIENCES
1.	
2.	
3.	

List the three skills you have chosen to develop next to the numbers 1, 2, and 3 in the skills column. Consider the first skill you listed. What can you do, what experiences might help you to learn and develop this skill? Here's an example:

Skill 99: classifying, recording, filing, retrieving. Where could I go, what could I do to build on this skill?

1. Volunteer to work in the school's main office.
2. Work in the office of the school newspaper.
3. Work part time after school or Saturdays in an office in my town or community.
4. Work in the local, school, church, library.

Get the idea? Be creative. Your experiences may be paid or volunteer work, hobbies or leisure experiences, educational activities, or personal and family experiences. Can you think of any others to add to the list above? How about organizing family papers (especially helpful when your parents might want to retrieve information for income tax purposes) or designing a recipe filing system? If you have a hobby of collecting things, how about a classifying system to find information about each item easily?

Here's another example: Skill 9: fixing or repairing. There are all kinds of things that need fixing and repairing: clothes, radios, clocks, lawn mowers, for example. Here are some ideas to develop this skill:

1. Ask a friend, parent, teacher, or store owner (most store owners love to talk about their products!) to show you how to repair something and then try it yourself.
2. Go to the library, take out a book, and read about fixing something. Try it and learn on your own through trial and error, following the directions.
3. Contact your local Y, continuing education center, church, rehab center, vocational high school, or community group. Find out what kinds of courses and workshops are being offered. Information about local activi-

ties will probably be in your community newspaper, too. Sometimes stores will offer a one- or two-hour workshop. For example, a store that sells sewing machines might offer a session on how to repair them or how to repair clothes.

As you can see, designing learning experiences can be easy and fun. Be creative. If you get stuck, ask for help. Your parents, counselors, and friends will probably enjoy helping you. If you are shy, find a friend who also wants to learn new things and develop new skills. Do it together. If you want to learn something, but can't find anywhere to learn it, try to form a group of people who share your interest; talk to your guidance counselor about getting together some students from your school to form a group. Maybe one of the existing clubs in your school would be interested in sponsoring a workshop. For example, first aid would be a natural interest for the Future Nurses of America Club; auto repair would be of interest to a driver education class or club; typewriter repair for a secretarial club; camera repair for a photography club. You get the idea. Think about what kinds of organizations or clubs might share your interest, and go speak with them. Tell them your idea for a workshop, program speaker, or field trip. See if you can't get other people interested in sharing this learning experience with you. You'll be amazed at how much fun you'll have and how many new people you'll meet.

Once you have explored learning experiences to develop the three skills you have chosen, take another look at your skills chart. Choose two or three more skills from the "Skills I want to develop" column and seek out ways to explore them. Keep learning and growing. One word of caution. If a skill looks interesting, but you don't think you can do it because of your disability, spend some time making sure that you *really* won't be able to do it before you eliminate it as a learning option. Call your rehabilitation counselor, and check it out. Your counselor knows about all kinds of aids and appliances available to help you overcome the limitations of your disability. And there are new ones designed every day. You won't know for sure until you ask. For a start, review the references in the appendix that deal with your specific physical disability.

EXERCISE 8: *Skills for Your Future Career*

As you design new learning experiences and seek ways to develop your skills, you will find that you enjoy using some skills more than others. You will begin to get a better sense of which skills you would like to use and build on in the future. As you determine which skills you would like to use in your future career, check them in the last column on your skills chart, "Skills for my future work." You may need to return to this chapter to complete the final column in six months, a year, or longer. The more time you allow yourself for learning and developing skills, the surer you will be about which ones you want to build into your career.

EXERCISE 9: *Exploring the World of Work*

As you are learning about your transferable skills, you can also be exploring different career options. Occupations can be looked at from a "skills" point of view, too. If you examine a job, you will find that it is composed of many tasks and responsibilities. The performance of each of these tasks and responsibilities requires a particular set of skills. Two seemingly unrelated jobs —surgeon and car mechanic—have several transferable skills in common. See the chart on the next page.

Can you find other transferable skills needed for both jobs? Add them to the list. There are many other occupations which would require most of the same transferable skills: lathe operator, welder, and medical laboratory technician, to name three. I am *not* suggesting that the identification of the transferable skills you most enjoy using is the *only* way to choose your career. Your interests, values, and goals, your ability, desire, and opportunity to pursue further education must be considered as well. I am also *not* suggesting that the surgeon and car me-

Transferable skills	surgeon	car mechanic
operating tools	✓	✓
operating machinery	✓	✓
showing manual or finger dexterity	✓	✓
fixing or repairing	✓	✓
diagnosing, determining	✓	✓
showing attention to detail	✓	✓
showing foresight	✓	✓
quickly sizing up a person or situation accurately	✓	✓
analyzing, dissecting	✓	✓
problem solving	✓	✓
separating important from unimportant	✓	✓
diagnosing	✓	✓

chanic could or would desire to switch jobs. But transferable skills assessment, analyzing your skills and which skills are needed for different occupational options, is the place to begin.

EXERCISE 10: *Developing a Master Career Exploration List*

Before you can narrow your career possibilities, you must expand your options. In order to make an intelligent and knowledgeable career decision, you will need to gather information about a variety of career possibilities. You are going to develop a list of careers that you would like to explore further. Title a piece of notebook paper "Master Career Exploration List."

To begin, think of what other people have told you—your parents, teachers, counselors, friends. Have they ever said, "You really ought to be a _____"? You may not like the idea, but include it anyway. Although parents and others often give you a lot of pressure to follow a particular career direction, don't dismiss their ideas immediately. Research them; investigate these possibilities. You may find that they were good suggestions for you, or you may decide to eliminate them from your list. If you do choose to reject these suggestions after researching them, you will have many good reasons why they are not the best choices for you. You will have good information for explaining why you decided against them. You will have accurate, well-thought-out reasons to back up your decision.

Most of the ways we learn about careers do not provide accurate, impartial information. Aunt Ernestine is a nurse and hates it; you'll never be a nurse, right? Whatever your disability, you may have a stereotyped idea about what might be "appropriate" for you. Perhaps everyone thinks you "should be" a special education teacher or rehabilitation counselor. Avoid making quick decisions on the basis of stereotypes for women or men or people who are blind or in wheelchairs.

The other ways we usually learn about careers, through radio, television, and movies, are equally bad. These media glamorize careers for the sake of entertainment. Perhaps you thought you might like to be a big-city detective because you saw "Kojak" on television. One person may find the job appealing because Kojak had a lot of power, or he helped people, or he got a great deal of respect, or the work was dangerous or exciting or whatever. You rarely see him doing the hours of paperwork that are typical of police work; you rarely see him working on many cases at one time, also truer to reality. So think again. What does police work really involve? What skills do you need to perform the tasks necessary for the job?

You can also expand your list by thinking about your ideal job. If I had magic fairy dust and could go *pooooof*, what would you like to be? What would you like to be doing? Forget the educational requirements, the money needed to make it happen, or your disability. Think of two or three things or more. What would you be if you could be anything? Remember, now is the time to include *every* possibility; you can eliminate later.

Another way of expanding your list is by using the "help wanted" section of your Sunday newspaper. Although you will find advertisements for employment every day in the paper, Sunday's paper contains the largest amount each week. If you live in a small town or rural area, buy a Sunday paper from the largest city near your home. Read every advertisement in the "help wanted" section carefully. Circle the ads which look interesting to you, even if you don't know anything about the position being advertised and you don't have the education or experience to qualify for it. Then look at each ad you circled, and ask yourself, "What skills might a person need to perform this job?" Try to imagine the tasks and responsibilities required for the job and what skills would be needed to perform these tasks. The advertisement may not provide enough information to do this completely, but it's a beginning. Add the job titles to your exploration list.

EXERCISE 11: *Collecting Information about Careers*

There are four ways to begin your search for information about careers: by reading, by talking with people, by watching people work, and by trying it out, experiencing it for yourself.

1. Reading: Many printed resources are available to provide you with further information about different careers. J. S. Mitchell's paperback books *I Can Be Anything: Careers and College for Young Women* (Bantam, 1978), *The Men's Career Book: Work and Life Planning for a New Age* (Bantam, 1979,) and *The Work Book: A Guide to Skilled Jobs* (Bantam, 1978) are three good ones. Some schools have extensive resource centers with a variety of books, filmstrips, and tape cassettes. Some even have computerized career information. Perhaps you are lucky enough to have such information available to you. If your high school doesn't have a career resource center, try a local college or state employment or training agency. Your local library is another good place to

begin your search. Resource librarians are information detectives. They can get you practically anything you want. And if they can't get it through interlibrary loan, they'll surely tell you how to find it and where. Ask your librarian for the *Occupational Outlook Handbook.* This huge paperback book is published every other year by the United States Department of Labor and is the basic resource for career information. The *Occupational Outlook Handbook* contains information about hundreds of careers: what kind of training is needed, how many people in the United States work in each career area, what the average salary is, what the prospects for the future are and where to get further information about each career. Browse through it!

If you have a visual disability, there are large-print and braille books available through the American Printing House for the Blind and the American Foundation for the Blind. Write to these organizations, and ask them what is available.

Although there will be some occupations which you may not be able to enter, there will be many more which are available to you. The federal government, for example, does not allow diabetics who take insulin to enter the military service, to pilot airplanes, or to drive trucks or buses in interstate commerce. Check with your rehabilitation counselor about the legal limitations for your disability. But if you can legally perform a job, there are only three other issues to consider:

a. Is the job hazardous to you?

b. Will you be jeopardizing the safety of others?

c. Will the job aggravate your disability? Your disability need not be a limitation if it can be overcome by specialized training, equipment and devices, or medical restoration. Before you eliminate any possibility (as long as it is legally feasible,) find out from your rehabilitation counselor what kind of help you can get. For example, the American Foundation for the Blind publishes *Sensory Aids for Employment for the Blind and Visually Impaired* ($7.50). Your local commission for the blind or rehabilitation commission may already have a copy of this book. If it doesn't, it will surely be interested in obtaining one for your reference and for use with other visually disabled people.

2. Talking with people: One of the very best ways to expand your list and also to learn about different careers at the same time is by talking with people. Look at the first career idea on your list. Think of where you can find someone who is doing that job so that you can discuss the work with him or her. Nervous, shy? Take along a friend who is also interested in the career to interview the person. Don't know anyone who does that job? Don't know where to find one? Here are some suggestions:
   a. Parents, friends, relatives.
   b. Teachers, counselors.
   c. People in your church or temple.
   d. People in groups to which your parents belong: Chamber of Commerce, fraternal organizations, political groups, unions.
   e. Local business people: the shoemaker, cleaner, grocery store manager, dentist, doctor.
   f. Look in the Yellow Pages of your telephone directory.
   Look around your community. Everyone is a potential resource!

The *most* important person to contact is your rehabilitation counselor, who may know of people with your disability who are already doing the work in which you are interested. These are the best people to visit. These people will realistically describe just what the limitations and difficulties of your disability are in performing their job. You will also be able to see what kinds of adjustments they have made, what kinds of appliances and aids they have found to perform their job better and more easily. If your counselor does not know of anyone with your disability doing the job, perhaps he can find someone. He has a lot of contacts throughout your community or city. He should be the first person you call.

Well, you now have a name of a person who is doing the job you are considering. What do you do then? Call and tell the person you are interested in learning more about what a _____ does; you are considering pursuing it as a career. You'd like to talk about it with them, at his or her convenience, for thirty minutes. Could you make an appointment? (Ask specifically for a short period of time; otherwise, the person may be afraid that you will take up too much time. My own and my students' experiences, however, have been that once people get involved talking about their work, they'll just go on and on and forget about the time!)

You may be thinking, "Why would they want to talk with me? What's in it for them?" The answer is that most people enjoy talking about what they know best—themselves and their work. Oh, some people will be abrupt or rude because they are short of time or having a bad day, but you will find that most people will be cordial and happy to speak with you. In fact, I bet you'll be amazed at how many people will spend time with you and share information with you once you get started!

You have an appointment. What do you say when you get there? Explain why you are there, and try to get the person to start talking about the work. Perhaps the following suggestions will be helpful:

a. How did you get into this career?
b. What did you perceive before you got into it? Is it different? How?
c. What do you like *most* about your work?
d. What do you like *least* about your work?
e. Why did you choose this type of work?

f. What are the skills necessary to perform your job? And if the person shares your disability:
g. What adaptations have you made, if any, in order to perform your job?
h. What are the greatest problems and pressures of having a physical disability in your job?

You might also choose to ask these questions near the end of your conversation:

a. Would you make the same career choice again? Why?
b. Where else, besides the environment in which you work, could someone perform your work?
c. Are there other careers I might investigate that are related to yours? At the end of the interview, always ask the following question:
d. Is there anyone else you know who also does your kind of work and who might be willing to speak with me? MAY I USE YOUR NAME WHEN I CALL?

The last part of the question is very important. It is always easier to get an appointment with someone if you say a friend or colleague suggested that you call. This question can be particularly helpful in locating someone who shares your physical disability. The person with whom you are speaking probably knows many other people in that career field and may know someone who shares your disability.

You won't need to ask all the questions suggested above. They are guidelines. Perhaps you can think of others which are of more interest to you.

Within a few days after your interview, remember to send a thank-you note. The person you interviewed has been generous with his or her time and taken an interest in your career planning. The note can be short, but the courtesy and appreciation will always be welcome.

If your mobility is limited, you can still make opportunities to speak with people about their careers. Your guidance department at school or rehabilitation center might be willing to invite people to speak with a group of students. A school club might be willing to sponsor such a visit. Taking a group of students on a field trip to a company to discuss careers is another possibility. The opportunities are limited only by your ability to be creative.

The more people you speak with, the more referrals to others doing the same work or variations of that work you will hear about. Perhaps you have explored the field of veterinary medicine and learned that it requires graduate school training. You might also have learned that a veterinarian's assistant requires only two years of post high school education. With each interview, you will have a better idea of whether or not this career is a possibility for you. You will not only be expanding your list but also be gathering information with which to narrow it. As you continue interviewing and get a clearer picture of a particular career, you will be better able to decide which careers to cross out on your list.

3. Watching people work: A school or community group field trip is an easy way to see people working. Keep your eyes and ears open; ask questions. What skills are needed to perform this job? Get the information you need, particularly as to the limitations of your disability.

Some schools offer a "shadowing" experience to enable you to watch people work. Schools with such a program have developed relationships with community businesses whereby a student visits the business organization for a day (or longer) and watches people work. You can actually see what is involved in doing a job and have the opportunity to ask questions as well. Ask your guidance counselor about the possibility of a shadowing experience.

4. Experiencing work: Before you make any decisions about pursuing further education or training, try to find a way to experience the job you are considering as a career. Volunteering is one way. If you are interested in

a medical career, volunteer in a hospital or clinic after school. If you want to teach elementary school children, volunteer as a teacher's aide in a school near you. Talk to your counselor about other volunteer opportunities in your community.

Some schools and rehabilitation facilities have paid work experience programs. You are paid in either school credit or money. Ask your counselor for help in finding a job. Jobs may be available in nonprofit community agencies, schools, or local businesses.

If your school or rehabilitation facility does not have such a program, perhaps you can find your own work experience. After speaking with people in your community about their careers, you may have many resources for finding employment. Call the people whom you interviewed. Tell them that you are considering a career choice which might be similar to theirs. See if they have any suggestions for locating an after-school, weekend, or summer job. Provide opportunities for yourself to learn as much as you can about a career before preparing for it.

Bravo!

If you have come this far, BRAVO! I know the work has required a great deal of time and thought. My experience has been that most people who spend the time and energy evaluating their strengths (transferable skills) and limitations in terms of realistic career information have felt that the effort expended was well worth the results in personal growth and career insights. I hope you feel the same way.

Exploring career options can be fun; it can be an adventure. You will learn more about yourself and what you are capable of doing and will meet new and interesting people as well.

Good luck.

Appendix

Teenage Sexuality

TEENS

Eagan, Andrea Boroff. *Why Am I So Miserable If These Are the Best Years of My Life?* Philadelphia: Lippincott, 1976. A lively straightforward guide to sex and relationships for young women.

Hamilton, Eleanor. *Sex, with Love: A Guide for Young People.* Boston: Beacon Press, 1978. A liberal view about sex for sophisticated teens.

Johnson, Eric W. *Love and Sex in Plain Language.* Rev. ed. New York: Bantam, 1979. A traditional view of complete sex facts for early teens.

Lieberman, E. J., and Peck, F. *Sex and Birth Control: A Guide for the Young.* New York: Crowell, 1973. A basic book about birth control especially for teens.

TEENS WITH DISABILITIES

Gordon, Sol. *Sexual Rights for the People . . . Who Happen to Be Handicapped.* Rev. ed. Syracuse, N.Y.: University of Syracuse, 1979. A ten-page article that deals with rights. Includes a reading list.

Heslinga, K.; Schellen, A. M. C. M.; and Verkuyl, A. *Not Made of Stone —The Sexual Problems of Handicapped People.* Springfield, Ill.: Charles C. Thomas Company, 1974.

Mooney, Thomas O.; Cole, Theodore M.; and Chilgren, Richard A. *Sexual Options for Paraplegics and Quadriplegics.* Boston: Little, Brown, 1975.

Also write to the national agency of your particular disability and ask for a list of publications about teenagers and sex. The agency address may be found on pages 242–247.

Visual

Ask the following national organizations for special materials for teenagers:

American Council of the Blind, Inc.
501 North Douglas Avenue
Oklahoma City, Oklahoma 73106   (405) 232-4644
American Association of Workers for the Blind
1511 K Street, NW, Suite 637
Washington, D.C. 20005   (202) 347-1559
American Foundation for the Blind
15 West Sixteenth Street
New York, New York 10011   (212) 924-0420
American Printing House for the Blind
P.O. Box 6085
1839 Frankfort Avenue
Louisville, Kentucky 40206   (502) 895-2405
Produces and distributes in braille, large type, and recorded formats: fiction and nonfiction books, textbooks, tests, magazines, and music. Also sells educational aids (e.g., relief maps and biological models) and equipment (e.g., braille writers and braille slates). Catalogues and brochures, which include prices, are available.
Instructional Materials Reference Center of APHB serves as a clearinghouse for educational materials for visually handicapped students (blind and partially sighted). Maintains the *Central Catalog of Volunteer Produced Textbooks,* which identifies the sources of these books. (*Central Catalog* is also available at other locations, such as regional libraries for the blind and physically handicapped and state departments of education.) Responds to requests for information about specific educational materials. Maintains mailing list to keep you informed about available materials.

National Association for Visually Handicapped
305 East Twenty-fourth Street, 17-C
New York, New York 10010   (212) 889-3141
National Blindness Information Center
Dupont Circle Building, Suite 212
1346 Connecticut Avenue, NW   (202) 785-2974
Washington, D.C. 20036   Toll-free (800) 424-9770
National Braille Association, Inc.
85 Godwin Avenue
Midland Park, New Jersey 07432   (201) 447-1484
National Federation of the Blind
218 Randolph Hotel Building
Des Moines, Iowa 50309   (515) 243-3169
National Society for the Prevention of Blindness, Inc.
79 Madison Avenue
New York, New York 10016   (212) 684-3505
Recording for the Blind
215 East Fifty-eighth Street
New York, New York 10022   (212) 751-0860

Hearing

When you write to the following national organizations, ask them for
special materials for teenagers:

Alexander Graham Bell Association for the Deaf, Inc.
3417 Volta Place, NW
Washington, D.C. 20007   (202) 337-5220
American Speech and Hearing Association
9030 Old Georgetown Road
Washington, D.C. 20014   (301) 530-3400
Gallaudet College
Seventh and Florida Avenue, NE
Washington, D.C. 20002   (202) 447-0475
Public Service Programs
Distributes publications to deaf young adults to help them better
understand deafness and hearing.
Attempts to respond to all inquiries relative to deafness.
Also, Gallaudet College Bookstore (same address, phone 447-0556)

stocks numerous books and visual aids for learning sign language as well as literature by and about deaf persons. (Catalogue and mail orders available.)

Junior National Association of the Deaf
    Gallaudet College
    Seventh and Florida Avenue, NE
    Washington, D.C. 20002   (202) 447-0741

National Association of the Deaf
    814 Thayer Avenue
    Silver Spring, Maryland 20910   (301) 587-1788
    Public Information Officer

National Center for Law and the Deaf
    Seventh and Florida Avenue, NE   (202) 447-0445
    Washington, D.C. 20002   Voice/TTY

Registry of Interpreters for the Deaf, Inc.
    P.O. Box 1339
    Washington, D.C. 20013   (202) 447-0511

Can assist you in locating interpreters in states where local RID addresses have changed or where no chapters exist.

Diabetes

When you write, ask for special materials for teenagers:
American Diabetes Association, Inc.
    1 West Forty-eighth Street
    New York, New York 10020   (212) 541-4310
    Booklets available at the above address include:
    1. *Diabetics Are Desirable Workers.*
    2. *Facts about Diabetes.*
    3. White, Priscilla. *What It Means to Be Female and Diabetic.*

Muscular Dystrophy

Write to:
Muscular Dystrophy Association
    810 Seventh Avenue
    New York, New York 10019

Send for:
Schock, Nancy. *The Child with Muscular Dystrophy in School.*
    Massachusetts Teachers Association

20 Ashburton Place
Boston, Massachusetts 02108

Cerebral Palsy

National Easter Seal Society
2023 West Ogden Avenue
Chicago, Illinois 60612   Information Center (312) 243-8400

Send for more information, and ask for special material for teens:
United Cerebral Palsy Associations, Inc.
66 East Thirty-fourth Street
New York, New York 10016   (212) 481-6350
Director of Program Services

Spinal Cord Injuries

Ask the following organizations for special material for teenagers:

National Center for a Barrier Free Environment
8401 Connecticut Avenue, NW
Washington, D.C. 20015   (703) 620-2731
National Paraplegia Foundation
333 North Michigan Avenue
Chicago, Illinois 60601   (312) 346-4779

Spinal Cord Injury Centers
Because of the pervasive nature of spinal cord injury, the federal government, through the Rehabilitation Services Administration, has designated eleven regional Spinal Cord Injury Centers to provide total care and rehabilitation. This includes not only medical treatment but also physical and occupational therapy, mobility training, psychological services, vocational counseling, and other services needed in order for the spinal-cord-injured individual to achieve maximum rehabilitation.

Locations of the regional centers are presented below. For further information on referral procedures and eligibility for services, contact the director at the nearest center.
Spain Rehabilitation Center
University of Alabama in Birmingham

1717 Sixth Avenue South
Birmingham, Alabama 35233   (205) 934-4155
Southwest Regional Spinal Injury Center
Good Samaritan Hospital
P.O. Box 2989
Phoenix, Arizona 85062   (602) 257-4533
Santa Clara Valley Medical Center
California Regional Spinal Cord
Injury Care System
Institute for Medical Research
751 South Bascom Avenue, H-8
San Jose, California 95128   (408) 998-4554 Ext. 37
Rocky Mountain Spinal Cord Injury System
Craig Hospital
3425 Clarkson
Englewood, Colorado 80110   (303) 761-3040
Northwestern Memorial Hospital and Rehabilitation Institute of Chicago
401 East Ohio Street
Chicago, Illinois 60611   (312) 649-4728
New England Regional Spinal Cord Injury Center
University Hospital
75 East Newton Street
Boston, Massachusetts 02118   (617) 247-5531
Regional Spinal Cord Injury Center
Department of Physical Medicine and Rehabilitation
University of Minnesota Hospitals
Minneapolis, Minnesota 55455   (612) 373-8990
Institute of Rehabilitation Medicine
New York University
400 East Thirty-fourth Street
New York, New York 10016   (212) 679-3200
Texas Institute of Rehabilitation and Research
1333 Moursund Avenue
Houston, Texas 77025   (713) 797-1440
Woodrow Wilson Rehabilitation Center
Fisherville, Virginia 22939   (703) 885-7281
University of Washington
CC 814 University Hospital
Seattle, Washington 98195   (206) 543-3300

Epilepsy

"Answers to the Most Frequent Questions People Ask about Epilepsy." Epilepsy Foundation of America, 1828 L Street, NW, Washington, D.C., 5 cents.

Hermes, Patricia. *What If They Knew.* Harcourt Brace Jovanovich, 1980.

"Medical and Social Management of the Epilepsies." Epilepsy Foundation of America, 1828 L Street, NW, Washington, D.C., 5 cents.

Silverstein, Alvin, and Silverstein, Virginia B. *Epilepsy.* Lippincott, 1975.

Getting Around

UNITED STATES ACCESS GUIDES

CALIFORNIA

Eureka
Access to Eureka for the Handicapped, prepared 1978 by the Architectural Barriers Committee. Available free from: Easter Seal Society for Crippled Children and Adults of Humboldt County, P.O. Box 996, 730 Fifth Street, Eureka, California 95501. Yearly updates are planned.

Fresno
The Source, prepared 1978 by and available free from: Fresno County Chapter, California Association of Physically Handicapped, P.O. Box 6094, Fresno, California 93703.

Los Angeles
Around Town with Ease, prepared 1979 and available for 46 cents (postage) from: Junior League of Los Angeles, Farmers Market, Third and Fairfax, Los Angeles, California 90036.

Oakland
A Guide to Oakland and Parts of Berkeley for the Physically Disabled and Aging, available free from: Easter Seal Society for Crippled Children and Adults of Alameda County, 2757 Telegraph Avenue, Oakland, California 94612.

Palo Alto
Getting Around in Palo Alto, available free from: City of Palo Alto, Office of Community Relations, 250 Hamilton Avenue, Palo Alto, California 94301.

San Diego
A Step in Time—San Diego Guide for the Handicapped, prepared 1977 and available free from: Community Service for Disabled, 4607 Park Boulevard, San Diego, California 92116.

San Francisco
Guide to San Francisco for the Disabled, prepared October 1976 by and available free from: Easter Seal Society of San Francisco, 6221 Geary Boulevard, San Francisco, California 94121.

San Jose
Wheeling Your Way Through San Jose, available free to disabled residents of Santa Clara and San Benito Counties, and for $3 to others from: Easter Seal Society for Crippled Children and Adults of Santa Clara and San Benito Counties, 1245 South Winchester Boulevard, Suite 304, San Jose, California 95128.

Santa Barbara
Open Doors for the Handicapped in Santa Barbara, prepared 1972 and available free from: Easter Seal Society for Crippled Children and Adults of Santa Barbara County, 31 East Canon Perdido, Santa Barbara, California 93101.

CONNECTICUT

Fairfield County (south)
The Directory, prepared January 1978 by and available for $1 (postage) from: Easter Seal Rehabilitation Center of Southwestern Connecticut, 26 Palmer's Hill Road, Stamford, Connecticut 06902.

New Britain
Your Key to New Britain, prepared 1977 by Junior League of New Britain. Available free from: New Britain Chamber of Commerce, 127 Main Street, New Britain, Connecticut 06051.

New Haven

Register of Architecturally Surveyed Facilities in New Haven Area, prepared April 1978 by and available free from: Woodbridge Rotary Club, c/o MITE Corporation, 446 Blake Street, Woodbridge, Connecticut 06515.

Waterbury

Access Waterbury, prepared January 1979 and available free from: Easter Seal Rehabilitation Center of Greater Waterbury, 22 Tompkins Street, Waterbury, Connecticut 06708.

DELAWARE

Rehoboth Beach

Welcome Handicapped Visitors, prepared 1977 and available free from: Rehoboth Beach Chamber of Commerce, 73 Rehoboth Avenue, Rehoboth, Delaware 19971.

Wilmington

A Guide to Northern Delaware for the Disabled, prepared 1974 by and available free from: Easter Seal Society of Del-Mar, 2705 Baynard Boulevard, Wilmington, Delaware 19802.

DISTRICT OF COLUMBIA

Washington, D.C.

Access Washington, prepared 1977 and available for $1 from: Information Center for Handicapped Individuals, Inc., 120 C Street, NW, Washington, D.C. 20001.

A Directory of Special Transportation Services in the Metropolitan Area, prepared 1977 by and available free from: Metropolitan Washington Council of Governments, Metropolitan Information Center, 1225 Connecticut Avenue, NW, Washington, D.C. 20036.

The Deaf Person's Quick Guide to Washington (D.C.), available free to the deaf from: Alice Hagemeyer, c/o Martin Luther King Memorial Library, 901 G Street, NW, Room 410, Washington, D.C. 20001.

Easy D.C. Touring for Handicapped, prepared by and available free from: Washington Area Convention & Visitors Association, 1129 Twentieth Street, NW, Washington, D.C. 20036.

Daytona

Guide to Daytona Beach Area, prepared 1978 by and available free from: The Palmetto Club Juniors of Daytona Beach, Florida, Palmetto Women's Club, 1000 S Beach, Daytona Beach, Florida 32014.

Jacksonville

Guide for the Handicapped—Jacksonville, prepared 1978 by the Jacksonville Junior Service League. Available free from: Easter Seal Society of Northeast Florida, 1056 Oak Street, Jacksonville, Florida 32204.

Gainesville

Access to Gainesville, prepared by and available free from: Chamber of Commerce, 300 East University, Gainesville, Florida 32602.

Orlando

Orlando's Guide for the Handicapped, prepared 1978 by the Orlando Area Tourist Trade Association. Available free from: Chamber of Commerce, P.O. Box 1913, Orlando, Florida 32802; also from: Easter Seal Speech & Hearing Center, 231 East Colonial Drive, Orlando, Florida 32801.

Pinellas County (lower)

Accessibility—Lower Pinellas County, prepared 1977 by the Committee on Assistance to the Physically Impaired. Available free from: Easter Seal Rehabilitation Center, 7671 U.S. Highway No. 19, Pinellas Park, Florida 33565.

Sarasota

Guide to Sarasota for the Handicapped, prepared September 1972 and available free from: Sarasota County Society for Crippled Children and Adults, 401 Braden Street, Sarasota, Florida 33580.

South Brevard

Accessibility Guide to South Brevard, prepared 1977 by and available free from: Easter Seal Rehabilitation Center, 450 East Sheridan Road, Melbourne, Florida 32901.

Tampa

1979 Guide to the Tampa Area for the Physically Handicapped, prepared 1979 by Hillsborough Community College. Available free by sending a stamped, self-addressed envelope to: Easter Seal Society for Crippled Children and Adults of Hillsborough County, A. Pickens Coles Easter Seal Center, 2401 East Henry Avenue, Tampa, Florida 33610.

GEORGIA

Albany

Guide for the Handicapped to the Greater Albany Area, prepared 1973 by the Junior Service League of Albany. Available free from: The Southwest Georgia Area Easter Seal Rehabilitation Center, 1906 Palra Road, Albany, Georgia 31705.

Athens

A Guide to Athens for the Handicapped and Senior Citizens, prepared 1974 and available free from: Georgia Easter Seal Society, 3254 Northside Parkway, NW, Atlanta, Georgia 30327.

Atlanta

Getting About Atlanta, prepared 1967 by and available free from: Georgia Easter Seal Society, 3254 Northside Parkway, NW, Atlanta, Georgia 30327.

Augusta

A Guidebook to Augusta for the Handicapped, prepared 1975 and available free from: Georgia Easter Seal Society, 3254 Northside Parkway, NW, Atlanta, Georgia 30327.

HAWAII

Hawaii Visitors Bureau Member Hotel Guide, 1978 (access indicated), prepared 1978 and available free from: Hawaii Visitors Bureau, 2270 Kalakauo Avenue, Honolulu, Hawaii 96815.

Honolulu

Pictorial Aloha Guide to Honolulu for Handicapped Travelers, available free from: Hawaii Visitors Bureau, 2270 Kalakauo Avenue, Honolulu, Hawaii 96815.

ILLINOIS

Carbondale

Carbondale Guide for the Handicapped, prepared 1978 and available free from: Easter Seal Society of South Illinois, P.O. Box 3249, 801 South Oakland, Carbondale, Illinois 62901.

Chicago

Access Chicago, prepared 1975 by Access Chicago. Available for $1 from: Rehabilitation Institute of Chicago, 345 East Superior Street, Chicago, Illinois 60611.

A Guide to Chicago Loop for the Handicapped, available from: Rehabilitation Institute of Chicago, 345 East Superior Street, Chicago, Illinois 60611.

A Resource Guide for the Physically Handicapped of Chicago, prepared 1978 by Access Chicago. Available for $1 from: Access Chicago, Rehabilitation Institute of Chicago, 345 East Superior Street, Chicago, Illinois 60611.

Access North Suburban Chicago, prepared 1977 by the League of Women Voters of Illinois. Available for $1 donation from: League of Women Voters of the Deerfield Area, Access, P.O. Box 124, Deerfield, Illinois 60015.

INDIANA

Evansville

A Guide for the Handicapped for Evansville, Indiana, prepared 1978 by the Junior League of Evansville, Indiana. Available free from: Vanderburgh County Society for Crippled Children, 3701 Bellemeade Avenue, Evansville, Indiana 47715.

Indianapolis

Navigation Unlimited in Indianapolis, prepared 1979 by and available free from: Marion County Muscular Dystrophy Foundation, 615 North Alabama Street, Room 221, Indianapolis, Indiana 46204.

KANSAS

Topeka

A Guide to Barrier-Free Establishments—1979, prepared by the Topeka Human Relations Commission. Available free from: Division for the Disabled, City Hall, Room 54, Topeka, Kansas 66603.

Wichita

A Guide for the Disabled of Wichita, prepared August 1975 by the Kansas Easter Seal Society, Kansas Paralysis Chapter, and Wichita Volunteers. Available free from: Easter Seal Society for Crippled Children and Adults of Kansas, 3701 Plaza Drive, Topeka, Kansas 66609.

LOUISIANA

Baton Rouge

Baton Rouge—A Guide for the Handicapped, prepared April 1978 by and available free from: The Junior League of Baton Rouge, 4950-C Government, Baton Rouge, Louisiana 70806.

New Orleans

A Guide to New Orleans for the Physically Disabled, prepared September 1978 and available free from: Easter Seal Society for Crippled Children and Adults of Louisiana, P.O. Box 8425, Metairie, Louisiana 70011.

Shreveport

A Guide to Facilities in Shreveport and Bossier City, prepared June 1973 by the Altrusa Club of Shreveport. Available free from: Community Council Office, 1702 Irving Place, Shreveport, Louisiana 71101.

MARYLAND

Baltimore

Ready/Set/Go!—Baltimore Guidebook for the Physically Disabled, prepared 1977 by Rhoda Eskivith and Ellene Christiansen. Available free from: The League for the Handicapped, 1111 East Cold Spring Lane, Baltimore, Maryland 21239.

MASSACHUSETTS

Boston

At Your Service, prepared June 1978 by and available for $1 from: Massachusetts Rehabilitation Hospital, c/o Recreational Therapy, 125 Nashua Street, Boston, Massachusetts 02114.

Cambridge
Access to Cambridge, prepared 1978 by and available free from: Alpha Chi Chapter, Alpha Phi Omega National Service Fraternity, Massachusetts Institute of Technology, Cambridge, Massachusetts 02108.

Springfield
A Guide to Springfield for the Physically Disabled and Aging, prepared 1971–72 and available free from: Easter Seal Society for Crippled Children and Adults of Massachusetts, 30 Highland Street, Worcester, Massachusetts 01608.

Worcester
Wheeling Through Worcester, prepared 1974 by and available free from: Easter Seal Society for Crippled Children and Adults of Massachusetts, 30 Highland Street, Worcester, Massachusetts 01608.

MICHIGAN

Travel Michigan . . . Handicappers Mini-Guide, prepared May 1978 and available free from: Michigan Travel Commission, P.O. Box 30226, Lansing, Michigan 48909.

Detroit
Guide to Detroit for the Handicapped, prepared 1973 by the Tau Beta Association. Available free from: Rehabilitation Institute, 261 Mack Boulevard, Detroit, Michigan 48201.

Flint
A Guide for the Handicapped, prepared 1972 by and available free from: Easter Seal Society of Genesee County, 1420 West Third Avenue, Flint, Michigan 48504.

Grand Rapids
A Guide to Grand Rapids for the Handicapped, available free from: Easter Seal Society of Grand Valley, 4065 Saladin Drive, SE, Grand Rapids, Michigan 49506.

Lansing
Access Lansing, prepared February 1979 and will be available from: The Center for Handicapper Affairs, 1026 East Michigan Avenue, Lansing, Michigan 48912.

MINNESOTA

Easy Wheelin' in Minnesota, prepared 1978 by and available free from: Robert R. Peters, 1 Timberglade Road, Bloomington, Minnesota 55437.

MISSISSIPPI

Jackson
A Key to Jackson for the Physically Limited, prepared 1975 by the Junior League of Jackson. Available free from: Mississippi Easter Seal Society, P.O. Box 4958, Jackson, Mississippi 39216.

MISSOURI

Kansas City
Accessibility Directory—Kansas City, Missouri, prepared 1975 by the Architectural Barrier Action Committee. Available free from: ACCESS, 3011 Baltimore, Kansas City, Missouri 64108.

St. Louis
St. Louis Has It A to Z for the Handicapped, prepared May 1975 by and available for $1 donation from: Easter Seal Society of Missouri —St. Louis Region, 4108 Lindell Boulevard, St. Louis, Missouri 63108.

NEBRASKA

Omaha
A Guide to Omaha for the Handicapped, prepared 1978 by and available free from: Easter Seal Society for Crippled Children and Adults, P.O. Box 14204, 12177 Pacific Street, Omaha, Nebraska 68114.

NEW JERSEY

Hackensack
A Guide to Hackensack for the Handicapped, available free from: Easter Seal Society for Crippled Children and Adults of New Jersey, 799 Main Street, Hackensack, New Jersey 07601.

New York State—I Love New York Travel Guide (access indicated), prepared June 1979 and available from: New York Department of Commerce, 99 Washington Avenue, Albany, New York 12245.

Albany—Schenectady—Troy

Access to Capitaland, prepared March 1978 by Junior Leagues of Albany, Schenectady, Troy. Available free from: Junior League of Schenectady, P.O. Box 857, Schenectady, New York 12301. New edition planned for 1981.

Buffalo—Lockport—Niagara Falls

Guide for the Disabled and Elderly, prepared 1974 by and available free from: Building Barriers Committee, Rehabilitation Association of Western New York, P.O. Box 74, Buffalo, New York 14205.

New York City

Access New York, prepared 1976 by and available for 50 cents from: Institute of Rehabilitation Medicine, New York University Medical Center, 400 East Thirty-fourth Street, New York, New York 10016.

List of Catholic Churches in Brooklyn and Queens Accessible to the Handicapped, prepared 1978 by the Tablet Blue Book. Available free from: Office for the Handicapped, Brooklyn Catholic Charities, 191 Joralemon Street, Brooklyn, New York 11201.

Tips for the Physically Handicapped Accessibility Guide (a guide to cultural facilities), prepared April 1979 and available free from: The Lincoln Center Public Information Department, 1865 Broadway, New York, New York 10023.

Syracuse

See Syracuse—A Guide for the Handicapped, available free from: Easter Seal Society, Room 204, State Tower Building, Syracuse, New York 13202.

NORTH CAROLINA

Asheville

A Guide to Asheville for the Disabled and Aging, prepared 1970 by and available free from: North Carolina Easter Seal Society, 1000-C Haywood Road, Asheville, North Carolina 28800.

Greensboro
Guide for the Physically Handicapped, prepared 1977 by the Council
on Conventions and Trade Shows, the city of Greensboro, and the
Easter Seal Society. Available free from: Accessibility Task Force,
Greensboro Chamber of Commerce, P.O. Box 3246, Greensboro,
North Carolina 27402.

NORTH DAKOTA

North Dakota Highway System—Rest Areas (access indicated), avail-
able free from: North Dakota State Highway Department, Capitol
Grounds, Bismarck, North Dakota 58505.
State Guidebook for the Handicapped, available free from: Governor's
Committee of Employment of the Handicapped, 207 Broadway, Box
568, Bismarck, North Dakota 58501.

Jamestown
A Guidebook to Jamestown for the Handicapped, available free from:
Easter Seal Society for Crippled Children and Adults of North
Dakota, Box 480, Bismarck, North Dakota 58501.

Valley City
A Guidebook to Valley City for the Handicapped, available free from:
Easter Seal Society for Crippled Children and Adults of North
Dakota, Box 480, Bismarck, North Dakota 58501.

OHIO

Akron
Akron Area Guide for the Handicapped, prepared 1979 by and avail-
able free from: The Junior League of Akron, 929 West Market Street,
Akron, Ohio 44313.

Canton
A Guide to Canton for the Handicapped, prepared 1977 by the Junior
League of Canton, Ohio. Available free from: Goodwill Industries
and Rehabilitation Clinic, 408 Ninth, SW, Canton, Ohio 44700.

Cincinnati
Greater Cincinnati Guidebook for the Handicapped, prepared September 1978 by the Junior League of Cincinnati. Available free

from: The Hamilton County Easter Seal Society, 7505 Reading Road, Cincinnati, Ohio 45237.

Dayton

A Guide to Dayton for the Handicapped, prepared 1977 by the Junior League of Dayton and Goodwill Industries. Available for 25 cents from: Dayton Goodwill Industries, 201 West First Street, Dayton, Ohio 45401.

Toledo

A Guide to Toledo for the Handicapped, prepared 1978 by the Junior League of Toledo, the Barrier Free Toledo Committee, and the Toledo Chapters of Junior Coterie. Available free from: Barrier Free Toledo, 218 Huron Street, Toledo, Ohio 43604.

PENNSYLVANIA

Bucks County

Access Bucks County, prepared summer 1978 and available free from: Bucks County Easter Seal Center, 2400 Trenton Road, Levittown, Pennsylvania 19056.

Delaware County

Guide to Delaware County for the Handicapped, prepared January 1976 by and available free from: Delaware County Easter Seal Rehabilitation Center of the Society for Crippled Children and Adults, 468 North Middletown Road, Media, Pennsylvania 19063.

Philadelphia

A Guide to Philadelphia for the Handicapped, prepared 1978 by and available free from: Mayor's Office for the Handicapped, Room 427, City Hall Annex, Philadelphia, Pennsylvania 19107.

Pittsburgh

Access: A Guide to the Campus of the University of Pittsburgh, prepared 1979 by and available for $1 from: Access, Office of Special Student Services, 507 Schenley Hall, University of Pittsburgh, Pittsburgh, Pennsylvania 15260.

A Guide to Pittsburgh for the Handicapped, prepared 1978 and available free from: Open Doors for the Handicapped, 1013 Brintell Street, Pittsburgh, Pennsylvania 15201.

State College

A Guide to Downtown State College for the Disabled and Aged, prepared 1976 by and available for $1 from: Easter Seal Society for Crippled Children and Adults of Centre and Clinton Counties, 1300 South Allen Street, State College, Pennsylvania 16801.

The Pennsylvania State University, University Park Campus—A Map for the Disabled, available from: Easter Seal Society for Crippled Children and Adults of Centre and Clinton Counties, 1300 South Allen Street, State College, Pennsylvania 16801.

RHODE ISLAND

A Guide to Rhode Island for the Handicapped, prepared 1980 and available free from: Easter Seal Society of Rhode Island, 667 Waterman Avenue, East Providence, Rhode Island 02914.

SOUTH CAROLINA

Columbia

Access Columbia, prepared 1978 by the Pilot Club of Columbia. Available free from: Columbia Chamber of Commerce, 1308 Laurel Street, Columbia, South Carolina 29201.

SOUTH DAKOTA

Wheelchair Vacationing in South Dakota, prepared 1980 by the South Dakota Division of Tourism and Handicapped Citizens of S.D., Inc. Available free from: Handicapped Citizens of South Dakota, Box 8005, Rapid City, South Dakota 57701; also from: South Dakota Division of Tourism, Joe Foss Building, Pierre, South Dakota 57501; also from: Black Hills, Badlands and Lakes Association, Box 539, Sturgis, South Dakota 57785.

TENNESSEE

Chattanooga

An Access Guide to Chattanooga is available from: Chattanooga Area Convention and Visitors' Bureau, Memorial Auditorium, 399 McCallie Avenue, Chattanooga, Tennessee 37402.

Memphis

A Guidebook to Memphis for the Handicapped, prepared 1966 by the Junior League of Memphis and the Easter Seal Society. Available free from: Easter Seal Society for Crippled Children and Adults of Western Tennessee Region, 3611 Midland Avenue, P.O. Box 11532, Memphis, Tennessee 38111. New edition planned for the near future, and orders for it are now being taken.

TEXAS
Dallas

Access Dallas '77, prepared by the Committee for the Removal of Architectural Barriers. Available free from: Easter Seal Society, 4429 North Central Expressway, Dallas, Texas 75205.

Houston

A Guide to Houston for the Handicapped, prepared January 1979 and available free from: The Coalition for Barrier Free Living, P.O. Box 20803, Houston, Texas 77025.

San Antonio

Access San Antonio, prepared fall 1977 by and available free from: Bexar County Easter Seal Society, 2203 Babcock Road, San Antonio, Texas 78229.

UTAH
Salt Lake City

Access Salt Lake, prepared 1978 by and available from: Division of Rehabilitation Services, Utah State Board for Vocational Education, 250 East 500 South Street, Salt Lake City, Utah 84111.

VIRGINIA
Roanoke

Guide for the Handicapped and Aging, prepared August 1972 by the Virginia Employment Commission. Available free from: Mayor's Committee on Employment of the Handicapped, P.O. Box 61, Roanoke, Virginia 24002.

Tidewater

Tidewater Access Guide for the Handicapped—1978, prepared September 1977 by and available free from: Mobility on Wheels, 1712

Glendon Avenue, Norfolk, Virginia 23518; also from: Norfolk Chamber of Commerce, Research Department, 475 Saint Paul's Boulevard, P.O. Box 327, Norfolk, Virginia 23501.

Williamsburg
Guide for the Handicapped to Colonial Williamsburg, prepared July 1978 by the Colonial Williamsburg Foundation. Available free from: Information Center, Colonial Williamsburg, Virginia 23185.

WASHINGTON

Seattle
Access Seattle, prepared 1977 and available free from: Washington Society for Crippled Children and Adults, 521 Second Avenue, West, Seattle, Washington 98119.

Spokane
A Guide to Spokane for the Handicapped, prepared 1972 by the Junior League of Spokane and the Easter Seal Society. Available free from: Easter Seal Society, West 510 Second Avenue, Spokane, Washington 99204.

WEST VIRGINIA

West Virginia Travel Guide for the Handicapped, prepared 1974 by and available free from: Travel Development, GOECD, State Capitol, Charleston, West Virginia 25305. New edition planned for August 1978.

Wheeling
Wheeling Through Wheeling, prepared September 1974 by Wheeling-Ohio County Planning Commission and West Liberty State College. Available free from: Wheeling-Ohio County Planning Commission, Room 305, City-County Building, 1600 Chapline Street, Wheeling, West Virginia 26003.

WISCONSIN

Madison
Wisconsin's Capital with Ease, prepared 1973 by the MOBILE Unit. Available free from: Easter Seal Society of Wisconsin, 2702 Monroe Street, Madison, Wisconsin 53711.

Milwaukee
A Guidebook to Milwaukee for the Handicapped, prepared 1970 by
and available free from: Easter Seal Society for Crippled Children
and Adults of Milwaukee County, 5225 West Burleigh Street, Milwaukee, Wisconsin 53210.

AIR AND RAIL TRAVEL

Access Amtrak, available free from: Amtrak's Office of Public Affairs,
400 North Capitol Street, NW, Washington, D.C. 20001.
Access Travel: Airports—A Guide to Accessibility of Terminals, prepared May 1980 by and available free from: Airport Operators Council International, 1700 K Street, NW, Washington, D.C. 20006; also
from Consumer Information Center, Pueblo, Colorado 81009.
Airlines and Disabled Travellers, prepared 1977 by and available for
18 Swedish kronor from: ICTA Information Centre, Fack, S-161 25
Bromma 1, Sweden. In English.
*Airport Guide for the Handicapped and Elderly: Chicago O'Hare In-
ternational Airport,* prepared December 1978 by and available free
from: Chicago Department of Aviation, City Hall, Room 1111, Chi-
cago, Illinois 60602.
Care in the Air—Advice for Handicapped Passengers, prepared 1977
and available free from: The Air Transport Users Committee, 129
Kingsway, London, WC2B 6NN, England.
*Carriage of the Physically Handicapped on Domestic and Interna-
tional Airlines,* prepared May 1972 by and available for $1.25 from:
United Cerebral Palsy Association of New York City, 122 East
Twenty-third Street, New York, New York 10010.
Flight Information for Blind Passengers, prepared 1978 by and avail-
able free from: Frontier Airlines, 8250 Smith Road, Denver,
Colorado 30207. In braille.
Flight Information for the Physically Handicapped, prepared 1978 by
and available free from: Frontier Airlines, 8250 Smith Road, Denver,
Colorado 30207.
How to Fly, prepared April 1976 by and available free from: Air Trans-
port Association of America, 1709 New York Avenue, NW, Washing-
ton, D.C. 20006.
Special Passengers, prepared 1978 by and available free from: Neal
Green, Passenger Sales Office, Eastern Airlines, Newark Interna-
tional Airport, Newark, New Jersey 07114.

Wheelchair Air Travel, available for $2.50 from: Clare Millar, Box 7, Blair, Cambridge, Ontario, Canada.

Access National Parks: A Guide for Handicapped Visitors (stock number 024-005-00691-5), prepared 1977 by the National Park Service, Department of the Interior. Available for $3.50 from: Superintendent of Documents, U.S. Printing Office, Washington, D.C. 20402.

Access to the World, written 1977 by Louise Weiss and available for $7.95 from: Chatham Square Press, Inc., 401 Broadway, New York, New York 10013.

Arts and the Handicapped: An Issue of Access (examples of accessible art programs), prepared 1975 by the National Endowment of the Arts. Available for $4 from: ARTS, Box 2040, Grand Central Station, New York, New York 10017.

Dialysis Worldwide for the Traveling Patient, prepared 1978 by and available free from: NAPHT, 505 Northern Boulevard, Great Neck, New York 11021.

Greyhound's Helping Hand Service for the Handicapped, from your local Greyhound office or: Greyhound International, 625 Eighth Avenue, New York, New York 10018.

Guide for Travelling Hemophiliacs: Directory of National Treatment Centers, prepared 1973 and available free from: World Federation of Hemophilia, 1170 Peel Street, Room 1126, Montreal, Quebec, H3B 2T4, Canada.

Highway Rest Areas for Handicapped Travelers, available free from: The President's Committee on Employment of the Handicapped, Washington, D.C. 20210.

New Programs and Facilities (describes recent art programs for the handicapped), prepared by the National Endowment for the Arts. Available free from: ARTS, Box 2040, Grand Central Station, New York, New York 10017.

1979 International Directory of Access Guides, Travel Survey Department, Rehabilitation/WORLD, 20 West Fortieth Street, New York, New York 10018.

Report of European Study Trip on Leisure Services for Disabled Persons, available from: Recreation Council for the Disabled in Nova

Scotia, Suite 308, 5516 Spring Garden Road, Halifax, Nova Scotia, B3J 1G6, Canada.

Travel for the Patient with Chronic Obstructive Pulmonary Disease, prepared by and available for $1.25 from: Rehabilitation Research and Training Center, George Washington University Medical Center, Ross Hall, Room 714, 2300 Eye St., NW, Washington, D.C. 20037.

Travel Tips for the Handicapped, prepared 1977 by and available free from: United States Travel Service, U.S. Department of Commerce, Washington, D.C. 20230.

The Wheelchair Traveler, written 1977 by Douglass R. Annand and available for $4.95 plus postage ($1.25 first class, 75 cents third class) from: Wheelchair Traveler, Ball Hill Road, Milford, New Hampshire 03055.

TOURS FOR THE DISABLED

Rambling Tours, Inc.
P.O. Box 1304
Hollandale, Florida 33009

Flying Wheels Tours
143 West Bridge Street
Box 382
Owatoona, Minnesota 55080

Handi-Tours
Calladine & Baldry, Ltd.
Yorkdale Shopping Centre Suite 153
Dufferin Street & Highway 401
Toronto, Ontario, Canada M6A 2T9

Travel Information Center
Moss Rehabilitation Hospital
Philadelphia, Pennsylvania 19141

Evergreen Travel Service
Forest Park Center
17171 Bothell Way, NE
Seattle, Washington 98155

Dynamic Travel Consultants
10050 Wolfe Road
Cupertino, California 95014

Sports

GENERAL

National Recreation Association
315 Park Avenue South
New York, New York 10010
No. 272, Table Football Game
No. 240, A Folding Table for Table Tennis
Oral Om Miller
6327 Thirty-first Place, NW
Washington, D.C. 20015
Inkprint manual on instruction and coach pointers
for blind bowling.
American Foundation for the Blind
15 West Sixteenth Street
New York, New York 10011
Aids & Appliances Division—Athletic assistance
equipment for the blind.
Audi-Ball, Balls Emitting Sound,
Bowling rail
National Wheelchair Athletic Association
40-24 Sixty-second Street
Woodside, New York 11377   (212) 424-2929
Organizes and governs competitive wheelchair sports, e.g.,
archery, swimming, track, weight lifting, for people who have
paralysis, amputations, and other orthopedic disabilities. Members
are thirteen years of age and older.
Provides information on sports and recreation for disabled persons; aids and equipment; and psychosocial factors related to disability.
National Handicapped Sports and Recreation Association
4105 East Florida Avenue
Denver, Colorado 80222   (303) 757-3381
An organization (with local chapters) of disabled persons who
enjoy participation in active recreational activities, such as skiing,
tennis, horseback riding, kayaking, bowling, etc.
Willing to share information about participation of persons with

all types of disabilities in sports. Supports the use of recreation and sports activities in all rehabilitation programs.

United Cerebral Palsy of Northwestern Pennsylvania
2230 Broad Street
Erie, Pennsylvania 16503
Information for construction of metal frame bowling device

BIKES AND TRICYCLES

Adulttrike Manufacturing Company (Division of Custom Cycle)
12209 Grand Avenue
El Mirage, Arizona 85335
J. J. Block
Aids for the Handicapped
1111 West Argyle
Chicago, Illinois 60640
Built-up chain velocipide and built-up chain atricycle
J. A. Preston Corporation
71 Fifth Avenue
New York, New York 10003
Tricycle with body support

GAMES AND ACTIVITIES

Geddes, Delores. *Physical Activities for Individuals with Handicapping Conditions.* St. Louis: C. V. Mosby Co., 1974. Practical information on modifying activities to meet the needs of those with prevalent handicapping conditions.

Craity, Bryant J. *Developmental Games for the Physically Handicapped Children.* Palo Alto, Calif.: Peek Publications, 1968. Covers string ball games and grid games.

SWIMMING—*Movies*

Focus on Ability. American Red Cross (no charge).

Keep on Walking. Modern Talking Picture Service, National Foundation March of Dimes, 1275 Mamaroneck Avenue, White Plains, N.Y. 10605. A film featuring a young amputee with two prosthetic arms and how he has adjusted to his handicap. Short portion on swimming.

Splash! Documentary Films, Aptos, California 95003. $25/day. Excellent film incorporating a number of activities of a lead-up nature when working in the water.

SWIMMING—*Books*

American National Red Cross. *Adapted Aquatics.* Garden City, New York: Doubleday, 1977.

Counsilman, James. *Science of Swimming.* Englewood Cliffs, N.J.: Prentice-Hall, 1968. Excellent in giving instructor stroke analysis. Sequential pictures of each stroke.

Reynolds, Grace, ed. *A Swimming Program for the Handicapped.* New York: Association Press (YMCA Swimming and Diving Series), 1973. Discusses considerations when working with a number of frequently encountered handicaps. Bibliography is excellent.

EQUIPMENT

Proprio Paddles—Pull-Buoy, Inc.
2511 Leach
Auburn Heights, Michigan 48057

Life Survival Skills

READING LIST 1

PLAYS—*Shakespeare*
1. HAMLET
2. JULIUS CAESAR
3. KING LEAR
4. MACBETH
5. ROMEO AND JULIET

POETS—*British*
1. W. H. Auden
2. William Blake
3. Robert Browning
4. Robert Burns
5. Lord Byron
6. Geoffrey Chaucer

7. Samuel T. Coleridge
8. Thomas Hardy
9. Robert Herrick
10. Gerard Manley Hopkins
11. A. E. Housman
12. John Keats
13. John Milton
14. William Shakespeare
15. Percy B. Shelley
16. Alfred Lord Tennyson
17. Dylan Thomas
18. William Wordsworth
19. William Butler Yeats

POETS—*American*
1. e. e. cummings
2. James Dickey
3. Emily Dickinson
4. T. S. Eliot
5. Robert Frost
6. Allen Ginsberg
7. Langston Hughes
8. Robert Lowell
9. Marianne Moore
10. Edgar Allan Poe
11. Ezra Pound
12. Edwin Arlington Robinson
13. Theodore Roethke
14. Carl Sandburg
15. Walt Whitman
16. Richard Wilbur
17. William Carlos Williams

PROSE

1–2. Suggested, above all others in this section, the Bible—at least a substantial portion of it—and Homer's *Odyssey*
3. Jane Austen, *Emma* and *Pride and Prejudice*
4. James Baldwin, *Go Tell It on the Mountain*
5. Samuel Beckett, *Waiting for Godot*
6. Charlotte Brontë, *Jane Eyre*
7. Emily Brontë, *Wuthering Heights*
8. Albert Camus, *The Stranger*
9. Lewis Carroll, *Alice's Adventures in Wonderland*
10. Rachel Carson, *The Sea Around Us*
11. Willa Cather, *My Antonia*
12. Miguel de Cervantes, *Don Quixote*
13. Eldridge Cleaver, *Soul on Ice*
14. Joseph Conrad, *Heart of Darkness* and *Lord Jim*
15. James Fenimore Cooper, *The Pathfinder*
16. Stephen Crane, *The Red Badge of Courage*
17. Daniel Defoe, *Robinson Crusoe*
18. Charles Dickens, *David Copperfield, Great Expectations,* and *Oliver Twist*
19. Fyodor Dostoyevsky, *The Brothers Karamazov*
20. Ralph Ellison, *The Invisible Man*
21. Ralph Waldo Emerson, *Essays*
22. William Faulkner, *The Bear*
23. Henry Fielding, *Joseph Andrews*
24. F. Scott Fitzgerald, *The Great Gatsby*
25. Benjamin Franklin, *Autobiography*
26. William Gerald Golding, *Lord of the Flies*
27. Graham Greene, *The Power and the Glory*

28. Thomas Hardy, *The Mayor of Casterbridge* and *The Return of the Native*
29. Nathaniel Hawthorne, *The Scarlet Letter*
30. Joseph Heller, *Catch-22*
31. Ernest Hemingway, *A Farewell to Arms, Short Stories,* and *The Sun Also Rises*
32. Hermann Hesse, *Siddhartha*
33. Homer, *Iliad*
34. Victor Hugo, *Les Misérables*
35. Aldous Huxley, *Brave New World*
36. Henry James, *The Turn of the Screw*
37. James Joyce, *A Portrait of the Artist as a Young Man*
38. John Knowles, *A Separate Peace*
39. Malcolm X, *The Autobiography of Malcolm X*
40. Herman Melville, *Billy Budd*
41. Arthur Miller, *Death of a Salesman*
42. Mythology. Bulfinch's or Hamilton's collection
43. Eugene O'Neill, *Long Day's Journey into Night*
44. George Orwell, *Animal Farm* and *1984*
45. Francis Parkman, *The Oregon Trail*
46. Alan Paton, *Cry, the Beloved Country*
47. Plutarch, *Lives* (selections)
48. Edgar Allan Poe, *Tales*
49. Ole Edvart Rölvaag, *Giants in the Earth*
50. Edmond Rostand, *Cyrano de Bergerac*
51. J. D. Salinger, *Catcher in the Rye*
52. Bernard Shaw, *Androcles and the Lion, Pygmalion,* and *Saint Joan*
53. Sophocles, *Antigone* and *Oedipus Rex*
54. John Steinbeck, *The Grapes of Wrath*
55. Jonathan Swift, *Gulliver's Travels*
56. Henry David Thoreau, *Walden*
57. J. R. R. Tolkien, *The Lord of the Rings*
58. Mark Twain, *Huckleberry Finn* and *Life on the Mississippi*
59. Virgil, *Aeneid* (especially Books 2, 4, and 6)
60. Thornton Wilder, *Our Town*
61. Tennessee Williams, *The Glass Menagerie*
62. Richard Wright, *Black Boy*

AMPUTATION—*Biography*

Brickhill, Paul. *Reach for the Sky: The Story of Douglas Bader, Legless Ace of the Battle of Britain.* New York: W. W. Norton, 1954.

Edgar, Betsy Jordan. *We Live with the Wheelchair.* Parsons, W. Va.: McClain Printing Co., 1970. $5, plus 40 cents postage.

McCormick, Donald. *The Incredible Mr. Kavanagh.* Old Greenwich, Conn.: Devin-Adair, 1961.

Waugh, Eileen. *No Man an Island: A Biography of Peter Spencer.* New York: Doubleday, 1970.

Wolf, Bernard. *Don't Feel Sorry for Paul.* Philadelphia: Lippincott, 1974.

BLIND—*Biography*

Krents, Harold. *To Race the Wind: An Autobiography.* New York: Bantam, 1973.

Mehta, Ved. *Face to Face: An Autobiography.* Boston: Oxford University Press, 1957.

Potok, Andrew. *Ordinary Daylight.* New York: Holt, Rinehart and Winston, 1980.

Putnam, Peter. *"Keep Your Head Up, Mr. Putnam."* New York: Harper & Row, 1952.

Robinson, Leonard A. *Light at the Tunnel End.* Silver Springs, Md.: Foundation for the Handicapped and Elderly, Inc., 1975.

Russell, Robert. *To Catch an Angel: Adventures in the World I Cannot See.* New York: Vanguard Press, 1962.

Ulrich, Sharon, with Anna W. M. Wolf. *Elizabeth.* Ann Arbor: University of Michigan Press, 1972.

Yates, Elizabeth. *The Lighted Heart.* Dublin, New Hampshire: W. L. Bauhan, 1974.

Zook, Deborah. *Debby.* Scottdale, Pa.: Herald Press, 1974.

CEREBRAL PALSY—*Biography*

Carlson, Earl Reinhold. *Born That Way.* New York: John Day, 1941.

Henscheid, Henry. *View of Life.* National Easter Seal Society for Crippled Children and Adults, 2023 West Ogden Avenue, Chicago, Illinois 60612, 1975. 25 cents, plus 25 cents postage and handling.

Killilea, Marie. *Karen.* New York: Dell, 1952.
————. *With Love from Karen.* New York: Dell, 1963.
Miers, Earl S. *Why Did This Have to Happen?* New York: St. Martin's Press, 1958. Also available in pamphlet form from the National Easter Seal Society for Crippled Children and Adults, 2023 West Ogden Avenue, Chicago, Illinois 60612. 25 cents, plus 25 cents postage and handling.

CEREBRAL PALSY—*Drama*

Nichols, Peter. *Joe Egg.* New York: Evergreen, 1968.

CEREBRAL PALSY—*Fiction*

Brown, Christy. *Down All the Days.* New York: Stein and Day, 1970. Also available from the same publisher is *The Poems of Christy Brown.*

DEAF—*Biography*

Levine, Edna S. *Lisa and Her Soundless World.* New York: Human Sciences Press, 1974
Powers, Helen. *Signs of Silence: Bernard Bragg and the National Theatre of the Deaf.* New York: Dodd, Mead & Co., 1972.
West, Paul. *Words for a Deaf Daughter.* New York: Harper & Row, 1970.

DEAF—*Fiction*

Greenberg, Joanne. *In This Sign.* New York: Avon Books, 1970.
Robinson, Veronica. *David in Silence.* Philadelphia: Lippincott, 1965.
Steward, Dwight. *The Acupuncture Murders.* New York: Harper & Row, 1973.

HANDICAPPED—*Biography*

Blank, Joseph P. *19 Steps Up the Mountain: The Story of the Debolt Family.* Philadelphia: Lippincott, 1976.
California Society for Crippled Children and Adults. *An Exceptional View of Life: The Easter Seal Story.* Available from the Easter Seal Society of California, 742 Market Street, Suite 202, San Francisco, California 94102. $7.95.

Eareckson, Joni. *Joni.* New York: Bantam, 1978.

Gauchat, Dorothy. *All God's Children.* New York: Hawthorn Books, 1976.

Gelfand, Revina, and Patterson, Letha. *They Wouldn't Quit: Stories of Handicapped People.* Minneapolis: Lerner Publications, 1962.

Lotz, Philip Henry, ed. *Unused Alibis.* New York: Arno Press, 1951.

Viscardi, Henry, Jr. *Give Us the Tools.* New York: Eriksson-Taplinger, 1959.

_____. *The Phoenix Child: A Story of Love.* New York: Paul S. Eriksson, 1975.

_____. *The School.* New York: Paul S. Eriksson, 1964.

Wallace, Archer. *In Spite of All.* New York: Arno Press, 1944. Now reprinted by Books for Libraries, $10.25.

HANDICAPPED—*Fiction*

Gallico, Paul. *The Snow Goose.* New York: Alfred A. Knopf, 1941.

Greenberg, Joanne. *Rites of Passage.* New York: Holt, Rinehart and Winston, 1972.

Kellogg, Marjorie. *Tell Me That You Love Me, Junie Moon.* New York: Farrar, Straus & Giroux, 1968.

Menotti, Gian-Carlo. *Amahl and the Night Visitors.* New York: McGraw-Hill, 1952.

Savitz, Harriet May. *On the Move.* New York: Avon, 1980.

Smith, Lillian. *The Journey.* New York: W. W. Norton, 1965.

HYDROCEPHALUS—*Biography*

Patterson, Katheryn. *No Time for Tears.* Chicago: Johnson Publishing, 1965.

MULTIPLE SCLEROSIS—*Biography*

Gilbert, Arlene E. *You Can Do It from a Wheelchair.* New Rochelle, N.Y.: Arlington House, 1973.

PARAPLEGIA—*Biography*

Campanella, Roy. *It's Good to Be Alive.* Boston: Little, Brown, 1959.

Epstein, June. *Mermaid on Wheels: The Remarkable Story of Margaret Lester.* Sydney, Australia: Ure Smith, 1967. Distributed in the

United States by Taplinger Publishing Co., 29 E. 10th St., New York, N.Y. 10003.

Valens, E. G. *A Long Way Up: The Story of Jill Kinmont.* New York: Harper & Row, 1966.

————. *The Other Side of the Mountain.* New York: Warner Books, 1975.

Willis, Jack and Mary. *". . . But There Are Always Miracles."* New York: Fawcett, 1974.

Wilson, Dorothy Clarke. *Handicap Race: The Inspiring Story of Roger Arnett.* New York: McGraw-Hill, 1967.

————. *Take My Hands: The Remarkable Story of Dr. Mary Verghese.* New York: McGraw-Hill, 1963.

PARAPLEGIA—*Fiction*

Nasaw, Jonathan Lewis. *Easy Walking.* New York: Lippincott, 1975.

POLIOMYELITIS—*Biography*

Kirkendall, Don, and Phraner, Mary. *Bottom High to the Crowd: The Story of One Man's Fight Against a Crippling Disease.* New York: Walker and Co., 1973.

Marx, Joseph Laurence. *Keep Trying: A Practical Book for the Handicapped by a Polio Victim.* New York: Harper & Row, 1974.

POLIOMYELITIS—*Fiction*

Barber, Elsie Oakes. *The Trembling Years.* New York: Macmillan, 1949.

Beim, Lorraine. *Triumph Clear.* New York: Harcourt Brace Jovanovich, 1946.

Sheed, Wilfred. *People Will Always Be Kind.* New York: Farrar, Straus & Giroux, 1973.

REHABILITATION—*Biography*

Kessler, Henry H. *The Knife Is Not Enough.* New York: W. W. Norton, 1968.

Index

Access guides, general, 263–264
Access guides, U.S., 115
 by states, 247–262
Achievement tests, 88, 89, 90, 91
Advanced Placement Examinations, 91
Advocate (newsletter), 109
Ageism, 102
Air travel, guides to, 262, 263
Alexander Graham Bell Association for the Deaf, 243
American Association of Workers for the Blind, 242
American Coalition of Citizens with Disabilities, 107, 108
American College Testing Program (ACT), 90, 91
American Council of the Blind, 242
American Diabetes Association, 53, 244
American Foundation for the Blind, 234, 235, 242, 265
American Printing House for the Blind, 37, 234, 242

American Red Cross, 141, 266, 267
American Sign Language (ASL), 42, 43, 45, 46, 185
American Speech and Hearing Association, 243
Amputation, reading list for, 270
Aptitude tests, 88, 89, 90
Architectural accessibility, as IEP accommodation, 180
Attitudinal climate, as IEP accommodation, 181
Avery, Chester Pike, 6
 quoted, 6–7, 35

Badminton, balloon, 134
Ball toss, 131–132
Balloon badminton, 134
Balloon volleyball, 138
Barrel ball toss, 132
Baseball, target, 138–139
Basketball, 130
Bicycling, 135, 266
Biklen, Douglas, quoted, 13
Biofeedback, 74–75

Birth control (contraception), 15, 16–17
Blindness, 3–4, 21, 31, 32, 34, 36, 37, 85, 206, 242–243
  "legal," 33
  and mobility, 111–112
  orientation instruction for, 111–112
  reading list for, 270
  and school tests, special considerations in, 94–95
  stereotypes of, 31
  teachers helped to deal with students', 36–37
  See also Braille; Limited vision
Body image, loss of, and rehabilitation, 22
Bogdan, Robert, quoted, 13
Books for You, 151
  See also Reading, and reading lists
Boris, Harold N., quoted, 120–121
Bowe, Frank, 101, 108, 197
Bowling, 135
Braille, 33, 34, 35, 36, 84, 88, 91, 95, 164, 181, 242
Braillewriter, 34
Bulletin (Interracial Books for Children), 13, 108

Career goals, 53, 58, 63–65, 70, 73, 78, 171, 174, 175, 176, 194, 208, 209, 210
  collecting information about, 233–239
  and getting appointment for interview, 236, 237
  and interview, suggestions concerning, 236–237, 238

work experience for testing, 192, 230–231, 238–239
  See also Life experience; Master Career Exploration List; Skills
Cassettes, use of, 34
Center for Independent Living (CIL), 103, 108, 109
Central Catalog of Volunteer Produced Textbooks, 242
Cerebral palsy, 12, 23, 60–66, 129, 177, 178, 245
  and appearance as factor in career possibilities, 64–65
  and career plans, 63–65
  dyskinesia in, 60
  helping teachers of students with, 61
  perceptual capacity in, 64
  reading list for, 270–271
  and reality testing in work situation, 63
  risk-taking in, importance of, 62–63
  spasticity in, 60
  therapy for, 64
Checking account, use of, 199
Class size, as IEP accommodation, 181
Closer Look Report, The, 108
Coalition, The (newsletter), 109
College Board Achievement Tests, 90–91
College choice, 188–191
College Guide for Students with Disabilities, 189
College Handbook, The, 89, 189
College-Level Examinations, 91–92

Coma, diabetic, 51
Communication skills checklist, 184–185
Contraception (birth control), 15, 16–17
Coping, 18–28, 68–69
by accepting physical differences, 19–20
and dependency, getting used to, 20
with fright of nondisabled, 25
potential for, 18
with recent disabilities, 20–21
and rehabilitation, 21–25
and self-concept, positive, building, 26–28
See also Handicapism
Council on Exceptional Children, 109
Counsilman, James, 141, 267
Course selection, 187–188
Croquet, 136

Deafness, 38, 39–40, 41, 42, 243, 244
and finger spelling, 42–43, 48, 185
friend's help in supplying knowledge curtailed by, 46–47
and interpreter, use of, 44, 48, 49
and lipreading, 42, 43, 44, 45, 48, 184
reading list for, 271
and school tests, special considerations in, 92–94
and sign language, 42, 43, 45, 46, 185

stereotype of, 47
teachers helped to deal with students', 44–45, 47–50
teletype machine for use in, 49
See also Partial hearing loss
DeLellis, John, 114
Diabetes, 51–55, 96, 205, 206, 244
and career plans, 53
diet in, 52, 53
and exercise, 52
explanation of, 52
helping teachers of students with, 53–55
insulin reaction in, 54
stereotypes of people with, 53
Diabetes Association of Greater Chicago, 54
Diabetic coma, 51
Dictionary, use of, 149–150
Dillenbeck, Douglas D., 81
quoted, 82, 98
Disabilities, physical, getting tested for. *See* Tests for physically disabled students
Disability rights movement, 102–109, 117, 169
organization of, 102–106, 169
terms used by, 106–107
See also Handicapism
Disabled in Action (DIA), 103, 105, 106, 109
Disabled Women's Coalition of Berkeley, 104–105
Driving by disabled, 9, 110, 173
education for, 112–114, 173
Dyskinesia in cerebral palsy, 60
Dystrophy, muscular. *See* Muscular dystrophy

Education
  guaranteed by law to disabled
    children, 103, 161, 163–164,
    167, 170
  and placement choices, 179–
    180
  specialized or mainstream,
    176–179
Employment. *See* Career goals;
  Work experience
Epilepsy, 19, 74–80, 106, 112,
    206, 207, 247
  acceptance of, 76
  biofeedback used with, 75
  and career planning, 78
  confidences about, 75, 76, 78,
    79, 80
  explanation of, 76
  medication for, 76, 77, 79, 96
  not a disease, 76
  teaching others about, 77
Epilepsy Foundation of America,
    77, 78, 106, 247
  job training and placement
    programs of (TAPS), 78, 193

Federation of Children with Spe-
    cial Needs, 109
Finger spelling, 42–43, 48, 185
*Free to Choose: Decision Making
    for Young Men* (Mitchell), 82,
    120, 128
Friends (friendship), 46, 47, 116–
    127, 193–194, 224
  blaming disability for lack of,
    117–118
  and evaluation of self, 122–125
  high school, 118, 119, 120, 122,
    127
  need for, 121–122

with self, 126
  sharing interests with, 127
  skill in developing, 125–126
  teenage, 118–121

Gallaudet College, 243–244
Games and sports, 128–141, 265–
    267
Glare shields for limited vision, 32
"Grabber" for muscular dystro-
    phy, 57
*Guide to College/Career Pro-
    grams for Deaf Students,* 189

Handicap, definition of, xv
Handicapism, 23, 24
  fighting, 101–109
  See also Disability rights move-
    ment
Handicapped Driver's Guide, The
    (DeLellis), 114
Handicapping America (Bowe),
    101, 108, 197
Hard-of-hearing, the. *See* Partial
    hearing loss
Health, Education, and Welfare
    (HEW), U.S. Department of,
    165, 167
Hearing aid, 43–44, 184
Hearing loss, partial. *See* Partial
    hearing loss
High Interest, Easy Reading,
    151–152
Hydrocephalus, 272

*I Can Be Anything: Careers and
    College for Young Women*
    (Mitchell), 233
In the Mainstream (publication),
    109

Independence
and life survival skills, 142,
145–146
making money as contribution
to, 196
Independent, The (newsletter),
103, 108, 109
Individualized education program (IEP), 161, 164, 176,
178, 179, 180
accommodations for, 180–183
Instructional materials and support services, as IEP accommodation, 181
Instruments, technical, brailled,
34–35
Insulin, 52, 53
Insulin reaction, treatment of,
54
Intelligence tests, 84, 86–87, 94
Interest tests, 87–88

Junior National Association of the
Deaf, 244

Kuder Occupational Interest Survey, 88

Labor, U.S. Department of, 175,
197, 234
Large-type textbooks for limited
vision, 32–33
Law
due process of, 162, 163
education of disabled children
guaranteed by, 103, 161,
163–164, 167, 170
on mainstreaming students,
164

on testing, 164, 170. *See also*
Tests for physically disabled
students
work. *See* Work law
Leiter International Performance Scale, 87
Levine, Edna S., 45, 271
Life experience
choosing, 211–213
educational, 223, 228
and family, 224, 228
and friendship, 224
in hobbies, 223, 228
leisure, 223, 228
"shadowing," 238
in volunteering, 223, 228, 238–239
in work, paid and unpaid. *See*
Work experience
See also Career goals; Skills
chart
Life survival skill(s), 142–158
and independence, 142, 145–146
center, 147
learning as, 157–158. *See also*
Studying, to learn
reading as. *See* Reading
studying as. *See* Studying
and testing. *See* Tests for physically disabled students
where to learn, 146
Limited vision, 32, 33, 34, 36,
37
Limits, acceptance of, 8–9
Lipreading (speechreading), 42,
43, 44, 45, 48, 184

Magnifiers for limited vision, 32,
33, 94, 180

Mainstream, Inc., 4, 5, 8, 107, 109
Mainstreaming or specializing, 176–179
Manipulation skills checklist, 186
Master Career Exploration List, 231–233
Mead, Margaret, quoted, 118–120, 127
Men's Career Book, The: Work and Life Planning for a New Age (Mitchell), 233
Mental retardation, 60
Milk, Leslie B., 4, 8, 9, 107
Mitchell, Joyce Slayton, 82, 118, 120, 128, 233
Mobility of disabled, 110, 186–187
Money
  disincentives for making, 197
  making, 196, 197–198, 201
  managing, 198–199
  saving, 199
Multiple sclerosis, 272
Muscular dystrophy, 56–59, 244–245
  and career possibilities, 58
  "grabber" for use in, 57
  helping teachers of students with, 58–59
  physical dependence in, 56–57
Muscular Dystrophy Association, 57, 244

National Association for Visually Handicapped, 243
National Association of the Deaf, 244
National Blindness Information Center, 243

National Braille Association, 243
National Center for a Barrier Free Environment, 245
National Center for Law and the Deaf, 244
National Council of Teachers of English, 150, 151
National Easter Seal Society, 152, 245
National Federation of the Blind, 243
National Handicapped Sports and Recreation Association, 265–266
National Information Center for the Handicapped, 108
National Merit Scholarship Corporation, 89
National Paraplegia Foundation, 72, 245
National Recreation Association, 265
National Society for the Prevention of Blindness, 243
National Wheelchair Athletic Association, 265

Occupational Outlook Handbook, 233–234
Office of Handicapped Concerns, 6, 7, 35
On the Move (Savitz), 68, 69, 70, 71, 128
Osteogenesis imperfecta, 174
Other Choices for Becoming a Woman (Mitchell), 118

Palsy, cerebral. *See* Cerebral palsy

Paraplegia, 67, 68, 70, 112
  reading list for, 272–273
  See also Spinal cord injuries
Partial hearing loss, 38–39, 40,
  41, 42, 43, 48, 112, 178,
  206
  hearing aid for, 43–44
  and school tests, special consid-
  erations in, 92, 93
Partial (limited) vision, 32, 33, 34,
  36, 37
Peabody Picture Vocabulary Test
  (PPVT), 87
Perlman, Itzhak, 111
Personality tests, 92
Physically disabled students, tests
  for. *See* Tests for physically
  disabled students
Ping-Pong, 136–137
Pitch back, 132–133
Poliomyelitis, 206
  reading list for, 273
Porter, Sylvia, 199
Pregnancy, teenage, 16–17
Preliminary Scholastic Aptitude
  Test/National Merit Scholar-
  ship Qualifying Test
  (PSAT/NMSQT), 89, 90
PRG Interest Inventory for the
  Blind, 88

Quadriplegia, 67, 68, 70, 112
  See also Spinal cord injuries

Racism, 24, 102
Rail travel, guides to, 262
Reading, 147–152
  improving, 148–149
  learning from, 152

and reading lists, 150–151, 152,
  267–273
  vocabulary developed by, 149–
  150
Recording for the Blind, 34, 243
Registry of Interpreters for the
  Deaf, 244
Rehabilitation, 21–25, 63, 198,
  273
Rehabilitation Act, Section 504
  of. *See* Work law
Rehabilitation counselor, 234
Rehabilitation Services Adminis-
  tration, 104
Resting platform for swimmer,
  140
Risk-taking, importance of, 62,
  172–173, 175
Roberts, Edward, 113, 171, 172,
  173
Roget's New Pocket Thesaurus,
  150

Savitz, Harriet May, quoted, 68,
  128
Schneider, Edith, 12
Scholastic Aptitude Test (SAT),
  89, 90
Scholastic Magazines, Inc., 151
Science of Swimming (Counsil-
  man), 141, 267
Seeing Essential English (SEE),
  42, 43
Self-concept, positive, building,
  26–28
*Sensory Aids for Employment for
  the Blind and Visually Im-
  paired,* 235
Sexism, 24, 102, 104

Sexuality, teenage. *See* Teenage sexuality
Shepard, Natalie M., 128
Shock, stages of recovery from, 69–70
Shuffleboard, 137
Siglish, 43
Sign Language, American (ASL), 42, 43, 45, 46, 185
Skiing, 129, 130
Skills
　in analytical thinking, 217–218
　artistic, 220–221
　bodily, 214
　checklist of, 183–186
　creativity in, 218, 228
　enjoyable, 226, 227
　expanding, through new experiences, 227–230
　finding, 210–213
　and follow-through, use of, 222
　for future career, 230
　with hands, 214, 228–229
　in helpfulness, 219–220
　and intuition, use of, 216–217
　in leadership, 221–222
　life survival. *See* Life survival skill(s)
　and logic, use of, 217–218
　manual, 214, 228–229
　new, learning, 226, 227
　with numbers, 216
　old, developing, 226–227
　originality in, 218
　in repairing, 214, 228–229
　sensory, 215
　transferable, 192–193, 210, 211, 226, 230–231, 239
　word, 215

See also Career goals; Life experience; Work experience
Skills chart, 214–222, 226
　completing, 223–225
　See also Career goals; Life experience; Work experience
Skills Development Chart, 227
Spasticity in cerebral palsy, 60
Spectacles, telescopic, 32
Speech disability, 65–66
Speechreading (lipreading), 42, 43, 44, 45, 48, 184
Spinal cord injuries, 67–73, 245–246
　acceptance of, 70
　and career plans, 70, 73
　coping with, 68–69
　helping parents of teenagers with, 71–72
　helping teachers of students with, 72–73
Spinal Cord Injury Centers, 245–246
Sports and games, 128–141, 265–267
Stereotypes, 4–7, 12–13
Strunk, Winifred, 62
Studying, 152–157
　and interest in subjects, 156
　to learn, 154–155, 157
　memorization in, 156–157
　time for, effective use of, 155
Subnormal (limited) vision, 32, 33, 34, 36, 37
Suggested Precollege Reading, 151
Support group, importance of, 193–194
Support services, as IEP accommodations, 182

Survival skills, life. *See* Life survival skill(s)
Swimming, 129, 130, 139–141, 266–267

Table tetherball, 137
Tape recorder, use of, 34, 37, 180, 184
Target baseball, 138–139
Target tennis, 133
Target throw, 133–134
Teenage friendship, 118–121
Teenage sexuality, 9, 10, 11–17, 47, 241–242
  and learning about sex, 15–16
  and pregnancy, 16–17
  and stereotypes, asexual, 12–13
Telescopic spectacles, 32
Tennis, target, 133
Tests for physically disabled students, 81–98, 157, 164
  achievement, 88, 89, 90, 91
  adaptations of, 84–85, 96–97
  Advanced Placement Examinations, 91
  American College Testing Program, 90, 91
  aptitude, 88, 89, 90
  College Board Achievement Tests, 90–91
  College-Level Examinations, 91–92
  intelligence, 84, 86–87, 94
  interest, 87–88
  Kuder Occupational Interest Survey, 88
  Leiter International Performance Scale, 87
  not sole basis for decision, 98

Peabody Picture Vocabulary Test, 87
  personality, 92
  Preliminary Scholastic Aptitude Test/National Merit Scholarship Test, 89, 90
  selection of, 83–84
  Scholastic Aptitude Test, 89, 90
  with specific disabilities, 92–97
  standardized, 86
  teacher, 86
  Wechsler Adult Intelligence Scale, 84, 87
  Wechsler Intelligence Scale for Children, 84, 87
Tetherball, table, 137
Textbooks, large-type, for limited vision, 32–33
Therapies, as IEP accommodations, 182
Tips on Car Care and Safety for Deaf Drivers, 114
Tollifson, Joan, 106
Tours for the disabled, 264
Training and Placement Services Project (TAPS), sponsored by Epilepsy Foundation of America, 78, 193
TRANSBUS, 103
Transferable skills, 192–193, 210, 211, 226, 230–231, 239
Transportation, public, 111
Transportation, U.S. Department of, 114
Travel guides, 262, 263, 264
Tricycling, 135, 266
Typewriters, large-print, electric, 180

Unemployment, and the disabled, 174–175
United Cerebral Palsy Association, 105, 245, 266

Vermont, driver education in, for handicapped, 112–113, 114
Veterans Administration hospitals, group counseling by, for teenagers with spinal cord injuries, 72
Vietnam War veterans, disabled, 102, 103
Vision, limited, 32, 33, 34, 36, 37
Vocabulary, developing, 149–150
Vocational rehabilitation (VR) agencies, 189
Volleyball, balloon, 138

Wallach, Ellen J., special section by, 205–239
Washington Square Press, 151
Water Safety Instruction teaching manual, Red Cross, 141

Wechsler Adult Intelligence Scale (WAIS), 84, 87
Wechsler Intelligence Scale for Children (WISC), 84, 87
What Happens After School? A Study of Disabled Women and Education, 105, 108
Wheelchair, power, 110
Wheelchair sports, 129, 132, 133, 134, 135, 136, 265
Women's Educational Equity Communications Network (WEECN), 105, 108, 197
Work Book, The: A Guide to Skilled Jobs (Mitchell), 233
Work experience, 223–224, 228
to test career goal, 192, 230–231, 238–239
See also Skills
Work law, 102, 103, 165–167
and access, meaning of, 167
getting copy of, 168

Yellow Pages, use of, 200, 235